Researching the Country House

Batsford Local History Series

Researching the Country House

A Guide for Local Historians

Arthur Elton   Brett Harrison   Keith Wark

B. T. Batsford Ltd · London

To Tessa, Felicity and Andrea

© Arthur Elton, Brett Harrison, Keith Wark 1992

First published 1992

All rights reserved. No part of this publication
may be reproduced, in any form or by any means,
without permission from the Publisher

Typeset by Deltatype Ltd, Ellesmere Port, Cheshire
and printed in Great Britain by
Billing and Sons Ltd, Worcester.

Published by B.T. Batsford Ltd
4 Fitzhardinge Street, London W1H 0AH

A CIP catalogue record for this book is
available from the British Library

ISBN 0 7134 6440 2

CONTENTS

CONTENTS

LIST OF ILLUSTRATIONS

LIST OF ILLUSTRATIONS

ACKNOWLEDGEMENTS

This work has grown out of a project initiated by the History Publications Group of Leeds University School of Education. We are very grateful for the support and encouragement of other members of the Group, particularly Michael Collinson, Elizabeth Foster, Bill Stephens and Keith Laybourn.

We would also like to acknowledge the assistance of Bill Connor of Leeds District Archives, Peter Morrish of the Brotherton Library, Leeds University, and Carol Boddington of Humberside County Record Office, Beverley. Thanks are due to Maureen Williams, Bessie Stott and Neil Betteridge for their individual contributions to the work.

Particular gratitude is, of course, accorded to the Earl of Harewood (5, 12, 24), J. R. Chichester Constable (16–18, 20, 22, 27, 33 and 41), the Duke of Buccleuch (32), Lord St Oswald (6), and Duff Pennington Ramsden (43) for permission to use copies of documents from their family archives as illustrations.

The following illustrations also appear by courtesy of the West Yorkshire Archive Service, Leeds (5, 6, 10, 12, 14, 23, 24, 37–40, 43, 45, and 47–49), Humberside County Record Office (16–18, 20, 22, 27, 29, 33), Special Collections, Brotherton Library, Leeds University (frontispiece, 19, 25, 26, 34, and 46), Brynmor Jones Library, Hull University (28 and 44), Cumbria Record Office, Barrow-in-Furness (32), Leeds City Libraries (36) and Buckinghamshire Record Office (50).

NAMES

OF THE

ACTING MAGISTRATES & PRINCIPAL OFFICERS,

WITHIN THE WEST-RIDING OF THE COUNTY OF YORK.

WILLIAM WENTWORTH FITZWILLIAM,

Earl Fitzwilliam, Viscount Milton, and Baron Fitzwilliam, in England; Earl Fitwilliam, Viscount Milton, and Baron Fitzwilliam, in Ireland; Lord Lieutenant and Custos Rotulorum of the said West-Riding, City of York, and County of the same, or Ainsty of York; and One of the Lords of HIS MAJESTY's Most Honourable Privy Council.

Names.	Places of Abode.	When Oath of Qualification taken.
Sir John Beckett, Baronet...	Gledhow, near Leeds...	1784, April 19th.
Francis Edmunds, Esquire..................................	Worsbro', near Barnsley............	... ... September 24th.
John Dixon, Esquire	... ,, ... ,,...... ... ,,...	1785, July 28th.
The Reverend James Geldart, Clerk... .. .., ...	Kirkdeighton, near Wetherby	1793, January 15th.
The Reverend Robert Darley Waddilove, D.D.....	Ripon ... ... ,,...... ...,,...... ... ,,... ...	...... Ditto.
Bryan Cooke, Esquire...	Owston, near Doncaster ,.....................	1795, October 14th.
The Reverend William Wood, Clerk	Woodthorpe, near Wakefield	1796, January 14th.
The Reverend Jeremiah Dixon, Clerk..............	Woolley, near Wakefield	...... Ditto.
Benjamin Brooksbank, Esquire...	Healaugh-Hall, near Tadcaster	February 19th.
The Reverend Henry William Coulthurst, D.D.....	Halifax	1797, January 18th.
Walter Fawkes, Esquire	Farnley-Hall, near Otley ,,...	... .. April 24th.
The Hon. Granville Anson Chetwynd Stapylton...	Wighill-Park, near York	... ... October 3d.
Godfrey Wentworth Wentworth, Esquire	Woolley-Park, near Wakefield......	1798, January 11th.
Hugh Parker, Esquire ;... ... ... ,,......	Woodthorpe, near Sheffield	1799, September 2d.
The Reverend John Lowe, Clerk	Wentworth, near Rotherham	...... Ditto.
John Dearden, Esquire	Hollings-Hall, near Halifax	1801, July 16th.
The Reverend Thomas Dunham Whitaker, L.L.D...	Holme, near Colne	1802, May 27th.
Joseph Priestley, Esquire	Whitewindows, near Halifax	... .. July 15th.
Thomas Horton, Esquire......	Howroyd, near Halifax	...... Ditto.
James Archibald Stuart Wortley, Esquire, M.P. ...	Wortley-Hall, near Sheffield	1803, January 19th.
The Reverend William Robert Hay, Clerk............	Ackworth, near Pontefract	1804, April 9th.
The Reverend John Myers, Clerk	Shipley, near Bradford ,.........................	...... May 17th.
The Reverend Lamplugh Hird, Clerk	Low-Moor-House, near Bradford	...... Ditto.
Matthew Wilson, Esquire .... ,,......	Eshton-Hall, near Skipton... .,.	... .. November 8th.
The Reverend Stuart Corbett, D.D	Wortley, near Sheffield	1805, January 23d.
The Reverend Thomas Drake, D.D......................	Rochdale	... .. July 18th.
The Honourable Frederick Lumley......	Tickhill-Castle, near Worksop......	1807, January 21st.
William Wrightson, Esquire	Cusworth, near Doncaster.....................	...... Ditto.
The Right Honourable Lord Viscount Milton, M.P.	Wentworth-House, near Rotherham	... ... October 14th.
Thomas Athorpe, Esquire	Dinnington, near Worksop	1808, January 20th.
Edward Ferrand, Esquire	St. Ives, near Bradford	... .. April 25th.
Sir William Chambers Bagshaw, Knight.............	The Oakes, near Sheffield	...... Ditto.
Benjamin Dealtry, Esquire.................	Lofthouse-Hall, near Wakefield	...... Ditto.
The Reverend John Forster, Clerk.	Ryther, near Selby .,.	1809, January 10th.
Michael Stocks, Esquire......	Catherine-House, near Halifax.............	...... Ditto 12th.
Samuel Wilkes Waud, Esquire	Camblesforth, near Selby ....,...	...... Ditto.
Christopher Nevile, Esquire	Scaftworth, near Bawtry... , ...	... .. Ditto 18th,
The Reverend Richard Lacy, Clerk	Whiston, near Rotherham ...,,...	...... Ditto.
Ralph Creyke, jun. Esquire	Rawcliffe-Hall, near Snaith	...... April 22d.
Sir William Ingilby, Baronet...	Ripley, near Knaresbro'...	1812, January 14th.
John Williamson, Esquire	Ripon..........	...... Ditto.
Joseph Scott, Esquire...... ... . ,,......... ...	Badsworth, near Pontefract......................	...... Ditto 16th.
Godfrey Higgins, Esquire ... ...,,.........	Skellow-Grange, near Ferrybridge...... ...	...... Ditto 22d.
John Fullerton, Esquire...... ... .,.	Thribergh, near Doncaster	... ,,. Ditto.
The Reverend Henry Stephen Milner, L.L.D... ...	Thribergh, near Doncaster	...... Ditto.
The Reverend George Chandler, Clerk	Treeton, near Rotherham... ,....................	...... Ditto.
John Henry Smyth, Esquire, M.P........	Heath, near Wakefield	...... May 14th.
William Vavasour, Esquire......	Weston-Hall, near Otley	... .. July 14th.
St. Andrew Warde, jun. Esquire	Melton, near Doncaster .... ,......	...... October 8th.
Ellis Cunliffe Lister, Esquire	Calverley, near Bradford	...... Ditto.
Sir Francis Lindley Wood, Baronet.....	Hemsworth, near Pontefract...	... .. Ditto.
The Reverend Alexander Cooke, Clerk	Loversall, near Doncaster...	...... November 12th,

List of West Riding magistrates, 1812–13.

FOREWORD

Country house visiting continues to be among the most popular of today's pastimes, but for most visitors, the pleasures gained come from architecture, landscaped gardens and parks, and admiring works of art. Likewise books on country houses tend to be devoted to these more familiar aspects. This book provides a new key; it leads us past the farm buildings and stables through servants quarters, into the estate office, and unlocks the secrets of the family archives often languishing in the muniment room.

Happily, many historic houses still preserve their estate papers intact and employ archivists. Additionally in recent years an increasing number have been made more accessible through being deposited in county record offices, universities and libraries. *Researching the Country House* provides practical guidance to the often bewildering task of locating estate papers, and then finding a way into them (especially those legal documents with complex preambles and subclauses). For those with limited time, it is an essential tool to help research the historical material.

The social history of country houses and their great estates has often been explored, but here we also have a concise survey of the major issues (ranging from finding homes for souvenirs of the Grand Tour to the servant problem) vividly evoked through an abundance of engaging anecdotes and other accounts quoted from documentary sources as diverse as diaries, marriage settlements, builders' contracts, maps, wage sheets, gamebooks and paintings. We are reminded of the importance of great houses to the economic and political life of the communities, as employer, landlord and as patron of local institutions and industry. Documents from country house archives reveal how tedious and uncomfortable life in a great house could really be for the family, especially when the master was away. Life below stairs had a distinct hierarchy, as distinct as the levels of the peerage and gentry, as is clearly set out in this study. It will appeal equally to the leisured historian, keen to seek out the history of a particular family or local community, to the academic of all ages in need of the tools of the trade (especially if visiting from overseas), and to the lover of great homes and estates keen to discover an alternative perspective to even the most familiar and famous houses.

Visiting country houses is itself part of our history. Beaulieu Abbey for example, has been open to the public since the 1890s but more buildings were opened in earnest in 1952 – just three years after the Marquis of Bath opened Longleat, and three years before the Duke of Bedford opened Woburn. In addition to seeing the growth of public interest at my own home, I have had the pleasure as Chairman of

FOREWORD

English Heritage of assisting the survival of great houses, their contents and parks. Today's visitors are better informed, more curious and enthusiastic than ever before. Thanks to popular research and publications such as this, the standards of country house maintenance, preservation and research are improving all the time.

Well-trod material can yield endless new evidence provided each generation brings its own fresh appraisal; I hope that this book will help to recruit many to the pleasures and potential of archival research and country house visiting.

LORD MONTAGU OF BEAULIEU

INTRODUCTION

Of the many books written about country houses very few have attempted to explore the vital relationship that exists between the house and its estate.[1] The tendency is to view them in isolation from the wider world; to see them as treasure houses sealed from the realities of daily life. This apparent obsession with the architecture and furnishings is closely related to the necessity of attracting visitors to houses in ever increasing numbers. But the price is a high one. The public does not see a family home but rather a museum or pastiche. In fact, in many cases, the country house has been adapted to modern conditions and reduced in size; the house admired today is often a mere shadow of its former self.

Country houses are still being built, as has recently been demonstrated, by old, established landowners.[2] Owners have either moved out of their old houses or demolished them and built on the foundations. In this way they are perpetuating the historical process of adaptation which, in the sixteenth century, saw the abandonment of castles and, in subsequent centuries, the demolition and rebuilding of country houses to the prevailing standards of taste and comfort.

The important and often ignored role of the country house is that of the headquarters of a functioning agricultural estate. While today that may appear to be of very limited significance, before the First World War and during the period with which this book is concerned, the sixteenth century onwards, it meant something quite different. The ownership of land was the key to political power, and estates grew with the ambition and wealth of the landowner. The country house blossomed or decayed in accordance with his fortunes and character, and those of his successors. The process, which had feudal origins, was greatly accelerated by the Crown's sale of monastic lands after 1537. The height of ambition of the wealthiest in the land was to build a country seat on a large estate, obtain a political appointment and establish a dynasty. Opportunities for such men flourished in the seventeenth century and many aristocratic families were founded at this time. When the government searched for an appropriate reward for great service to the nation, it was a title, together with a country estate, that, above all, demonstrated its gratitude. As his reward for winning the battle of Blenheim in 1704, the Duke of Marlborough was presented with the royal manor of Woodstock and 2000 acres on which Queen Anne intended to build him a palace to commemorate the achievement. Similarly, Stratfield Saye was purchased for the Duke of Wellington after the battle of Waterloo.

For the local historian the country house has generated and preserved a vast amount of evidence. As the parish church has served as the repository for records, not only of the church, but also of the community it serves, so the country house has held, not only the material relating to housekeeping and furnishing, but also the central records of, in many cases, a vast estate. Country houses stood at the centre of large, if fluctuating, estates, ranging from 1000 to 100,000 acres or more. The great estates could be widely dispersed. The Duke of Buckingham owned some 56,823 acres in 1837 of which 26,838 acres were in Buckinghamshire around his country house at Stowe, 17,282 were in Ireland, 9225 in Hampshire, 1836 in Cornwall, 1640 in Middlesex, together with a plantation of unknown size in Jamaica. Similarly, the Fitzwilliam estate in the 1870s comprised three large blocks of land, an Irish estate of 80,000 acres in county Wicklow, a small estate in North Yorkshire, 19,000 acres around the family seat at Wentworth Woodhouse in West Yorkshire and some 24,000 acres in the East Midlands.[3] The smaller estates on the other hand might be confined to a single county. The administration of great estates was complex and dispersed among numerous agents, solicitors and surveyors but the landowner, of necessity, kept central control over all activities. He was ultimately responsible for the employment of farm managers, gamekeepers, woodmen, house servants, etc., the letting of land and the leasing of mineral rights. The houses, since there was often more than one country seat and, perhaps, a town house in London, needed housekeepers, butlers, footmen and other servants. As the most influential figure in the neighbourhood, the landowner had a wider responsibility as patron and arbiter. The position could be formal, as where the landowner was a Member of Parliament, a Justice of the Peace or lord of the manor, or less formal as general benefactor and patron of local charities, schools or, in the nineteenth century, agricultural societies. The words of the seventh Duke of Bedford to the seventh Duke of Devonshire in May 1858 reflect the widely held view of the landowner's role:[4]

> The duties and responsibilities of such an estate as yours and mine are very great – we must discharge them as best we can, and make a good amount to look back upon at the close of life – I am pleased to see you paying so much attention to yours – it will afford a fund of satisfaction to others as well as to yourself – and conduce to the well being of those who live upon them.

Hardly any aspect of country life was, therefore, untouched by the influence of the landowner of the great estates and even lesser landowners played their parts.

The purpose of this book is to reveal and exemplify the range and richness of the records of most significance for the country house. In general, the main types of material to be found amongst family and estate records have been well analysed elsewhere.[5] The difficulty for the local historian is that series of records of an area may be located amongst the family and estate papers of a landowner held many miles away. In the case of the estates of the Duke of Buckingham from Stowe, they are held by the Huntington Library in San Marino, California, USA. Few local historians would feel the need to make such a journey. Alternatively, some family and estate records are still held in the country houses to which they relate and research is positively discouraged. Increasingly, since the last war, however, the records of great and small landed estates have come to be deposited in county record offices and university and other libraries and numerous stately homes have been more prepared to enable serious research to be undertaken on their papers. Thus it is possible, for example, to see the records of the Duke of Devonshire at Chatsworth, on request. Serious research amongst the family and estate collections in local record offices and libraries is generally free of charge.

In many cases, the most difficult aspect of the problem for the local historian is establishing the existence of material of relevance to his or her interest or locality. As with most historical investigation, clues are required to assist the search. One of the most useful starting points is a recent publication by Michael Holmes, indexing articles on country houses in *Country Life* and similar basic sources.[6] Although mostly aimed at the art historian, the index has its value for those attempting to

THE
VICTORIA HISTORY
OF THE COUNTIES
OF ENGLAND
HAMPSHIRE AND
THE ISLE OF WIGHT

WESTMINSTER
ARCHIBALD CONSTABLE
AND COMPANY LIMITED

1 Title page of first volume of *Victoria County History* to be published, 1900.

identify families associated with particular houses. Naturally, many other possible methods are available, not least a simple enquiry at your local reference library or record office. But, in the case of a long vacated house or one that has been destroyed, the task may be more difficult. It will certainly be more problematical in a locality where the landowners were non-resident. Not all landowners were as determined to mark their connection with a place as the Marquesses of Bute, who gave family names to so many streets and parks in the city of Cardiff. Nevertheless, surviving public-house names or street names can provide clues. Memorials in churches can also reveal family links with a parish.

A number of other basic sources should be mentioned, not least the volumes of the *Victoria County History* that have been published. They aim to provide an overview of the local history of a county and have particularly useful parish histories. The histories of 12 counties have been completed since 1899, 12 are currently being worked on, 16 have been begun but remain unfinished. The texts of their parish histories alone have expanded over the years. Originally conceived at 900 words, they had risen to 2000 by 1910 and 9700 by 1968. Today the average is 11,000 words, reflecting the enormous increase in accessible source material.

Each county also has a record or archaeological society which has been producing transactions since the mid-nineteenth century. From the Cambridge Antiquarian Society, founded in 1840, to the Record Society for the publication of original documents relating to Lancashire and Cheshire, founded in 1878, they have been producing articles of significance for local history. Amongst these articles, footnotes and references can reveal the identities of noted families in the past and their link with local country seats. Above all, there is the Royal Commission on Historical Manuscripts, which has published 238 Reports and Calendars of privately owned collections of historical papers since its establishment in 1869. Despite the concentration on pre-1800 material and the omission of personal and private papers, they can be both fascinating and frustrating sources of information. The recent update of the locations of collections is invaluable and reveals the predation to which family papers can become subject over time.[7] A recent article on the Portland Archive, accepted for the nation in lieu of tax in 1986, reveals how much more material survives than was reported upon in the ten volumes published 1891 to 1931. It shows how the family built up its estates and accumulated its papers and the way in which the papers are distributed among five repositories: Nottingham-shire Archives Office; Nottinghamshire University Library MSS Dept.; the British Library, Dept. of Western MSS; Hampshire Record Office; and the Bodleian Library, Oxford, Dept. of Western MSS. Yet more material, not part of that accepted for the nation, is noted, particularly the Ayrshire estate papers in Strathclyde Regional Archives, Ayr, and the Scottish Record Office, and 60 trunks of Welbeck estate records (not yet catalogued) deposited in the Nottinghamshire Archives Office in 1985. Most particularly, the article demonstrates that the papers are not a closed collection as the Cavendish-Bentinck family continues and the Welbeck and other estates still generate records.[8] The local historian needs determination and imagination to unearth relevant material in an archive whether on this or a smaller scale. Organically related, they nevertheless become fragmented by carelessness, whim and administrative convenience, even war damage. Some vital records of title may remain with solicitors, some items of particular interest may have become exhibits in the houses themselves. There will be frustrating gaps in surviving evidence, but, for those interested in reconstituting their community in the past, the records of the country house are invaluable.

HISTORICAL MANUSCRIPTS COMMISSION.

THIRTEENTH REPORT, APPENDIX, PART II.

THE

MANUSCRIPTS

OF HIS GRACE

THE DUKE OF PORTLAND,

PRESERVED AT

WELBECK ABBEY.

VOL. II.

Presented to both Houses of Parliament by Command of Her Majesty.

LONDON:
PRINTED FOR HER MAJESTY'S STATIONERY OFFICE,
BY EYRE AND SPOTTISWOODE,
PRINTERS TO THE QUEEN'S MOST EXCELLENT MAJESTY.

And to be purchased, either directly or through any Bookseller, from
EYRE AND SPOTTISWOODE, EAST HARDING STREET, FLEET STREET, E.C., and
32, ABINGDON STREET, WESTMINSTER, S.W.; or
JOHN MENZIES & Co., 12, HANOVER STREET, EDINBURGH, and
90, WEST NILE STREET, GLASGOW; or
HODGES, FIGGIS, & Co., LIMITED, 104, GRAFTON STREET, DUBLIN.

1893.

[C.—6827.–I.] *Price 2s.*

2 Title page of part II of Historical Manuscripts Commission Report on the records of the Duke of Portland, published as an appendix to the Thirteenth Report in 1893.

Chapter One

THE ARISTOCRACY: LANDOWNERSHIP, STATUS AND TITLE

Aristocracy

There is an old Yorkshire saying which runs as follows: Lord Rockingham built a house at Wentworth fit for the Prince of Wales; Sir Rowland Winn built a house at Nostell fit for Lord Rockingham and Mr Wrightson at Cusworth built a house fit for Sir Rowland Winn. Whoever entertained these thoughts had observed an important characteristic of eighteenth-century landed society; namely, that country house owners were differentiated in terms of income and status and their homes were intended to be visible symbols of their wealth, political standing and social aspirations. Rockingham, Winn and Wrightson represent three important groups – the hereditary peerage, the baronetcy and the gentry. Between them were distinctions of political function, wealth and privilege and yet they had sufficient in common to be counted members of the same estate, the aristocracy. The shared interests of aristocrats can be summarized as follows:

> They were landed – ownership of land was a chief requirement for entry into the aristocracy.
> They subscribed to roughly the same ideals.
> They saw themselves as a ruling class.
> They had a high regard for birthright and inheritance.
> They were part of a kinship network through intermarriage and social mobility.

To explain the origin and development of the aristocracy would require a chapter in itself; only the briefest outline is possible here. The eighteenth century is the high point in the story. It was at that time that the most potent of all the forces that had shaped the British aristocracy, the Crown, ceased to control government policy and patronage. Following the political and constitutional struggles of the seventeenth century, those powers were firmly in the hands of the great landowning families. In order to understand how the Rockinghams, Winns and Wrightsons came to dominate British society it is necessary to go back to the thirteenth and fourteenth centuries.

The peerage

The origins of the peerage are to be found in the feudalism of the early Middle Ages. Under the Norman and early Angevin kings, tenants-in-chief had the duty of attending the king's court, the *Curia Regis*. In the thirteenth century it became

Henry Lascelles,

EARL OF HAREWOOD,

VISCOUNT LASCELLES and **BARON HAREWOOD,**
of HAREWOOD-HOUSE, in the County of York ;

Lord Lieutenant *and* Custos Rotulorum
of the West-Riding of the County of York, and of
the City of York, and County of the same, or
Ainsty of York ;

To Godfrey Wentworth Junr Esquire   Woolley

By Virtue of the Power and Authority in me vested, **I DO HEREBY
APPOINT** and **COMMISSION** you, to be a **DEPUTY-LIEUTENANT** of
the West-Riding of the County of York, City and County of the City of York ;
(your Qualification having been delivered in to the Clerk of the Peace for the
same Riding, and your Name having been by me certified to his Majesty, who
has not signified his Disapprobation of you within Fourteen Days after the
laying of such Certificate before him :) You are therefore hereby required to
execute the Office of a Deputy-Lieutenant within the above-mentioned
Precincts ; and in all Things to conform yourself to the Duties thereof.

Given under my Hand and Seal the *Eighteenth* of *June*
in the Year of our Lord 183*1*

ROBINSON AND HERNAMAN, PRINTERS, LEEDS.

Harewood

---

3 Commission of Godfrey Wentworth as Deputy Lord Lieutenant of the West Riding,
1831.

---

customary for the king to issue personal writs of summons to his great landowning barons to attend Parliament on a regular basis, and their heirs likewise. By 1300 there were 13 families that could be described as being an hereditary peerage. They formed a powerful and distinctive group. From the time of Richard II any new peerage was formally confirmed by Letters Patent. The patent defined the peerage and its mode of descent, usually to direct male descendants by primogeniture. By the Tudor period the number of peers had increased to 60; in 1714 there were 170 and at the end of the nineteenth century there were over 500. Today, the peerage consists of five ranks – duke, marquess, earl, viscount and baron, which titles can be of England, Scotland, Ireland or the United Kingdom. Details of peers and their living relatives have been published periodically since 1713 in Debrett's *Peerage and Baronetage*. A later series, Burke's *Peerage, Baronetage and Knightage* (from 1826) gives paragraph pedigrees of all living peers and baronets. One very ancient peerage is that of Lord Mowbray. The entry in Burke reads as follows:

> The 26th Baron Mowbray, 27th Baron Segrave and 23rd Baron Stourton. His Lordship is heir general of the House of Howard and Talbot (of which his heirs male are the Duke of Norfolk and the Earl of Shrewsbury) and is senior co-heir to the earldom of Norfolk (1312) and to the baronies of Talbot, Howard, Strange de Blackmere, Broase of Gower, Greystock, Dacre of Gillesland, Ferrers of Wemme, Verdon, Darcy of Darcy, Giffard of Brimmesfield, and co-heir to the baronies of Kerdeston, Dagworth, Fitz-Warine, Fitz-Payne, Argentine, Darcy of Darcy, etc.

Lord Mowbray claims to be Premier Baron of England and can cite a judgement of his fellow peers in support of his claim:

> The House of Lords on 26 July 1877 resolved that it was proved by the Writ of Summons addressed to Roger de Mowbray in 11 Edward I (1283) and the other evidence that the Barony of Mowbray was in the reign of Edward I vested in Roger Mowbray. It was therefore regarded as proved that Roger Lord Mowbray was summoned to parliament by one of the earliest Writs which could create a peerage.[1]

Peerages can be controversial; they can also be dormant or extinct. More than half the peerages created by James I were extinct within a century. The most reliable account of peerages, current, extinct, dormant and in abeyance, is to be found in the *Complete Peerage* (1887) edited by George Edward Cokayne. For subsequent developments it is necessary to consult the House of Lords Record Office.[2]

The gentry

The origins of the gentry are also to be found in feudal society. Knights, the fighting men who followed the Conqueror into England in the eleventh century, were rewarded with grants of land for their services. They held these lands directly from the king or, more often, from a baron, in return for military service. The male descendants of a knight served as esquires in their teenage years and were dubbed when they came of age. A landowner who did not take up his knighthood remained an esquire all his life. As in the case of peers, military service in return for landholding gradually disappeared and by 1300 a money payment was the norm. Consequently, instead of being primarily a professional soldier, the knight became a man of substance with considerable landed resources. Increasingly, knights, squires and gentlemen were drawn into serving the Crown as local government officials. The coat of arms, once an indicator of military status, became the status

THE

Peerage of *England :*

OR, AN

·Hiftorical and Genealogical

A C C O U N T

Of the Prefent

N O B I L I T Y.

CONTAINING,

The DESCENT, CREATIONS, and moft Remarkable ACTIONS of them and their ANCESTORS.

Alfo, the Chief Titles of Honour *and* Preferment *they now enjoy* ; *with their* Marriages *and* Iffue ; *conti- nued to this* Time, *and the Paternal* Coat of Arms *of each* Family, *Engrav'd and Blazon'd.*

Collected as well from our beft Hiftorians, Publick Records, and other fufficient Authorities, as from the perfonal Informations of moft of the Nobility.

In Two P A R T S.

The THIRD EDITION Corrected, and very much Enlarg'd with many Valuable Memoirs, never before printed. And an Account of thofe Families advanc'd by his prefent Majefty King *George.* To which is alfo added, a General Index of the feveral Families of *Great Britain* and *Ireland,* &c. allied by Marriage or Inter-marriage to the Noble Families mention'd in this Work.

V O L. II.

LONDON : Printed by *E. J.* and fold by *Arthur Collins* at the *Black-Boy* in *Fleet-ftreet,* and *J. Morphew* near *Stationers·Hall.* MDCCXV.

4 Collins' *Peerage of England*, 1717, title page.

symbol of the landed aristocracy and in the fourteenth century the same privilege was extended to the lesser nobility, esquires and gentlemen. The hereditary connection gradually disappeared and knighthood became very much a personal honour, a reward for services to the Crown. The legal obligation dating from 1306 which required a landowner worth £40 a year to claim the privilege was finally abolished in 1646.

The title of baronet dates from the early seventeenth century. It was a title created by James I in 1611 to raise money for the maintenance of troops in Ulster. A baronet is the highest rank of the gentry and the lowest of the hereditary dignities. In terms of precedence, the baronet comes above the knight and below the baron. Baronets and knights both have the formal title, Sir, but a baronet includes after his name the abbreviation Bart. or Bt. For over 200 years, from 1616 to 1827, the eldest sons of baronets were entitled to claim knighthood on coming of age.

Because peerages are awarded by royal grant it is a relatively easy task to calculate the numbers of peers reign by reign. The demography of the baronetcy is more complex. It is possible that between 1611 and 1800 no less than 1226 baronetcies of England and Great Britain were granted, and the best time for obtaining one would seem to have been the reign of Charles II. By 1665 Charles II had awarded 304 English and 51 Scottish and Irish titles. Queen Victoria was enthusiastic about knighthoods and between 1840 and 1900 she dubbed no less than 1275 knights bachelor. It is even more difficult to make confident statements about the numbers of esquires and gentlemen. Thomas Wilson at the end of the sixteenth century, Gregory King in the later seventeenth and Patrick Colquhoun at the beginning of the nineteenth century each attempted a careful calculation but their figures have been called into question by present-day historians. In the words of one authority, 'such is the disparate and inconclusive nature of surviving evidence, that any attempt to assess the size of the aristocracy through time cannot hope to offer more than trend guidelines'.[3]

The ideal of the landed gentleman dates from the decay of feudalism in the fourteenth century. It lasted until the middle decades of the nineteenth century when, in the context of industrialization and urbanization, the entrepreneurial or middle-class ideal gained the ascendancy. For roughly 500 years the aristocracy (nobility and gentry) dominated British society and determined its values and standards.

The revolution in landownership in the sixteenth century

The growth in the size of the gentry was a remarkable feature of the late sixteenth and early seventeenth centuries. The increase was due, in large measure, to the ability of the commoners to purchase suitable estates and the willingness of the Crown to admit new armorial bearings. In the 200 years 1500 to 1700 it is estimated that the gentry tripled whilst the population doubled and that the gentry's share of the land increased from roughly 30 to 50 per cent.[4] The most striking feature of the Elizabethan age was the number of gentlemen and their power in relation to other sections of the community. As G. R. Elton has observed, it was the middling sort of people – those between the Crown and the great magnates on the one hand and the landless and small farmers on the other – who came into their own.[5] How did this come about?

Calke Abbey in Derbyshire, like many other country houses, stands on the site of a medieval religious house secularized in the reign of Henry VIII. In common with a much smaller number of houses, it actually incorporates some of the fabric of that house. Calke was a priory, not an abbey, but the name serves as a reminder of the revolution in landownership that occurred in the sixteenth century. At the dissolution of the monasteries this small cell or estate belonging to the Augustinian canons at Repton was confiscated by the Crown and the property eventually came on to the market. What happened at Calke happened nationwide between 1536 and 1540 and in the great shift in the balance of property owning the beneficiaries were royal servants, local gentry, wealthy merchants and lawyers.

To have worked for Thomas Cromwell and the King in bringing an end to the monasteries brought rich rewards for some. Sir John Tregonwell, one of Cromwell's commissioners, obtained the site and most of the possessions of Milton Abbey in Dorset. Richard Rich bought Leighs Priory in Essex and had it converted into a country house. In the north of England Dr Thomas Legh acquired Nostell Priory and its large estates. The descendants of some of the older medieval lordships did not ignore the opportunity to expand their territories. Henry Clifford of Skipton Castle in Yorkshire bought large estates in Craven and a major part of the Bolton Priory estate. The Talbots, Earls of Shrewsbury, acquired many monastic properties – Glossop in Derbyshire, Worksop Priory and Rufford Abbey in Nottinghamshire and Rotherham in Yorkshire. Amongst the interesting new-comers to the ranks of the aristocracy were the Russells, the Wriothesleys and the Levesons. James Leveson of Wolverhampton had begun a policy of systematic land purchase in the south Staffordshire area from 1528 onwards and the dissolution of the monasteries provided him with a golden opportunity to found a landed dynasty. Between 1537 and 1540 more than 20,000 acres of land from Trentham Priory, Stone Priory, Lilleshall Abbey and Wombridge flowed into his hands. As J. R. Wordie has observed, he must have made a considerable fortune in the wool trade, for when it came to buying estates his purse seemed bottomless. Leveson made his family major landowners·in two counties and still managed to die a very wealthy man.[6] In the seventeenth century the family improved its pedigree by marrying into the Gower family with its authentic Norman ancestry.

Another newcomer, John Russell, achieved prominence in the reign of Henry VIII as a soldier and diplomat. He married a rich, propertied Buckinghamshire widow and in 1539 became Lord Russell of Chenies. He held many high offices and in 1550 received the title Earl of Bedford. When he died in 1555 Russell had a vast estate of former monastic lands in Devon, Cornwall, Nottingham and Bucking-hamshire, as well as the territories formerly belonging to Woburn Abbey.

Thomas Wriothesley, first Earl of Southampton, was equally successful in the service of Thomas Cromwell. As Lord Chancellor he used his substantial income to invest in monastic and other properties as well as receiving substantial grants from his royal master. Between 1536 and 1550 he took possession of the abbeys and estates of Titchfield and Beaulieu, eighteen manors in Hampshire, three in Devon and three in Dorset.[7]

The peak years in the scramble for ecclesiastical properties were the 1540s and 1550s. By the end of the reign of Edward VI a good three-quarters had been disposed of by the Crown. Sales continued in the reigns of Elizabeth I and James I. The first of the Stuart kings was ably assisted in this by Arthur Ingram. Between 1605 and 1614 nearly three-quarters of a million pounds' worth of land came on to the market. Ingram was the middleman, bringing together the investors and negotiating the terms of the contracts. He received a knighthood for his services to the Crown in 1613. Using his growing wealth, this son of a London merchant began to finance property deals in Yorkshire. He purchased the estate and mansion of Temple Newsam, near Leeds, and made it the principal family seat.[8]

The fortunes of those who joined the ranks of the aristocracy from the sixteenth to the eighteenth centuries were based on one or more of three main sources – the favours of the court, the spoils of the monasteries and profits from trade. The wealth of the Fitzwilliam family of Milton in Northamptonshire owed much to the mercantile achievements of London alderman Sir William Fitzwilliam. Sir William, a prominent Merchant Taylor and Merchant of the Staple of Calais, used his wealth to purchase Milton in 1502, and before his death in 1534 he had accumulated lands and manors in Essex, Lincolnshire and Hertfordshire.[9] Edwin Lascelles was able to finance the purchase of the Yorkshire estates of Gawthorpe and Harewood in 1739 with money that his father had made in colonial administration and the West Indies trade.[10] The progress of the Spencers of Althorp in Northamptonshire was exceptional. They acquired great wealth and status through a century of successful sheep-farming. When Sir Robert Spencer was created Baron Spencer of Wormleighton in 1603 it was generally recognized that he was one of the wealthiest men in England. The huge profits from farming enabled him to acquire additional properties in the brisk land market of the early seventeenth century. The Wormleighton block of estates was consolidated by the acquisition of the Warwickshire manors of Priors Marston, Priors Hardwick and Radbourn, the manor of Hinton in Woodford and the manor of Byfield in Northamptonshire. Additions were also made to the Althorp estates with the purchase of the manor of Muscott and the lordship of Nobottle and Little Brington.[11]

The Civil War and landownership

Whilst there are few today who would hold the view that the primary cause of the Civil War was the rise of the gentry and the accumulation by them of substantial landholdings at the expense of the Crown and nobility, the economic circumstances of the gentry in the early seventeenth century continue to provide historians with a compelling area of study. There can be no doubt, however, that civil war in the mid-seventeenth century brought about another major disturbance in the land market, the last before the twentieth century. Royalists suffered either confiscation of property or heavy fines. Many did recover their losses but the pressure of mortgages and taxation encouraged land sales.

The fortunes of individual families throughout the two centuries from the Reformation to the Civil War provide fascinating studies. For many it was a series of up and downs. Take the Ashburnham family, for example. The Ashburnhams were small landowners in Sussex from the twelfth century. By the reign of Elizabeth I they were prospering modestly and the College of Heralds recorded for them a pedigree of doubtful reliability but befitting their station and antiquity. Sir John Ashburnham was knighted by James I and the family looked set for fame and fortune. But Sir John wasted his resources and died in the Fleet Prison in 1620. His eldest son, John the Cavalier, restored the family fortunes through a career at Court

5 Terminal part of a rental for the estate of Gawthorpe and Harewood drawn up at the time of purchase by the Lascelles family in 1739.

where he enjoyed the patronage of the Duke of Buckingham. The Civil War proved a major setback. Ashburnham was required by the Parliamentarians to compound for half the value of his estate and was generally harassed for supporting the king. At the Restoration in 1660 he recovered his place as Groom of the Bedchamber and Charles II rewarded the family with the gift of a house at Chiswick and preferential leases as compensation for the loans made to his father. Ashburnham was succeeded by his grandson, another John, who continued the tradition of royal service but combined it with successful business ventures. John's enthusiastic support for William of Orange earned him the title Baron in 1698. The family estates at this time were not extensive but through a series of well-planned marriages they grew rapidly; for example, the second Baron, William, married a Bedfordshire heiress. Yet within five months of the marriage both fell victim to smallpox. The third baron, another John, continued the tradition of service at Court and was created Earl of Ashburnham in 1739. He managed to outlive three wives, each of whom brought dowries in the region of £10,000. Moreover, there were few children to complicate the family inheritance. The second Earl's marriage in 1756 to Elizabeth Crowley, granddaughter of Sir Ambrose Crowley, the great ironmaster and financier, further enhanced the Ashburnham fortune. Within less than a century the Ashburnhams had risen from the ranks of the Sussex gentry to an earldom and extensive properties in Wales, Bedfordshire, Suffolk, Dorset, Lincolnshire and elsewhere.[12]

Muniments of title

In general, the great landowning families have been fascinated by and respectful of their past achievements and down the centuries the muniment rooms and chests of country houses have accumulated large quantities of family archives. Title-deeds, or muniments of title, make up a substantial part of most collections. They are an invaluable source of detailed information about relationships between families, the history of property, continuity of ownership and variations in the physical size of estates. The best-preserved collections offer great potential to the historian. Put simply, a title-deed is a legal document drawn up to transfer property and/or rights from one person to another. West Sussex archivist J. M. L. Booker had this to say about the 5000 title-deeds which form the bulk of the Wiston archives:

> they range from grants of land in the medieval deeds of Billinghurst in Sussex and Seal in Kent to the sale and exchange in 1869 of the town of Steyning. Most of the farms in the Wiston area are covered by original bundles of deeds in which every stage of the build up can be traced. The coverage of the deeds is wide and encompasses more than 60 places in Sussex as well as properties in Derbyshire, Huntingdonshire, Kent, London, Staffordshire, Surrey and Yorkshire.[13]

Continuous coverage such as this over many centuries is rare. More commonly, the historian will run into serious gaps. A. A. Dibben, an authority on title-deeds and editor of the Cowdray archives, relates a sad tale of neglect and destruction.

The muniment room at Cowdray House was in the Kitchen Tower and survived the fire which destroyed the main part of the building in 1793, but, apparently, no attempt was made to rescue the documents, which for more than half a century were left entirely to the mercy of the elements and human predators. In 1873 the chamber floor was reported to have been strewn with papers and parchments, all damp and decaying and many items mutilated by collectors of autographs and seals. Fortunately, a large number of deeds survived and they appear to be complete from 1717 onwards.[14]

Title-deeds can be missing for a variety of reasons. The likelihood increases when estates change hands by sale and when they are acquired through marriage.

Marriage settlements

Reference has already been made to the Ashburnham family's fortunes in the sixteenth and seventeenth centuries. An excellent catalogue of the family archives was published in 1958 which lists many marriage settlements and associated documents dating from 1601. These, as the editor notes, are of great value when trying to establish a chronology of estate accumulation. Some indication of the sort of detail contained in them is provided in the following summary of the marriage settlement of the second Earl to Elizabeth Crowley in 1756:

  (i) how John Crowley senior derived a great personal estate from his business as a dealer in iron goods;
 (ii) how his widow will continue the said business;
(iii) details of the intended marriage of John, Earl of Ashburnham, and Elizabeth Crowley;
 (iv) details of part of the fortune to be transferred to Elizabeth on her marriage;
  (v) a detailed account of the Crowley estates in Suffolk;
 (vi) details of estates in Sussex, Bedford, Dorset and Lancashire to be held in trust to provide a jointure for Elizabeth.[15]

The importance of marriages to heiresses in the building up of estates and restoring family fortunes should not be underestimated. Lord William Howard (1563–1640) married Elizabeth Dacre in 1577 when he was fourteen and she was eight. The alliance brought the Howards the great Dacre estate at Naworth in Cumberland and Henderskelfe (later Castle Howard) in Yorkshire. The fortunes of the main Howard line in the late sixteenth century were so reduced that Thomas Howard was born penniless in a cottage in Romford in Essex. His title of second Earl of Arundel and Surrey was restored in 1604 but it was his marriage to Altheia Talbot, third daughter and eventually sole heiress of Gilbert seventh Earl of Shrewsbury, in 1606 that transformed his finances.[16] It was through marriage settlements that another Roman Catholic family, the Throckmortons of Coughton Court in Warwickshire, accumulated estates in Worcestershire, Warwickshire, Berkshire and Devon. It was through the marriage of George Throckmorton (1721–62) to Anna Maria Paston, for example, that the Throckmortons inherited the Courtnay estate at Molland in north Devon. Appropriately, portraits of Maria and her parents are displayed at Coughton Court. What surely must have been the marriage of the year in 1819 was that of Lord Stewart, the future third Marquis of Londonderry, to Emily Frances Anne, only daughter of Sir Henry Vane-Tempest. Frances Anne was a ward of Chancery from the time of her father's death in 1813 until her marriage. All her father's estates in County Durham, including Seaham Harbour and a number of collieries, had passed to her. Not only was she one of the greatest heiresses in England at that time, she was described as being tall, elegant, very beautiful and possessing a fascination of manner few could withstand.[17] Marriage settlements can be lengthy documents and this one is no exception, there are 22 volumes!

Accounts of the making of marriage settlements are sometimes to be found in letters, diaries, memoirs or even solicitors' bills. Samuel Pepys records in his diary in 1665 how he helped to arrange a marriage between Jemimah, the daughter of his patron, Lord Sandwich, and Sir George Carteret's eldest son. Pepys was well briefed about the matter:

> My Lord, I perceive, entends to give £5000 with her, and expects about £800 per annum joynture . . . My Lord would have had me have consented to leaving the young people together tonight to begin their amours . . . but I advised against it, lest the lady might be too much surprised. So they led him up to his chamber, where I stayed a little to know how he liked the lady; which he told me he did mightily, but Lord, in the dullest insipid manner that ever lover did. So I bid him goodnight . . .[18]

The progress of a marriage settlement is described in the memorandum book of Sir Walter Calverley Bt. Sir Walter gives a detailed picture of the careful negotiations that preceded his marriage to Julia Blackett, the eldest daughter of Sir William Blackett of Newcastle, in 1707. It took two months of intensive deliberations before a settlement was reached. Sir Walter had this to say about his visit to Newcastle:

> I went over and took Samuel Hemingway with me to assist about matters, and the settlement, drawing etc., and staid most of three weeks; and the draught was made very long, but not then fully agreed to, though we had counsil of both sides, and severall meetings both of Mr Wilkinson, Mr Thomlinson and the counsil, and at some of them I was also present myself. They made use of Mr John Ord for drawing the writings, and Mr Barnes counsil for my Lady, and I had Mr John Cuthberts, the recorder of Newcastle, for my counsil. But the matter was not then concluded, upon account of some scruples about the young lady's portion, when it would be due and payable . . .[19]

Lady Blackett decided to seek advice in London about the payment of the portion and other matters and it was some time before everything was ready to be signed and sealed.

Wills

Having acquired an estate and invested heavily in its development and in the building of a house, understandably, the owner wanted the inheritance to pass intact to his descendants. The oldest and most common method of doing this was to make a will. Sir Edward Coke's affairs provide a useful example. The distinguished Chief Justice laid the foundation of what was to become a vast landed estate in the 1570s when he purchased a messuage with ten acres adjoining it in the parish of Tittleshall. He was called to the Bar in 1578 and two years later was able to lay out £3600 to purchase the estate of Godwick adjoining the parish of Tittleshall. Here he built himself a house just a few miles from the modest family home at Mileham. Thereafter, as C.W. James has observed, his investments in land went on with almost monotonous regularity. Sir Edward also married an heiress in 1583, Bridget, the eldest daughter of the ancient family of Paston in Suffolk. Estimates vary as to her inheritance but it was a substantial one. Sir Edward in 1614 was in a position to purchase the Paston family home at Huntingfield and the entire estate for £4500.

In 1612 Sir Edward Coke made his will, giving all his real and personal estate, 'chattels', etc. (except such as were settled on his wife) to certain trustees for the use of his eldest son, Robert, and his heirs, in tail male. In his lifetime the Chief Justice had provided an estate for each of his sons, and the remainder of his possessions (except Stoke Poges and certain other lands that formed the portion of his daughter, Frances – offspring of his second marriage) were strictly entailed on his heir male. So concerned was he that his possessions should descend in the right course that he went so far as to indicate the eldest daughter of his third son, Arthur, as the heiress in case of complete failure of the male line. In later years the large estates given to John, Henry and Clement Coke were added to the 'Grand Estate' of the family, as well as properties which their wives brought with them.[20]

Another great member of this family, Lord Leicester (1697–1759), the creator of Holkham, also left a will. He left all his real estate in the hands of trustees who were directed to raise money to pay off debts not on mortgage. The descent of the house and estates was laid down by the will. His wife, Margaret, was to have the estates for life. After her death they would go to Anne Roberts, his sister, who had contracted a runaway marriage with an officer in the Blues. It was emphasized in the will that the profits of the estate were to go into her hands. After her the estates were to go to Lord Leicester's nephew, Anne's son, Wenman Coke. Anne died before she could benefit but her son succeeded to the estates when Lady Leicester died in 1775. Wenman Coke held the estates for only one year. He died in 1776 and his son, Thomas William Coke, succeeded him as his great-uncle's will had directed. Since then Wenman's direct descendants have lived at Holkham.[21]

Strict settlement

Settlement is crucial to understanding the whole process by which estates have remained intact and it is a subject which in recent years has attracted a good deal of interest and debate amongst historians.[22]

At the beginning of the seventeenth century a variety of forms of settlement were in use. For example, it was not uncommon for a landowner to settle on his eldest son an entailed interest in the estate. In order that the eldest son should not deprive any younger brothers of their provision, they were provided with estates carved from the main inheritance. This is what happened in the case of Sir Edward Coke and his sons. But such a method of provision could seriously reduce the estate, and lands cut off to provide for younger sons were not easily recoverable. Having a large family was often a mixed blessing: too many daughters or younger sons could spell ruin. Of all the legal devices aimed at restricting the power of alienating land, the one attributed to the ingenuity of a mid-seventeenth-century conveyancer, Sir Orlando Bridgeman, received the greatest respect in the courts. It became known as strict settlement and it meant that a landowner could not dispose of his house and lands outright, he was simply the life-tenant. Following Bridgeman, lawyers were careful to include in settlements the clause 'trustees to preserve contingent remainders', which went a long way to ensuring that the estate would pass from the son to the grandson and not leave the son in unfettered possession and able to destroy the grandson's interest.

Settlements are not easy documents to understand and it does help to know where the preamble ends and the new information begins. As Barbara English and John Saville have pointed out in their most helpful monograph on the subject, the real starting point is 'NOW THIS INDENTURE WITNESSETH'.[23] The dominant feature of a settlement is the entail, or pattern of succession it establishes. A typical arrangement was that the estate was conveyed to Lord A for life, then to his son B for life, with remainder in tail to B's eldest son and similar remainders to B's younger children. It was impossible for B to destroy his life-tenancy and gain full powers of alienation over the estate since the settlement included a limitation in favour of trustees, whose duty it was to preserve the interests of B's unborn sons, i.e. the contingent remainders. Eventually, however, B's son would become the tenant in tail and, thus, would have power to dispose of the estate. Before this could happen, however, B and his son would normally agree to resettle the estate, continuing B as life-tenant, with a life-tenancy in remainder to B's son, and with remainder in tail to B's grandson.[24] Once in each generation a time came to resettle the estate. The pressure of family tradition weighed heavily upon father and son, as well as the obligation to maintain and carry forward the family inheritance to future generations. There were also the interests of other members of the family to be taken into account, provision for a bride's jointure (the annuity she would receive if she outlived the bridegroom), for example, and the portions of the children yet to be born. The estate might already be saddled with jointures, portions and pensions arising from a former life-tenant's will and these would have to be respected in any resettlement.

One of the most vivid and detailed accounts of a resettlement on the coming of age of an heir is to be found in the archives of the Sykes family of Sledmere. The marriage of Sir Tatton Sykes, fifth Baronet, and Lady Jessica was, to say the least, a turbulent one. In the 1890s Lady Sykes spent much of her time in London and piled up debts which her husband refused to pay. A crisis developed when Mark Sykes came of age in 1900. For the first time since 1847, the disentailing and resettlement of the estate was possible. Sir Tatton was reluctant to act and was only persuaded to do so when Mark told his father that he was leaving to take part in the South African War. A detailed account of what happened survives in the letters written by Mark Sykes to his future wife, Edith Gorst. The following is a summary of what happened on the evening of Friday 20 April 1900:

> . . . two sitting rooms were engaged at the Hotel Metropole in London, where the elder Sykes usually stayed; in the first were Sir Tatton Sykes, his London solicitor, a head clerk and five other clerks, a conveyancing specialist, the Sledmere agent, and a solicitor for the Allied Assurance Company (the company was to lend £110,000); in the other room were Lady Jessica's solicitor and his two cousins. Negotiations lasted until early the next morning, 'arguing, fighting, changing, erasing, quarrelling, cursing, go to-ing and fro-ing' from 9.45 pm until 1.00 am. By the morning of the 21st, when Mark left for South Africa, the resettlement was made: the estates had been disentailed and resettled once more, in the traditional manner but also including a mortgage of £110,000 to pay off Lady Jessica's debts.[25]

The second Marquess of Bute's father died before signing his will and his marriage articles which meant that when Bute inherited in 1814 he was not the life-tenant but the owner in fee simple of almost the whole of his landed estates. He therefore had full power to dispose of them as he wished. However, when the Marquess married in 1818 he restricted his own freedom of action by granting all his estates in England and Wales to be held in trust for the eldest son of the marriage and to raise portions for the other children and a jointure for the marchioness. But the inclusion of rapidly developing land in the settlement caused problems because it restricted the owner's freedom to mortgage, lease or sell. As a result, land in the vicinity of Cardiff was released from the bonds of settlement through Acts of Parliament in 1827 and 1837.[26]

Pedigrees and coats of arms

Wealth and the ownership of land were the basic qualifications for entry into the aristocracy, but no one had really arrived until he could provide evidence of pedigree and the right to bear arms. Edward Baildon of London's letter to his cousin, Robert Baildon of Baildon in Yorkshire, in 1589 indicates the concern about family history among the sixteenth-century gentry:

> Right deare & well beloued in ye Lord,
> . . . My earnest requeste & suite unto you is that yow would be soe friendly unto me as to send by my Cozen Perslow your Petigree & ours, & how they have beene & arr matched, soe farre as yow may, untill this time. I have viewed the Harrolds' [Heralds] booke Concerning this matter, & as yett I cannott finde itt to be any further than from Watter Baildon. If I Could I would have itt frome ye first of ye name untill this day. I will doe what I Can to bring this to passe. The Harrold of armes will doe whatt he can or may for me, I hope . . . Yr. poor Loving Cozen, ever to Command, Edward Baildon.[27]

Establishing a pedigree was no problem for a family like the Ferrers of Baddesley

S.ʳ Rowland Winn Baronet

6 A coat of arms in flamboyant rococo designed by James Paine. From the period of the 4th Sir Rowland Winn's marriage to Susannah Henshaw, 1729–42.

Clinton in Warwickshire. The Ferrers were an ancient Norman family and Henry de Ferrers had served as Master of the Horse to William the Conqueror at the Battle of Hastings. Staunch Catholics, the Ferrers kept a low profile in the post-Reformation period. Henry Ferrers, squire from 1564 to 1633, was a great enthusiast for family and local history. The fine armorial glass and heraldic overmantels at Baddesley Clinton are memorials to his antiquarian pursuits. The great hall there is dominated by a splendid chimneypiece, carved in stone with shields commemorating the Ferrers' family marriages placed round a coat of arms quartering Ferrers of Baddesley Clinton, Brome, Hampden and White. The glass celebrates the antiquity and history of the Ferrers family. The shields record family marriages up to that of William Ferrers, sixth Lord Ferrers of Groby, who died in 1445 and was great-grandfather of Sir Edward Ferrers, the first of his family to live at Baddesley in 1509. Henry Ferrers, the antiquary, kept a diary in which he recorded in 1629 the making of an elaborate heraldic carved wooden chimneypiece for his bedroom and his personal supervision of the work. He expressed dissatisfaction with the way the joiners handled the unicorn. It was, he said, '. . . made to big and the horne to big and upright, and the eyes set ill and sidelonge'.[28] Henry Ferrers spent a lifetime in antiquarian pursuits and much of his local research was later used by Sir William Dugdale in his *Antiquities of Warwickshire* (1656), the first of the great county histories. Dugdale's *Warwickshire*, like many similar volumes that appeared in the late seventeenth and eighteenth centuries, is a rich source for pedigrees, heraldry and engravings of family seats.

Sir Edward Coke (1552–1634) took a great interest in the story of his ancestors and in genealogical and heraldic studies in general. His library catalogue shows that he possessed some fourteen manuscripts of heraldry, nine printed works on the subject and twenty pedigrees, including two of his own family. One Coke pedigree by Camden is very elaborate, with 97 coloured coats of arms and many annotations in Edward Coke's fine script.[29]

The fashion for heraldic decoration was a feature of early nineteenth-century landed society. The extent of the craze has been well summarized by John Martin Robinson and Thomas Woodcock:

> the landowner marked all the tied cottages on his estate with tablets bearing his crest or coat of arms. At Holkham in Norfolk, the iron door of every cottage oven was embossed with the ostrich crest of the Cokes. At Arundel, the cast-iron bollards in the streets of the town bear the ducal lion of the Norfolks, and even the tokens for the toll bridge at Shoreham, built by the 12th Duke, were stamped with the Norfolk crest.

The use of heraldry to mark the owner's possessions, as a form of display, was so widespread that it was taxed in the eighteenth century as a form of income tax, and licences to display arms, similar to the dog licence, survived until 1945.[30]

The proper arrangement of armorial bearings to denote rank and condition, connection by marriage or representation of families, had developed by custom from the thirteenth century to the fifteenth century. In the sixteenth century these arrangements were recorded in books of precedents by heralds. By this time it had been fully worked out who was entitled to an escutcheon. Peers, knights, esquires and plain gentlemen were all expected to display a coat of arms and the process was, and still is, controlled and regulated by the College of Arms. The senior heralds of the college, called Kings of Arms, made tours of the country from 1530 onwards to examine gentlemen's claims. Family muniments and family traditions, together with any evidence of a previous visitation, were scrutinized before a claim was allowed. The heralds' visitations continued until 1686 but did not prevent the emergence of a large number of family trees of doubtful reliability. The Fitzwilliam family of Milton, for example, claimed descent from the ancient Yorkshire family of that name settled in Sprotborough and Emley but, according to M.E. Finch, this is open to doubt. She points out that not only is there no record of evidence to prove that Sir John Fitzwilliam of Emley who died in 1417 was in fact the father of John Fitzwilliam of Greens Norton, Northamptonshire, but the matter is further complicated by two other factors: the willingness of the College of Arms to invent a fabulous descent for a new man when he rose in wealth, and the possibility of partisan researches by a member of the family, Hugh Fitzwilliam, the sixteenth-century antiquary.[31] An even more incredible pedigree was provided for the Russells of Woburn in the nineteenth century. In 1821 the sixth Duke of Bedford engaged a Quaker named Jeremiah Wiffen to be his librarian at Woburn. Wiffen worked for eight years writing a history of the Russell family. Among the Woburn manuscripts which he used was an illuminated pedigree roll of the Russells that had

ARMS.—Four grand quarters, 1. HOWARD. Gules on a bend between 6 cross-crosslets fitchee argent, an inescutcheon or charged with a demi-lion rampant pierced through the mouth with an arrow, within a double tressure floreè counterfloreè gules.
2. PLANTAGENET. Gules 3 lions passant guardant in pale or, a label of 3 points argent.
3. WARREN. Checkie or and azure.
4. MOWBRAY. Gules a lion rampant argent.
Behind the whole two marshal's staves in saltier or, enamelled at each end sable.
CREST.—On a chapeau gules turned up ermine a lion statant guardant or, gorged with a ducal coronet argent.
SUPPORTERS.—On the dexter side a lion argent, and on the sinister a horse of the same holding a slip of oak fructed proper.
MOTTO.—Sola virtus invicta.

THOMAS HOWARD, earl of Arundel, Surrey, and Norfolk, &c., = Lady ALETHEA TALBOT, heiress of Hallamshire, descended in the seventh degree from John Howard, created duke of Norfolk anno 1483. Restored in 1603 to all the honours lost by the attainder of his father Philip earl of Arundel. Installed knight of the Garter 13 May 1611 : Earl marshal of England 29 Aug. 1621 : Earl of Norfolk 6 June 1641. Died 4 Oct. 1646, and was buried with his ancestors at Arundel in Sussex. // youngest of the three daughters and co-heirs of Gilbert earl of Shrewsbury, and the only one who left issue. She died on the 24th of May 1654.

| Sir JAMES HOWARD K.B. commonly called Lord Mowbray and Maltravers, eldest son and heir apparent. Died at Ghent, his father still living. | HENRY-FREDERICK, earl of Arundel &c. summoned to parliament by the title of Lord Mowbray 21 Mar. 1639. Died at his house in the Strand, London, 7 Apr. 1652, and was buried at Arundel. = Lady ELIZABETH STUART, daughter of Esme duke of Lenox. | THOMAS HOWARD, died unmarried. | GILBERT HOWARD, died unmarried. | CHARLES HOWARD, died unmarried. | Sir WILLIAM HOWARD, K.B. and viscount Stafford, so created 11 Nov. 1646, having married Mary sister and heir of Henry Stafford Lord Stafford. Beheaded 29 Dec. 1678. |

| THOMAS, fifth duke of Norfolk of the family of Howard, to which title he was restored by act of parliament 13 Chas. II. lord of Hallamshire. Died at Padua, unmarried, 1 Dec. 1677. | Lady ANN SOMERSET, first wife, dau. of Edward marquis of Worcester and sister to Henry first duke of Beaufort. = HENRY, sixth duke, lord of Hallamshire. Created baron Howard of Castle-Rising and earl of Norwich, and in 1672 earl marshal and hereditary earl marshal of England. Died at Arundelhouse, London, 11 Jan. 1684, and was buried at Arundel. = JANE, second wife, dau. of Robert Bickerton, son of Jas. Bickerton lord of Cash in Ireland. She survived the duke, took to her second husband col. Thomas Maxwell, and died at the Holmes near Rotherham 28 Aug. 1693. | PHILIP HOWARD, third son, commonly called Cardinal of Norfolk. Born at Arundelhouse anno 1629. Died at Rome 16 June 1694. | CHARLES HOWARD, fourth son. 8th son. Of whom hereafter, as ancestors of the second and third house of Howard of Norfolk. | ESME HOWARD, ninth and youngest son. Died 14 June 1728, aged 82, and was bur. in the churchyard of St. Pancras, Middlesex, as were also his wife Margaret, and an only dau. and heir named Elizabeth Howard. | TALBOT HOWARD. EDWARD HOWARD. FRANCIS HOWARD. 5th, 6th, and 7th sons, all died unmarried. | CATHERINE, wife of John Digby of Gothurst co. Bucks, esq., son and heir of Sir Kenelm Digby. ELIZABETH, wife first of col. Alexander Macdonald, secondly of Sir Bartholomew Russel. ANN, died in her infancy. |

| HENRY, seventh duke of Norfolk, lord of Hallamshire. The protestant duke.K.G. Born 11 January 1653-4. Died without issue at his house in St. James's-square, London, 2 April 1701, and was buried at Arundel. = Lady MARY MORDAUNT, dau. and sole heir of Henry earl of Peterborough, married in 1677. Divorced in 1700, and took to her second husband Sir John Germain. She died in Luswick St. Peters cu. Northampton, 16 Oct. 1705. | THOMAS HOWARD, of Worksop,esq., second son. Accompanied James II. to France: was with that king in Ireland, and lost in his passage from that country to Brest on the 9th of Novem. 1689. = ELIZABETH-MARIA, only dau. and heir of Sir John SavileofCopley co. York, baronet. Died 10 Dec.1732, and was bur. at Arundel. | ANN-ALETHEA, died in her infancy. ELIZABETH, wife of George marquis of Huntley, afterwards duke of Gordon. FRANCES, wife of the marquis Valperaizo, a Spanish nobleman. | GEORGE HOWARD, married Arabella dau. & sole heir of Sir Edward Allen of Hatfield-Peverel co. Essex, relict of Francis Thompson of Humbleton co.York, esq. and died without issue 6th Mar. 1720-1. | JAMES HOWARD, drowned at Sutton-wash, 12 Aug. 1702. Never married. | FREDERICK-HENRY HOWARD, of the Holmes near Rotherham, a posthumous child. Married Catherine dau. of Sir Francis Blake, of the county of Oxford, knight, relict of Sir Richard Kennedy of Ireland, bart. and dying without issue 16 March 1726-7, left the Holmes, the manor of Rotherham and other property, to the Effingham branch of the family of Howard. | JOHN HOWARD, died in his infancy. CATHERINE. ANN. Both nuns in Flanders. PHILIPPA wife of Ralph Standish of Standish co. Lane. esq. |

a

been compiled by Le Neve, the York Herald, in 1626, for the third Earl of Bedford. It traced the Earl's descent from Hugo de Rosel, one of William the Conqueror's knights. The imaginative Wiffen went further and traced the lineage of the Russells to Olaf, a seventh-century king of Rerik. J. H. Round demolished Wiffen's story at the beginning of this century and the more plausible version today is that the first ancestor of the Bedford line was Stephen Gascoigne (alias Russell) of Weymouth and Bordeaux, a fifteenth-century wine merchant.[32]

Landed estates in the nineteenth century

The opportunity to purchase large estates outright diminished significantly from the early years of the eighteenth century. Edwin Lascelles had indeed been fortunate to be able to buy Harewood in the 1730s. Purchases continued to be made but for the most part they were piecemeal attempts to consolidate existing estates, especially the family seat. At Woburn the fourth Duke of Bedford pursued such a policy. He acquired the Ampthill estate in 1738; Houghton and Oakley were added about the same time and farms and small areas of land were bought when the opportunity occurred. By the end of the century the Woburn estate comprised six villages and many tenant farms.

In order to consolidate the family estate an owner might be prepared to sell off more distant holdings to raise the necessary capital. Coke of Holkham sold his outlying estates in Oxfordshire, Buckinghamshire and Lancashire in order to buy more land adjoining his own at Holkham.[33] William George Spencer Cavendish, the sixth Duke of Devonshire, inherited extensive estates in Yorkshire, Derbyshire, Lancashire, Sussex and Ireland in 1811 when he was 21. Although rather deaf and shy, he had extravagant tastes which included collecting books and enhancing the house and estate at Chatsworth. The estate had been neglected in the time of the fifth Duke and his successor employed Wyatville and Paxton to make many alterations to the house and gardens. Even with an income of over £125,000 a year, the sixth Duke spent so much on building and reconstruction that he was heavily in debt and had to sell a number of properties. As early as 1824 the manor of Wetherby in Yorkshire was put under the hammer. The sale of this estate – over 1000 acres, manorial rights and more than 200 business and domestic premises – aroused interest over a wide area. Numerous printed sale catalogues were distributed, and contemporary newspapers throughout the county included a complete account of the auction details. Needless to say, such a turnover of property produced voluminous conveyancy material. When he died in 1858 the sixth Duke left debts of £1 million and an estate diminished by almost 200,000 acres.[34]

By the 1870s, and in a context of severe agricultural depression, there was growing criticism of the concentration of landed property in the hands of so few people. The decade saw the first official survey of landownership since the Domesday Book and the publication of an influential book, J.W. Bateman's *The Great Landowners of Great Britain and Ireland*, in 1876. Bateman himself acknowledged that the book contained inaccuracies and in subsequent editions

DEVONSHIRE, Duke of, K.G., F.R.S., Chatsworth, Bakewell, &c. 🌳.

			acres.		g. an. val.
Coll. Eton, Trin. Cam.	Derbyshire	.	89,462	.	89,557
Club. Ath., Ox. and Cam.,	York, W.R.	.	19,332	.	16,958
Jun. Ox. and Cam.	Lancashire	.	12,681	.	12,494
b. 1808, s. 1858, m. 1829.	Sussex . . .		11,062	.	14,881
	Somerset . .		3,014	.	4,918
	Lincoln . .		1,392	.	2,657
	Cumberland .		983	.	1,925
	Middlesex . .		524	.	3,079
	Notts . . .		125	.	130
	Stafford . .		26	.	40
	Cheshire . .		28	.	21
	Co. Cork . .		32,550	.	19,326
	Co. Waterford		27,483	.	15,000
	Co. Tipperary		3	.	4
			198,665	.	180,990

Sat for Cambridge University, for Malton, and for North Derbyshire.
Included in the above is a Derbyshire rental of 6,257*l.* standing in Lord Hartington's name.

DE WINTON, Mrs., of Maesllwych Castle, Hay.

s. 1878, m. 1867.	Radnor . .	4,955	.	6,193
	Glamorgan .	2,458	.	6,333
	Brecon . . .	2,485	.	3,115
	Hereford . .	2	.	1
		9,900	.	15,642

** TENNYSON-D'EYNCOURT, Admiral Edwin Clayton, 🌳 C.B., of Bayons Manor, Market Rasen, &c.

Coll. Westm., Roy. Nav. C.	Lincoln . .	3,504	6,200
Club. Uni. Ser., Travellers'.	b. 1813, s. 1871, m. 1859.		

Served in Royal Navy.

DICCONSON, Thomas, of Wrightington Hall, Wigan.

b. 1819, s. 1862.	Lancashire .	4,380	.	9,983

8 The Duke of Devonshire's estates as listed in Bateman's *The Great Landowners* 1879.

there were substantial revisions. The author claimed that in the vast majority of cases the corrections were made by the owners themselves. Bateman's summaries indicated that some 12.5 million acres, or 41.5 per cent of the total 30 million acreage for England and Wales, were owned by peers and other 'great landowners'. The peerage held over 5 million acres and other persons owning at least 3000 acres worth a gross rental of at least £3000 a year accounted for nearly 7.5 million acres. Among the greatest estates recorded in Bateman were those of the Dukes of Sutherland, and Buccleuch and Queensbury. But whereas the former with 1,358,000 acres produced a gross rental of only £141,000, the Buccleuch and Queensbury estate with 460,000 acres produced £217,000. By contrast, the Duke of Bedford's 87,500 acres (not including his London property) had a gross annual value of £141,500. Bateman does not give any help with net incomes, and these were of crucial importance for the future of estates.

Continuity has been one of the themes of this chapter. The ties that have bound families, estates and houses together over many centuries have produced rich quantities of source material. Some houses have been in the hands of the same families throughout the entire period covered by this book. Beaulieu in Hampshire, the home of Lord and Lady Montagu, has been in the family since it was acquired

THE

GREAT LANDOWNERS

OF

Great Britain and Ireland.

A LIST OF ALL OWNERS OF

THREE THOUSAND ACRES AND UPWARDS,

WORTH £3,000 A YEAR,

IN

ENGLAND, SCOTLAND, IRELAND, & WALES,

Their Income from Land, Acreage, Colleges, Clubs, and Services,

CULLED FROM

THE MODERN DOMESDAY BOOK.

Corrected in the vast majority of cases by the Owners themselves.

BY

JOHN BATEMAN, F.R.G.S.

NEW EDITION:

With the Addition of 1,320 *Owners of* 2,000 *Acres and Upwards.*

LONDON:

HARRISON, 59, PALL MALL, S.W.,

Bookseller to Her Majesty and H.R.H. the Prince of Wales.

1879.

9 Title page of John Bateman's *The Great Landowners of Great Britain and Ireland*, 1879. A useful, albeit controversial, reference work for landownership in the second half of the nineteenth century.

after the dissolution of the monasteries. Althorp and Castle Ashby in Northamptonshire have been the residences of the Spencers and Comptons since the sixteenth century. Chillington Hall in Staffordshire, the home of the Giffard family, has passed down from father to son since 1178. There are a number of properties where continuity could be said to hang by a thread. Rather than dispose of a house, the family has assigned it to a private trust or to the National Trust whilst retaining a few rooms for its own use. One family at least is not thinking of giving up for many years to come. At Castle Howard there is a mausoleum where 19 members of that family are buried in the crypt. The practice of family burial in the mausoleum ceased after the interment of the eighth Earl of Carlisle in 1889 but was revived in 1972. As the Honourable Simon Howard observed in a television programme in 1987, there are some 63 niches still to be filled![35]

Chapter Two

BUILDING, LANDSCAPING AND IMPROVING

The country house was a symbol of the social and economic power of the landed classes. At its height it had few architectural equals. Its finest rooms were filled with the fashionable products of European art and craftsmanship and its garden and grounds had no immediate rival. These areas have consequently received an enormous amount of attention from historians, so the local historian who looks in this direction is unlikely to do more than dot the i's and cross the t's, unless for a minor house, though even there the ground will probably have been well tilled.

The compensation for any historian who ploughs this furrow is that there is a considerable range of relevant sources in the archives of the country house. He or she will find appropriate material in letters, journals and diaries, plans, paintings, drawings and prints, accounts, estimates, contracts, agreements, bills and receipts, inventories and travellers' descriptions, and even wills and epitaphs. As well as all this, there is the house itself, its contents and its grounds, which need, repeatedly, to be looked at by a fresh eye.

Attitudes to building

In his letter of 27 July 1708 to the Earl of Manchester, John Vanbrugh commented on several houses under construction:

> . . . I have not yet been at Kimbolton [the Earl's house] . . . where I believe I shall find all right, & as I hear very much Advanc'd . . . We have made a Vast Progress [at Blenheim], but it will Still take up to two Seasons More to finish. I met John Coniers there on thursday last, with Severall Virtuoso's with him; He made mighty fine Speeches upon the Building, And took it for graunted No Subjects house in Europe wou'd Approach it: which will be true, if the Duke of Shrewsbury judges right in Saying there is not in Italy so fine a House as Chattesworth, for this of Blenheim is beyond all Comparison more Magnificent than that, My Ld Carlisle has got his whole Garden Front up And is fonder of his Work every day than Other. The Duke of Shrewsbury's house will be About half up this Season; My Ld Bindon is busy to the Utmost of his Force in New Moulding Audley end, And All the World are running Mad after Building, as far as they can reach . . .[1]

Rivalry and emulation were obviously central motives in the building of country houses. When Arthur Young visited Castletown, some 30 miles from Dublin, he began his description of the house with, 'Mr Conolly's, at Castletown, to which all travellers resort, is the finest house in Ireland, and not exceeded by many in

England.'[2] Conolly, the son of a provincial innkeeper, made his fortune as a lawyer and a dealer in forfeited estates after the Battle of the Boyne. He bought the land on which Castletown was built from the attainted Earl of Limerick. He built it with the intention of outdoing the homes of all previous Irish landowners, and succeeded. It was the model for most of the grander eighteenth-century country houses in Ireland.

Emulation could be a powerful incentive even for those who, fundamentally, objected to it, as was the case with the Yorkshire gentleman, Sir Henry Slingsby. From 1638 to 1648 he kept a diary, in the early part of which he wrote disapprovingly of several of the ambitious country houses of his day:

> I may see by this vanity of all worldly things which men do so much rest upon. Let a man propose to himself never so great matters, yet shall another come that may exceed him . . . I shall ever dissuade my son from effecting building, unless it be with great moderation. But whatever one doth let him resolve to please himself, for it may be that it shall not please another.

But not long after he had written this he was entertained, in June 1640, by Lord Holland at Kensington. There he was:

> much taken with the curiosity of the house and from it I took a conceite of making a thorough house in part of Redhouse which now I build, and that by placing the dores so one against another and making at each end a balcony that one may see cleare thro' the house.[3]

Advice to resist the attractions of fashion and status was given in 1634 to Michael Wentworth of Woolley, Yorkshire, by his kinsman, Thomas, Viscount Wentworth:

> If you builde a new house remember that I tell you itt is a matter wherein you may shew a great deale or a great want of discretion, itt being nothing soe easy a thinge to build well as men take it to bee that knowe it not, & therefore at your perill looke well about you.[4]

Michael Wentworth had little option but to accept this advice for, as a recusant, he paid heavy annual fines. Such rebuilding as eventually took place at Woolley was the result of fire, which often forced the rebuilding, the contraction or the abandonment of a family home. But to reject the ambition to rebuild or to do so in the latest style could simply be a matter of taste or prudence. Thus, Sir John Lowther, scion of a hard-headed Cumbrian house, could suggest to his son (later the first Viscount Lonsdale) in 1697 that there were other considerations besides fashion in the rebuilding of Lowther Castle:

> The greatest part of our Lives is spent in our houses, and therefore ought to be made most pleasant and Easie . . . I have consulted Strength as well as Ornament, Suitable to the coldness of our Climate, and Necessare to defend us ffrom the Rigour off the Winter.[5]

It took money to build in any style, conservative or fashionable, and the acquisition or inheritance of a fortune could lead to it, but family pride could actually reject the necessity to rebuild an old family home. Shortly after the marriage of his daughter, Mary Elizabeth, into the Lucy family of Charlecote Park, Warwickshire, in 1823, Sir John Williams of Boddlewyddan, Flintshire, wrote to her:

> Any man with money can build a new house but an old respected mansion like Charlecote that is above price can only be found in the possession of the first families . . .[6]

The preservation of an old house could sustain family pride as powerfully as rebuilding in a fashionable style.

Architect and patron could wrangle endlessly during the time of building and the response to the completed house was not always one of pleasure. A variety of responses are recorded by Jill Franklin in her study of the nineteenth-century house and its plan, including that of Lord Overstone, the millionaire Manchester banker, to the rebuilding of Overstone Hall, Northamptonshire, by W.M. Teulon in 1861 to 1862. In a letter he wrote:

> The New House, I regret to say, is the cause of unmitigated disappointment and vexation. It is an utter failure – we have fallen into the hands of an architect in whom incapacity is the smallest fault. The House though very large and full of pretension – has neither taste, comfort nor convenience. I am utterly ashamed of it . . . the principal rooms are literally uninhabitable – I shall never fit them up . . . I grieve to think that I shall hand on such an abortion to my successors.[7]

Mark Girouard condemns it similarly as 'a terrible bastard Renaissance house'.[8] It survives as a school.

Costs

J.V. Beckett lists the expenditure involved in the building of 16 country houses at various times between 1694 and 1875. The sums range from £8533 for the smaller of two nineteenth-century projects at Thoresby to a quarter of a million pounds at Tottenham House, both in the 1820s. But he remarks that a modest country house could be built for £3000 in the late seventeenth century, while the lesser gentry built for hundreds rather than thousands of pounds.[9] The historian may find a more or less reliable figure of the cost of building a particular house in its archives, or he or she may venture on the hazardous task of estimating the cost by adding up the figures found in its building accounts. Those of the two Hardwick Halls, built by Bess of Hardwick in the closing decades of the sixteenth century, have been published and from them the editors, D.N. Durant and P. Riden, conclude that the second and most famous cost about £5000. Scores of detailed payments to masons, carpenters, plasterers, glaziers and others are recorded. In the masons' account there are many entries like the following:

> Payd to John Roads 28th June [1592] for hewing of tow hundred 65
> foots ashler at 1¼d the foot   1 7 7
> Payd to John Roods the same day for hewing of 18 foots of arkatravs at
> 1½d the foot for the 3rd story[10]   2 3

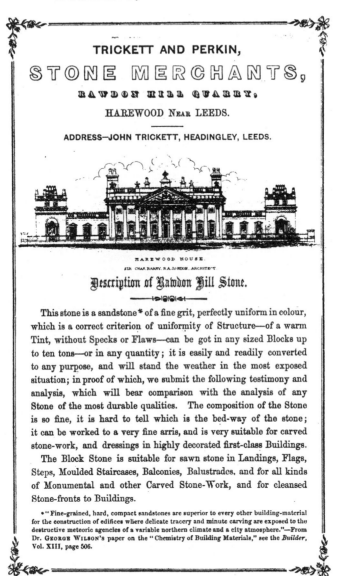

10 Nineteenth-century stone merchants' advertisement.

Determining the overall costs is not easy even where the accounts survive. Costs may or may not include that of land (hardly appropriate where the builder inherits) or interior decorations and furnishings, whilst some or all of the building materials were frequently drawn from the estate itself. When the great chamber at Petworth was being enlarged in 1619 for Henry Percy, ninth Earl of Northumberland, it was agreed with the masons that:

> . . . the ruff stone wilbe digged in the Liths and the ashler stone at Byworth Quarrey, your Lordshipp to paye for digginge, and the stones to be carryed by your Lordshipp's tenaunts, The lyme wilbe sent in from Sutton att v s the loade . . .[11]

Further, material from an older property being replaced might be used, as at the Earl of Manchester's Kimbolton, Huntingdonshire. To defend himself against the criticism that he was using neither pilasters nor columns externally, Vanbrugh wrote to the Earl on 18 July 1707:

> As to the Outside, I thought 'twas absolutely best, to give it Something of the Castle Air, tho' at the same time to make it regular. And by this means too, all the Old Stone is Serviceable again; which to have had new wou'd have run to a very great Expence . . .[12]

Whatever the economies, building and landscaping were regarded as dangerous liabilities for those who undertook them, and some landowners were certainly bankrupted by being over-ambitious. It is not surprising that John Aislabie, Chancellor of the Exchequer before the South Sea Bubble ruined his career, should have been cautious when he returned to Yorkshire to devote himself to the transformation of the gardens of Studley Royal. He had hoped to incorporate the neighbouring ruins of Fountains Abbey into his garden scheme, but was forced to abandon this ambition, as he informed his steward in a letter of 17 October 1720:

> . . . as to the buying Estates, I will not buy an acre more, nor give 20 years purchase for anything. if Mr Messenger design'd to sell his Estate, he has lost his market, I wou'd have bought it then but must never think of it now, tho' I might have it for 20 years purchase. if he design'd to sell it was extremely silly to go that way to work; the refusing to let me have an inch of ground to build my walls was very unkind, but cou'd never induce me to give a farthing more for Fountains since I can do as well without it, and if I cou'd buy it t'morrow I shou'd not want it . . .[13]

He went on to create the dramatic gardens to the north-west of the abbey, but it was left to his son to add the abbey itself to the estate in 1768.

Designing and building

In the National Trust survey of the history of Hardwick Hall, Mark Girouard points out Hardwick's good fortune in the survival of the greater part of its building accounts (quoted earlier in this chapter), as well as two more general account books from the building period and an inventory of 1601 which gives the original use of the rooms. Elsewhere in the sixteenth and seventeenth centuries the historian is unlikely to find so much material directly relevant to the building of a house; it is therefore easier to illustrate the types of source that throw light on it from the eighteenth and nineteenth centuries.

By the late seventeenth and early eighteenth century designing an aristocratic house was seen more and more to be the role of a professional architect rather than of a master mason on the one hand or a gentleman-amateur on the other. If the greatest of the latter, Lord Burlington, was yet to come, the finest of early eighteenth-century houses, like Castle Howard, Wanstead House or Cannons, were the work of professionals. They increasingly dominated the designing of such houses, so that by the nineteenth century the gentleman-amateur who designed his own house was rare and of no great significance in the development of country house architecture.

Material relating directly to the architect of a house may be found in bills or correspondence, like the bill tendered by the Yorkshire architect, John Carr, to Viscount Irwin of Temple Newsam.[14] The bill was for attendance at the house and for various drawings made in 1765, 1767 and 1768, including:

> *Sep[tembe]r 18th 1765* At Templenewsam with a drawing for finishing the Hall, and planned the alteration of the Great Stair Case, sketch'd the manner of altering the Cupola, made a plan of the Old Rooms as they are at present in the South Front and a Drawing for the Keepers Lodge.   15.15.0

Capability Brown and the Adam brothers were also consulted about the rebuilding of the south wing of the house, but nothing seems to have been done until a local architect was eventually employed to do so, and of Carr's submission all that seems to have been carried out was the building of a keeper's lodge.

Carr's Latin epitaph is to be found in the parish church of his birthplace, Horbury, near Wakefield, West Yorkshire. It concludes with a reminder of the non-architectural roles that a public figure like Carr fulfilled and (in translation) runs:

The duties of a JUSTICE OF THE PEACE
He managed with the utmost honesty and justice.
Twice he was mayor of the city of York.
If you want to know, reader, with how much liberality and devotion
And, equally, with how much talent and skill he excelled,
Look at this holy building,
Raised with his most praiseworthy generosity.
Died 23 February A.D.1807 Aged 83

In discussing the work of Vanbrugh at Castle Howard in his biography of the architect, Kerry Downes was able to use the correspondence between Vanbrugh and his patron, Lord Carlisle. In one letter, Vanbrugh pointed out certain dangers that had arisen from pressure to cut costs, commenting on discussions with the mason and carpenter about their prices:

> I talk't a great deal to 'em both, the morning I came away; but found 'em very unwilling to come to any abatement . . . I ask't Mr Hawksmoor alone, what he really thought on't; he said they were indeed come as low, as he ever expected to bring 'em; and yet perhaps it was not impossible for 'em to work lower, but . . . they might take this pretence, to perform the work ten per Cent: worse for five per Cent: [if] they were reduc't . . .

wheras, if they have the rates they have propos'd, they own themselves to do as good work as they receive twice as much for, at London, and by consequence they have no room left for evasion.[15]

Estimates, contracts and bills of artists and craftsmen, both famous and obscure, frequently survive. Thus, the accounts of Chirk Castle, North Wales, for 1702, record payments to Robert Davies of Bersham (later to be regarded as the greatest of the Welsh smiths) for the humdrum work of:

. . . makeing skrew pins, & a new handle, hamering and holeing 2 big plates to secure the beame on the gallary . . . for hookes & hinges for the stable weighing 29lb . . . & a new thomb lach to the stable doore.[16]

Such sources are almost inevitably matter-of-fact, though the occasional artisan breaks out of his mould. John Mackey, plasterer, burst into verse at the end of the bill which he submitted early in the eighteenth century to William Flower of Castledurrow in Ireland, with:

I wish your Honnour long life and health
Though this Will not increase my wealth
To Seall this wish he may not live one hour
That would not drink a health to Noble Colonell Flower[17]

Plans are useful to the social as well as to the architectural historian, for they usually provide an indication of the functions of the various rooms at a particular point in time. Of course, they may show no more than the architect's intentions, for they could be rejected or modified. Thus, the rectangularity of John Carr's initial plans for Harewood House was softened in certain key areas under Robert Adam's influence, and even his final plans[18] were altered during the building process. Nevertheless, the final plans show an interesting stage in the evolution of thinking about the nature of the country house. The offices and working areas for the servants were on the ground floor (in fact, a semi-basement), while the principal floor, slightly elevated, illustrates the eighteenth-century acceptance of relatively relaxed relationships within the landowning élite. Earlier houses had been designed with an eye to formality and ceremonial, while Harewood provided a series of rooms of varying size and style that permitted guests to circulate informally and to choose from a number of activities. The visitor entered the hall and circulated back to it via the saloon, drawing room, south dining room, gallery, common dining room and music room, all opulent rooms full of stylish furniture, pictures and *objets d'art* and offering striking views over the grounds. The circuit lay to the right of the main axis of the house, though by siting bedrooms and dressing rooms to the left of the axis rather than placing them on an upper floor Harewood retained an element of conservatism, as in the failure of the plan to provide for a library, which had become usual by this time.

11 John Carr's final plan for the principal floor of Harewood House.

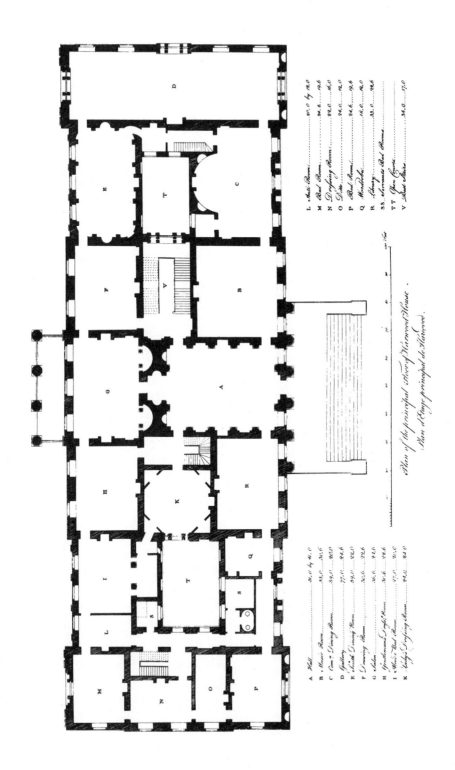

A Hall .... 31.0 by 41.0
B Music Room .... 33.0 .. 30.6
C Com.ᵗ Dining Room .... 34.0 .. 22.0
D Gallery .... 77.0 .. 24.6
E South Dining Room .... 34.0 .. 22.0
F Drawing Room .... 34.6 .. 22.6
G Salon .... 36.6 .. 24.6
H Gentleman's Dress.ᵍ Room .. 31.6 .. 40.6
I Ante Bed Room .... 17.0 .. 20.6
K Lady's Dressing Room ...... 24.0 .. 24.0

L Ante Room .... 20.0 by 12.0
M Bed Room .... 24.6 .. 19.6
N Dressing Room .... 24.0 .. 16.0
O Dit.ᵒ .... 24.6 .. 12.0
P Bed Room .... 24.8 .. 19.6
Q Wardrobe .... 12.0 .. 12.0
R Library .... 35.0 .. 24.6
SS Servants Bed Rooms
TT Open Courts
V Back Stairs .... 34.0 .. 17.0

Plan of the principal Story, Harewood House.
Plan d'Etage principal de Harewood.

The first Stone of Harewood—
— House laid March 23: 1759
Roof of East wing June 25: 1763
Roof of West wing Oct.: 1763
Roof of House Sep.: 1764
John Muschamp — Mason

12 John Muschamp, the master mason at Harewood House, records the main stages in the building of the house.

Plans for Allerton Park and Grimston Park, Yorkshire,[19] show the rather different disposition of rooms that marked the country house a century later. At Grimston an entrance hall was flanked by the dining room and the blue drawing room, with the library and the yellow drawing room beyond, the latter leading into a conservatory, while an orangery projected from the opposite side of the house. An extensive servants' wing lay to one side, with billiard room, smoking room, a study and a dressing room lying between. Allerton was more typical of its day in that each of two alternative plans provided a huge great hall instead of the relatively small entrance hall of Grimston. Halls like Allerton's were symbols of the revival of 'old English hospitality' that took place in the nineteenth century. They served as vast, informal living rooms, with armchairs, sofas, perhaps a writing table, a billiard table and even an organ, rooms on which the house party could centre as the informality of the previous century was taken even further. Bedrooms were all upstairs, those of the master and mistress adjacent to the nursery, together forming a family unit. The accommodation of some of the senior servants was on the same floor, as were guest bedrooms, whilst further guest and servant bedrooms lay in separate and distinct locations on a higher floor.

Travellers' descriptions and comments can sometimes be illuminating, like Arthur Young's description of Wentworth Castle, visited in the late 1760s. Unlike the houses just described, it was built to no single plan but consisted of three attached wings when Young saw it, a provincial gentleman's house from the 1680s, a baroque wing from the second decade of the eighteenth century and a palladian wing built 1759 to 1761. He begins with the entrance hall, moves on through a suite consisting of antechamber, bedchamber and drawing room, then on to the main drawing room, dining room, stairs and gallery, covering thus the main internal features of the baroque wing. This classical wing with its opulent interior had been built to mask the older, and largely unimpressive, house of the 1680s. Young was evidently not shown the latter, for he makes no mention of it, moving from the baroque wing to the palladian, where he mentions only 'Lord Strafford's library . . . Her Ladyship's dressing-room . . . reading-closet . . . bird-closet . . . and bed-chamber . . .', indicating the way in which the latest wing had added finer family accommodation and a library to the house.[20] Thirty years later changes in the nomenclature and function of certain rooms is apparent in the description of another traveller, Revd Richard Warner, who describes the former baroque antechamber and drawing room as gentlemen's and ladies' dressing rooms.[21] Thus even matter-of-fact or banal travellers' descriptions may throw light on the development of a house and changing attitudes towards it.

Like other travellers, Young and Warner comment on the furniture and works of art in the house, but another source, the inventory, is likely to throw even more detailed light on these. Inventories list rooms by the names in use at the time of compilation and give detailed catalogues of their contents. They were usually drawn up at the time of succession to a title or first possession of a house, or at the death of an owner. Most noble inventories were drawn up for probate, as required by law, and the valuations then included were generally low: such inventories are not necessarily complete, for they exclude fixtures and any property owned by the wife of the deceased. A non-probate inventory of Temple Newsam made in 1734 shows the old-fashioned Long Gallery just before the seventh Viscount Irwin transformed it. It was very different from the fashionable saloon that succeeded it, for it contained only:

A Long Settle
6 Pictures, Family pieces
60 Deal Boards
3 Marble Tables
7 Cannons fit for Use
2 Ranges[22]

Objets d'art and pictures are usually dealt with matter-of-factly. More detailed information is likely to be given and comment made by travellers or in sale catalogues, though the latter may well be of a house emptied of its contents, as in the case of Grimston Park when it was put up for sale in 1872. It had been restored in 1840 by Lord Howden, with Decimus Burton as the architect. The major rooms and features are described, for example:[23]

ENTRANCE HALL

The Mansion contains on the Ground Floor a handsome Entrance Hall, 30 feet by 18 feet, now used as the Armoury, the ceiling of which is supported by columns. The Floor is composed of Black and White Marble. The Hall is warmed by Hot Water Pipes, and an open Fire-place, with a handsome Carved Chimney-piece.

There can be few houses that have not received the attention of an artist at one time or another and paintings and prints can provide valuable evidence of the development of an exterior, interior or an estate. Remarkable collections of prints (of plans, elevations and grounds) were published in the eighteenth century, the various editions of *Vitruvius Britannicus* being the best known. Later on, other collections followed, some regional or local: for example, J.P. Neale's *Views of the Seats, Mansions, Castles, Etc. of Noblemen and Gentlemen in the County of York* appeared in 1847. Publications aimed at a different market, namely the professionals interested in the erection of country houses, contain architects' drawings, like E.W Pugin's extraordinary proposal for the transformation of Carlton House, Yorkshire, into Carlton Towers that appeared in *The Building News* of 20 February 1874; the tower and the adjoining gothic wings to the right were never carried out. A painting may reveal vanished aspects of a house or estate, as does one of the west front of Muckross House, County Mayo, painted by George Moore in 1761, which shows boats sailing up the river Carrowbeg from the sea to the stone bridge that now adjoins the house before this was made impossible by the creation of a lake.

This section may be concluded by citing the range of sources used by one historian as the basis of her analysis of a particular issue in the development of a house. The building account book was of central importance for Mary Mauchline when, in her *Harewood House*, she wrote of the alterations made to the house by Barry in the 1840s and 1850s. She also consulted the times and wages book of the plumbers, bricklayers and other workmen, Barry's account and the estimates and account of George Trollope & Sons, the London cabinet-makers responsible for the interior decorating and refurbishing. Barry's portfolio of drawings, elevations and plans was also used, along with correspondence between Barry and the Lascelles.[24] The exalted status of the successful architect is clear from a letter in which Barry coolly rejected criticism of his final account, which supplied little if any detail. He wrote to Lord Harewood's agent, W. Maugham, on 26 January 1855:

> I have received your letter of the 24th inst. requiring a more detailed account of my services at Harewood than that which has been delivered. [Although] I cannot defer to your judgement with reference to the value of my professional services, and should consider it derogatory to my position to depart from my usual custom in supplying you with all the details of my charges; I have no objection, as an act of courtesy, to answer your specific enquiries . . .[25]

On occasion, the lack of any other evidence may make a single source of crucial importance to the historian; the example of Mauchline, however, offers an insight into the way that, in investigating a problem, the historian consults a range of sources whenever possible. The source by source citation adopted here should not be interpreted as suggesting that any single source is likely to provide an adequate understanding of an issue.

---

13 E.W. Pugin's design for Carlton Towers, 1873. Only the wings to the left were completed.

The Building News, Feb. 20. 1874.

CARLTON TOWERS, YORKSHIRE.

THE LORD BEAUMONT.

E. WELBY PUGIN
ARCH[r] 1873

BIRDS-EYE VIEW OF CARLTON TOWERS, YORKSHIRE.

E. WELBY PUGIN ARCHITECT.

Gardens and grounds

Houses may be burned to the ground or knocked down and replaced, but gardens are even more likely to disappear completely as fashion succeeds fashion. On the other hand, since the introduction of the 'jardin anglais' in the eighteenth century, the larger landscape of the surrounding grounds frequently survives as a permanent element in Britain's scenery, even though its details may have perished. And where a garden or a man-made landscape has been lost it can often be 'seen' again via an aerial photograph taken at the right time of year. Even without it, close attention to current ground features with the aid of a large-scale map may also reward the walker in understanding long-lost landscape features.

Very little remains of the earliest gardens: formal country house gardens of the sixteenth and seventeenth centuries are almost wholly modern re-creations. Nor is the evidence for them plentiful. Occasional mention of garden features or plants may be found in correspondence, as in a letter from Sir Michael Hicks of Ruckholts to the Earl of Salisbury on 2 October 1609:

> Having been lately at Sir Edward Sulyard's [of Flemyngs, Essex], and finding his grapes as good as ever I tasted for the relish and sweetness, I prayed him to send you some to taste of, so that if you liked them you might have some grafts of the same vine. But he said if you liked them he would give you half a dozen roots to set, which he says are far better to take, and will bear in two years, where the other will not bear in three or four. Besides he will give you two nectarine plum trees and anything else he has in his garden or orchard . . .[26]

Obtaining new stock as presents from or exchanges with fellow landowners was usual at this time, whilst purchases were also made from commercial gardeners, and were recorded in accounts like those of Woburn later in the century – mainly fruit trees for the garden and vegetables for the kitchen-garden. Thus, in 1671, 'To him [Thomas Gilbank, gardener at Bedford House] more for 45 pear trees at 1s. 6d. each, and for 6 cherry trees and 3 plum trees, all sent to Woburn . . .', while, for December 1675 and February 1676, 'John Field the gardener's bill for seeds for Woburn Abbey' was for gilly flower, radish, cucumber, purslane, parsnip, red beet, cabbage, lettuce, carrot, leek, onion, celery, Canterbury bell, scarlet bean and pea seeds.[27]

After the Restoration the gardens of Le Nôtre and Louis XIV's France set the European fashion. British gardens began to conform to the new ideal, which, broadly speaking, took the components of the gardens of the Renaissance, subordinated them to grand vistas and arranged them in a rigidly formal and logical way. They are described by travellers, whose accounts became more and more frequent as roads and transport improved in the eighteenth century. Thus, grounds at Wentworth Castle which reflected the French influence were described by an unknown visitor in 1724:

> [in front of the house] the peice of water with the Cascade & 2 grottoes in the Court was very fine, & the Menagerie, with all the variety of close shady walks, & the noise of a fine cascade 30 feet deep and 300 feet long was very delightful. The Gardens are full of

Terrasses & wilderness, & the park of young Oaks, but my Lord shewed us . . . on Saturday morning 3 noble large woods with great variety of Shady alleys & great avenues, & all full of old Stout oaks; & the whole Prospect is enriched with vast plenty of Forrest. After this we saw my Lords 2 large square Kitchen gardens with the Stone walls for ripening Grapes.[28]

If parterres, fountains, statuary, pyramids and other garden ornaments are added to this, the main elements of the late seventeenth- and early eighteenth-century garden and park are apparent. However, if this description is compared with the prospect of the grounds of Wentworth Castle provided by two roughly contemporary prints (that of Holzendorf from 1714 and Badeslade's from the early 1730s),[29] the visitor clearly missed or ignored the extreme formality of the grounds, in particular, the way in which three broad, straight, tree-lined avenues led up to and converged on the house, making the stately home the dominant element in the landscape. The house was the hub of a hierarchy, the centre of an ordered way of life. The grounds were intended as a statement of this social philosophy in landscape, even if it escaped the visitor.

The same formal notions can be seen in the design for a single parterre that is preserved in the papers of Ingilby of Ripley. It was drawn by the gardener, Peter Aram (father of Eugene Aram, the eighteenth-century schoolmaster-murderer), and showed earlier work of his at Newby Hall. It is entitled:

The Plan of ye North East Q[uarte]r in the Garden to the North of the House at Newby. An[no] 1716 – consisting of Pyramid Yews and round Headed Variegated Hollies together with Flowr'g Decorations interm[ingle]d.[30]

These gardens represent the end of a lengthy tradition of garden and ground layout. They had scarcely been created before Kent began to move away from artificiality by using the natural lie of the land, and by the 1740s 'Capability' Brown had taken Kent's ideas further to develop the informal 'jardin anglais' that replaced French and Italian notions throughout Europe.

Until recently, all too many eighteenth-century landscaped grounds were attributed to Brown, but historians have eliminated several of these claims by testing them against estate correspondence, plans, drawings, accounts, bills and agreements, like the agreement made between Brown and George Lucy of Charlecote Park, Warwickshire, in May 1760:

Article 1. To widen the river Avon, and lay its banks properly, giving them a natural and easy level, corresponding with the ground on each side of the river.
Article 2. To sink the fosse quite round the meadow, of a proper width, to make it a sufficient fence against the deer, and of a proper depth to hide the pales from the terrace . . .
Article 3. To fill up all the ponds on the north front of the house, to alter the slopes and give the whole a natural, easy, and corresponding level with the house on every side.[31]

Sources may throw up unexpected evidence. Brown was notorious for sweeping away existing formal elements in the grounds that he landscaped but his 'Plan for the intended Alterations at Temple Newsham, Yorkshire The seat of Charles Ingram, Esq'[32] includes a wilderness with its intersecting walks left over from an earlier age of landscaping. The various kinds of maps that were produced for purposes connected with estate administration and the smaller-scale commercial maps, like Thomas Jeffery's map of Yorkshire of 1775, may all reveal details of parks and gardens. The whole range of nineteenth-century Ordnance Survey maps, particularly those of the six-inch scale, are of value. On the early twentieth-century Ordnance Survey map, Allerton Park, Yorkshire,[33] is shown surrounded by its landscaped park in the style of Brown or his most important successor, Humphrey Repton, with one clear departure from Brown's style that Repton was happy to accept. Surrounding the house are formal gardens of the kind that Brown would not allow and which, initially under Repton's influence, became the centrepiece of the Victorian style.

The Grand Tour

The rift with Catholic Europe brought about by the Reformation hindered travel on the Continent but from about 1620 young noblemen and gentlemen went in increasing numbers to France and Italy (their Mecca, because of its classical past) and sometimes elsewhere in western and central Europe. While abroad they corresponded with their families and friends and many kept journals or diaries. Such material survives in many country house archives, though the letters are usually more interesting and informative than the journals, which tend to be rather like holiday slide-shows without the slides.

The travellers usually carried, or were preceded by, letters of introduction to important persons or families so that the journey would be profitable socially as well as culturally. For William Constable of Burton Constable, who would subsequently achieve a fine reputation as a collector, cultural priorities marked the letter that was sent on his behalf to Georges Louis Leclerc, Comte de Buffon, the famous French naturalist, on 22 April 1770. The writer was J.T. Needham, the Catholic cleric and scientist:

> I request as the greatest favour you can bestow upon one of the most sincere of all your friends, that you would receive with distinction and your usual benevolence, Mr Constable . . . He is a gentleman of a very ancient family, and of considerable fortune, qualified in every respect to do honour to that reception, which I am persuaded you will give him at Montbard, a lover of arts and sciences, and I may say yet much more, a man of study, knowledge, taste, and application.
>
> You cannot oblige him more than by being communicative, and conversing freely with him upon every subject. He desires to be much acquainted with your person, as he is already conversant with your works, and one of his prime intentions in passing through Burgundy in his road to Italy is to make a personal acquaintance with you, Sir, most particularly . . .[34]

On the other hand, social priorities were reflected in one phase of the travels of

Walter Stanhope of Leeds, who was marked out to succeed his uncle at Cannon Hall, South Yorkshire. He wrote to his mother from Lausanne on 25 November 1769:

> To live at the house where I do is recommendation sufficient without any other. I have already been at most of the Families here and shall shortly go to them all. The Duchess of Courland, the Marquis of Gentilo & 3 or 4 others are the best Houses here, and besides we have a drove of German Princes, Barons, and Counts that come for the same end that I do . . .[35]

Accompanied by a tutor the travellers would acquire modern languages, culture and polish, and broaden their experience: some, like Thomas Coke of Holkham, set out as boys and returned as men. The aspiring virtuosi and dilettanti among them collected pictures, sculpture, *objets d'art* and anything that took their fancy. Like Sir Thomas Gascoigne of Parlington, West Yorkshire, they might have their portrait done by a fashionable painter, in his case Pompeo Batoni in Rome in 1779: already portly, for he was making the tour at a somewhat later age than most of his contemporaries, he holds a snuff-box in his left hand as he stands before portrait busts of two friends and travelling companions. The delight in exotic finds is apparent in the letter to his father written in Rome in 1760 by Thomas Robinson, the future second Lord Grantham of Newby Park:

> I am just sending off a case for Leghorn which in a few months will reach you. It contains two Tablets of Egyptian Granite, which I think are the first pieces of it I have ever seen; and not to make them useless I propose with your leave to desire you to set up a couple of busts that attend them upon them.[36]

On his return in the 1760s William Weddell of Newby Hall set up a sculpture gallery to house his collection of antique sculpture. It drew grudging admiration from even the jaundiced pen of Louis Simond in his *Journal of a Tour and Residence in Great Britain during 1810 and 1811 by a French Traveller*:

> Newby Hall is one of those innumerable fine houses, scattered over this country, which are allowed to be shown to strangers. This one, however, is distinguished from the crowd, by a collection of antique marbles of much reputation. Mr W. the last proprietor, took the trouble of collecting himself abroad, at a vast expense, these remains of Grecian art. His [Barberini] Venus alone, we were told, cost £15,000 sterling; a great price, undoubtedly; but the satire of Voltaire will not apply here, for although acheté cher, this is not a moderne antique.

In this way the core of the antiquities, genuine, touched up, doctored, copied and faked, that grace so many country houses today, entered Britain. Valuable heirlooms now, on occasion they had no lasting significance for their collector: the marbles bought in Rome by the young Duke of Bridgwater, whose energies later went into mining and canal building, were still in their packing cases when he died.

Of course, the worldly-wise never saw the Tour simply in terms of the acquisition of culture and sophistication by their sons. Introductions to aristocratic society abroad brought invitations to balls and parties, while, away from home and family, young men could run wild. Venice might be visited for its galleries and churches, but the masked Carnival promised licence. Further, the Tour was expensive, so that the poorer gentleman found the cost of pictures or antique marbles beyond his purse. Three years after he succeeded to the family estate in 1706 at the age of 19 Sir William Wentworth of Bretton, Yorkshire, set off. Advised by Lord Raby to buy antiquities in Rome he replied that he hadn't the money:

> . . . for want of which I shall be very well content with the walls of Bretton just as they are, so that I have but a good glass of Ale and Bear to make my friends welcome with when they honour me with his [sic] company, which is all that I desire. . . .[37]

The cultural aspirations involved in the search for *objets d'art* were never universal in the landed classes.

Patronage of the arts

The building, fitting, decorating and furnishing of a country house and the ornamentation of its grounds was a considerable enterprise which gave employment to a wide range of artists and craftsmen – masons, joiners and carpenters, blacksmiths, plasterers and painters (ranging from housepainters to artists), sculptors and carvers. The historian who admires their work and wishes to document it will find evidence in contracts, bills, accounts and receipts, advertisements and correspondence.

Among the artists and craftsmen involved, the most widely known is perhaps Thomas Chippendale, with his reputation as the finest cabinet-maker and furniture designer of his day. In beautiful line drawings his *Gentleman and Cabinet Maker's Director*, first published in 1754, illustrates rococo designs for furniture: chairs, tables, chandeliers, mirrors, clock cases, bed or window cornices, candle stands, basin stands, wine coolers. It soon became the authoritative pattern-book for cabinet-makers. In the following year Peter Thornhill, a craftsman, obtained a copy for John Aislabie of Studley Royal, drawing attention to it in a letter of 2 January 1756:

> My young man told me you was observing to Him about ye Bill for the large Fender – but Sir you paid Me for it yourself in the large Hall at the same time when you paid Me for Chippendales Book – so there is nothing more due to me but the last Acco't given In – £11 8 0.

The bill referred to lies in the Vyner archives along with the letter.[38]

Complete accounts of extensive collections of Chippendale's work survive for three houses in England: Harewood, Nostell Priory and Mersham le Hatch. Other owners bought particular pieces. A beautifully written, signed bill for three minor pieces – a hexagon table, a pole glass and a mahogany travelling strongbox – survives for Temple Newsam, the total price being £8.[39]

Bills and receipts are chiefly of value in establishing the provenance of their contents, whereas correspondence may also illuminate attitudes and introduce

Darlington Jan'y 2nd - 1756

Sir/ My young Man told Me you was observing
to Him about my Bill for the large Fender —
but Sir You paid Me for it Yourself in the
large Hall at the same time when You
paid Me for Chippendales Book —
so there is nothing more due to me but
the last Acc'. given Yr — £ 11 " 8 . 0
Sir I shall be very much Oblig'd to Yr Honour
if you please to order the Payment of it to
John Dowson Hatker in Ripon against
the 6th of this Instant being one of My
Neighbours will be their at y'. Time and
Sr What may be further wanted in My Way
at any time Sir I shall be thankfully Glad
to Receive yr Orders, it it shall be faithfully
Observed By yr most

H'ble Serv't

To Com'd

Peter Thornhill

14 Craftsman's bill mentioning purchase of Chippendale's *Gentleman and Cabinet Maker's Director*, 1756.

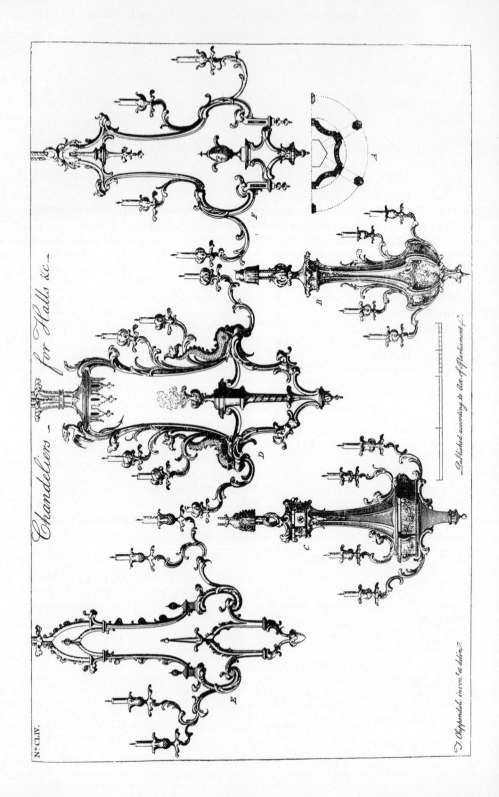

Chandeliers — for Halls &c.—

Published according to Act of Parliament.

T. Chippendale inven.t et delin.

issues of wider human interest. When the first Earl of Strafford of Wentworth Castle married in 1711, he commissioned portraits of Anne, the Countess, and himself from Charles Jervas. The result did not please Lady Anne, who wrote to the Earl on 27 November:

> I went last week to see our piktures and I like them worse than I ever did, for he has mad a Dwarfe of you and a Giant of me, and he has not tooched the dressing of them sence you went. I made Capt. Powell scold at hime to mend them, for they are nethere of them like. He is so ingaged with the Marlborough daughters that he minds no body elce.

By 21 March of the following year she was sufficiently mollified to write:

> I have been at Mr Jervises to see our pikturs; I think he has mended them both extremly and has made yours a good deal taller and the robes are well of them both . . .[40]

From small beginnings in the sixteenth and seventeenth centuries books became increasingly important in the fitting out of a house as the notion of the gentleman as a man of cultivated sensibilities became widespread. Eighteenth-century plans increasingly show a library, some of the most famous being long galleries, and eventually it became a *sine qua non*. Their contents offer an insight into the interests and the intellectual and cultural ideals of their owners. Catalogues were, in fact, compiled in the great houses that employed scholar-librarians, while when house contents were sold books would be listed in sale catalogues, though valuable items might be held back.

A catalogue and an index of the 900 or so titles at Temple Newsam were compiled in the mid-eighteenth century. Histories were more plentiful than any other type of book, followed by more or less equal numbers of works on philosophy and religion on the one hand and Greek and Latin classics (in both the original language and translation) on the other. Then came contemporary or recent writers, like Swift, Pope and Gay, native literary classics, travel, standard works useful for estate management, architectural works and collections of periodicals like the *Spectator* and the *Tatler*.[41] Perhaps Lord Warrington's library at Dunham Massey was more typical of the time. It contained sections on architecture and topography, natural history and botany, politics and philosophy, theology, literature, music and genealogy. But as well as books for current use, rare and beautiful books were collected, in line with the collections of books and rare and curious objects that had occupied the closets of earlier centuries.

Any analysis of the patronage of the arts in the nineteenth century would rest on similar sources, but one example in particular is worth quoting as it points to a useful source for the fitting out of the country house in relatively recent times. In the loggia of the marble staircase installed by William Bankes at Kingston Lacy is set a bronze relief of the siege of Corfe Castle in the Civil War along with monumental brass figures of Sir John and Lady Bankes, and Charles I. Sir John was Chief Justice

---

15 Chandeliers from Chippendale's *Gentlemen and Cabinet Maker's Director*, 1762 edition.

---

to the King and Lady Bankes withstood the siege. William Bankes commissioned both the relief and the figures from the Turin-born French sculptor Baron Marochetti. In March 1855 Bankes wrote to his sister:

> I scarcely ever received a letter that gave me more pleasure than one . . . from Marochetti, enclosing a photograph (which you know is a reduced representation produced mechanically on paper, and therefore exact to the utmost degree), of the basrelief executed by him . . . If the execution of the statues be comformable to this high standard of excellence . . . where will there be in any private house in England a family monument of equal magnificence.[42]

'Exact to the utmost degree', but as partial and fallible as any other source, the photograph offers its particular insights into the country house and its surroundings. The camera came into its own just as the dominance of landed wealth was under threat and provides a significant record of the subsequent fortunes of the country house.

Chapter Three

THE LANDED ESTATE: MANAGEMENT AND IMPROVEMENT

Manors and manorial records

From the Middle Ages to the twentieth century aristocrats were privileged to exercise seigneurial rights over their copyhold tenants. In practice, this meant that as lords of the manor they were entitled to hold a court. Like so many developments in feudal society after the Norman Conquest, the manorial system defies a simple explanation. A manor was an administrative unit of a landed estate. A large estate might comprise a number of manors. Sometimes the manorial unit coincided with a village but this need not be the case. Some villages contained several manors and some manors contained several villages. In short, there was infinite variety, but in England manors will be found in almost every place and at almost every time between the twelfth century and the fifteenth.[1]

In contrast to those of their Continental counterparts, the seigneurial rights of the English aristocracy had diminished significantly by 1550. In particular, the right to exercise criminal jurisdiction over their tenants had been surrendered to the Crown. However, where the lord had the right to hold a Court Leet he retained a jurisdiction in petty offences such as debt, trespass and nuisance as well as in the appointment of the lowest officials in local government.[2]

By the sixteenth century all land was held to be either freehold or copyhold. Copyhold tenure depended for proof upon a copy of an entry in the court rolls of the manor and copyholders were subject to manorial dues, small annual rents and heriots or fines of admission when inheriting or selling. Copyhold was already declining in the sixteenth century and by 1750 the great bulk of English agricultural land was let for money rent on leases of from three to fourteen years. On some manors copyholds were enfranchised with the tenant paying a lump sum to convert his tenure into a freehold. Indeed, it has been suggested that the growth of farm leases marks the most significant element in the history of English landholding from 1400 to 1750.[3] These changes were not only of enormous importance in transforming the character of rural society and the process of farming, they also determined to a considerable extent the survival of manorial records. As N.W. Alcock has pointed out:

> On manors without copyhold tenure, the keeping of manor courts generally came to an end in the seventeenth and eighteenth centuries, and it is all too common for most of the rolls to have been lost. Where copyhold persisted, the court rolls were of legal importance as the main record of land 'ownership' (as it was in effect). They were therefore generally both well-kept and well-preserved, and many copyhold manors have continuous runs from the sixteenth or seventeenth centuries down until 1922.[4]

The Manor of Burstwick. to wit **A Rental** of the Copyhold rents due to Francis Constable Esquire Lord of the Seigniory of Holderness Lord of the said manor at Michas 1805 for messuages lands tenements and hereditaments in the Township of Keyingham within the said manor to be collected by Robert Carlile Broadley Esquire Pennygrave for the said Township and to be paid in at the Court to be held in and for the said manor on Wednesday 16th October 1805

	£	s	d
Atkinson Robert Jur. ux. late Elletson			10
Bath Countess of		3	4
Burnes Matthw late Bell		1	6
Booth John late Hodge			1
Broadley Robert Carlile Esqr.	5	12	10¼
Burrill Peter		3	4
late Hollon			3
late Gray			1
Carr William Jur. ux. late Elletson			10
Carlin William late Bell	1	5	2
late Bell free Rent		3	4
late Wood		7	9
Carrick John late Waddingham			2
Carrick Lydia late Rooss			1
Christy Robert qu. house now Thos. Jackson jur. ux.			1
Collings Jane		4	11¾
Coleman John			1
Crawforth John & Samuel Suddaby			½
Elletson Elizabeth			9
Elletson Job late Scott		1	4
Fenby John late Ramsey		8	2
Same		1	7
Same		6	8
Hancock William late Skelton			6
late Colman		7	¾
Harrison John		1	2
Hildyard Sir Robt. D'Arcy seal late Rooss		4	5¼
Jackson Thomas Jur. ux. late Christy		13	2
Kemp Wilfred Jur. ux. late Arcy in reversion after the decease of Frances ux. Geo. Scott		1	

Carry over £ 10 4 3¼

16 A rental of the copyhold rents due to Francis Constable Esquire, Lord of the Seigneury of Holderness and Lord of the Manor of Burstwick. 1805.

THE LANDED ESTATE: MANAGEMENT AND IMPROVEMENT

Assuming that manorial records have survived in the archives of a landed family, what can one expect of them? They are among the most informative of all sources of local history; a mine of information about farming and rural life down the centuries. Originally, manor courts were held once a year. The freeholders of the manor came to do homage to their lord, to pay their rents, and to elect a constable, a hayward and a tithingman. A jury of 12 was sworn; deaths were reported and tenancies surrendered, entered into or renewed; rights of way were confirmed, rules of husbandry laid down and any matters of local interest discussed. Court rolls, the records of the transactions of the court, are usually found to be entered on membranes of vellum, measuring from 7 to 12 inches in width and about 20 to 24 inches in length, stitched together in a bulky roll many feet long. The entry for a single court may vary in length from two to three inches to two feet or more. The end of the proceedings of one court and the beginning of another are clearly spaced and titled. However, there are problems to be faced by would-be users of early court rolls. Most are yellowed, faded and damaged, often barely legible. The writing is in Latin and in a variety of hands.[5] There is some small comfort in that they ceased to be recorded in Latin fom 1722, and that some are available in translation and printed editions.

Most sets of manor court rolls and books are now in county record offices, but strays are frequent. The writer Elspeth Huxley, who lived for many years in the Wiltshire village of Oaksey, has described how she came to be shown the court books for Poole Keynes' Court Leet and Court Baron for the years 1845 to 1871. Apparently, when the first Lord Biddulph, lord of the manor of Poole and Kemble, died, his son sold off most of the farms to their tenants. One of the tenants inherited the court books and his son showed them to Miss Huxley. They relate to a period when Robert Gordon MP was lord of the manor, 1809 to 1865. The court had settled matters such as a dispute between Poole and Oaksey over their boundary, cases of ploughing up the footpath from Poole to Somerford, depositing rubbish by the highway and impounding stray sheep and fining their owners. Robert Gordon's daughter became lady of the manor in the mid-1860s and she convened the court only twice more before abandoning the tradition.[6] The story does illustrate how manorial records can turn up in private hands. A good way of finding out where to locate originals is to consult the up-to-date register kept by the Royal Commission on Historical Manuscripts.[7]

One of the richest collections of manorial records is to be found in the archives of Petworth House, West Sussex. These date from the reign of Edward III and are complete from the beginning of the seventeenth to the twentieth century. For the period from the accession of Charles I the proceedings of Petworth Manorial Court were also recorded in books and 25 volumes cover the 300 years from 1625 to the passing of the Law of Property Act in 1922.[8] Lord Leconfield researched them extensively in the 1950s to construct a detailed picture of Petworth Manor in the seventeenth century. The Honour of Petworth belonged to the Percy family, Earls of Northumberland, and comprised the manors of Petworth, Sutton, Duncton and Heyshott. In the seventeenth century each manor had its own court which combined the functions of:

90	ENFRANCHISEMENTS.	Copyhold in BONDAGE						Cop: With! Imp. of WASTE						Annual Cop. Rent			Year enfran-chised	Rec'd for Enfranchisem'		
		Qty			Value			Qty			Value									
		A	R	P	£	s	d	A	R	P	£	s	d	£	s	d		£	s	d
1	Prest. Mr. Iveson	6	9	34	4	2	6	33	1	16	21	3	6	~	13	3	1774	69	10	6
2	— Fran. Thompson Esq	120	~	0	93	5	~	29	~	30	25	2	~	6	7	~	—	060	7	~
3	— Mr. Bramley							76	1	12	50	10	~	2	13	~	—	130	~	~
4	— Mr. Bendall							1	2	~	1	6	~	~	~	9	...	2	7	10½
5	— Jos. Sykes Esq	31	~	~	27	~	~	92	2	20	90	~	~	4	14	9½	—	411	3	6
6	Shipwell Jos. Sykes Esq	68	1	17	22	~	~	69	3	0	32	~	~	5	7	0½	—	347	6	~
7	Bunstw. Mr. Standidge	139	3	30	75	~	~	43	1	13	20	~	~	6	16	0	—	750	~	~
8	Burst. Mr. Iveson	30	~	27	16	~	~	23	~	31	15	~	~	1	10	7	—	104	17	6
9	Prest. Jos. Williamson Esq	35	2	24	20	~	~	94	3	24	70	~	~	4	11	7½	—	309	0	9
10	Burst. Mr. Smith							10	1	1	7	~	~	~	10	1	1775	22	2	6
11	Prest. Mr. Smith	4	~	~	2	10	~	27	2	5	10	10	~	1	~	11	—	70	3	6
12	Eas. John Porter Esq	50	2	30	46	~	~	123	3	20	73	~	~	3	12	9	—	504	2	6
13	Sheffl. John Porter Esq	15	2	0	11	13	~	5	1	36	4	2	~	1	~	2	—	115	10	~
14	Prest. Christ. Scott Esq	12	2	34	14	10	~	22	3	26	15	~	~	1	5	7	—	154	17	6
15	Mackl. Tho. Appleby							1	2	36	2	10	~	~	1	11½	1776	5	0	3
16	Burst. Mr. Brown	36	2	30	23	~	~	39	1	39	33	10	~	3	10	9	1777	300	12	6
17	Sproat. Mr. Tho. Brown	16	1	12	0	~	~	10	1	4	10	~	~	1	3	11	—	106	17	6
18	Lell. Mr. Binnington	19	~	20	11	~	~	21	3	32	13	~	~	~	12	~	1778	100	~	~
19	Lell. Rob. Fisher	1	2	10	1	10	~							~	~	1	—	10	12	6
		602	3	26	304	10	6	1735	2	33	491	13	6	46	1	5	£	4552	3	10½

17 Enfranchisements for the Holderness manors of the Constable family, 1778.

(i) the Court Baron of the freehold tenants in which they were the judges.
(ii) the Customary Court of the copyhold tenants with the lord or his steward as the judge.
(iii) the Court Leet with jurisdiction over petty offences.

What sort of things did the Petworth courts deal with? The court rolls and later the books are a record of all the ordinances, duties, customs and conveyances that concerned the lord and his copyhold tenants. All transfers of copyholds had to be presented to the court as surrenders and admittances, as had deaths of tenants and admissions of heirs to be presented and recorded on rolls or in books. From these were written the copies of court roll that were the copyholders' title deeds. The deaths of freehold tenants and the reliefs paid by their heirs were recorded separately. The lord of the manor appointed three officials, the seneschal, who presided over the court, the bailiff, its executive officer who collected the rents, and

> Dec.r 12th 1804 Hornsea
>
> Sir
>
> This is to acquaint you that Four
> Men at Atwick. George Ulliot Matthew Dickeson
> John Collinson and John Milner. got a piece of wood
> at the Sea Side which was marked for Mr Constable.
> They are the Men who watches the Beacon. They
> catch all that comes thereabouts. and threatens to
> put into the Sea any who marks a piece of Wood
> for Mr Constable ——————
> I am
> Sir
> your Hble Servt.
> B Watson

18 Letter concerning right of wreck. As lords of the seigneury of Holderness, the Constable family had special claims of land reclaimed from the sea, wrecks and timber.

the reeve, who was head of a jury of 24. The business of the court originated with this trio. They were required to present whatever happened in the manor to the prejudice of the lord or the tenants and to recommend what was of advantage to the lord without injury to the tenants. Yet another official, the messor, was responsible for the lord's court perquisites and amercements, for example, fines and heriots recoverable on the estate transactions of copyholders, reliefs due on freeholds and royalties on the mining of iron ore. He or the hayward superintended the water meadows and commons. The ale-conners were kept busy reporting sales of beer on short measure and were also responsible for detecting breaches of the assize of bread and sales of butter on short weight. When the court sat as a Court Leet its main business was with keeping the streets of Petworth clean. A general presentment offered in September 1644 summed up the problem:

> That the streets and highways of the town are foul and full of dung and dirt to the common
> nuisance of the King's people in default of the inhabitants of the said town and therefore
> [we] do order that every inhabitant within the said town shall amend and reform the said
> nuisance so much as concerns every inhabitant respectively upon pain of every particular
> person as shall be found defective to forfeit 20s. to be amended before the feast day of All
> Saints next.[9]

The problem of wandering pigs in the town was a matter that frequently called
for action. In 1662 an ordinance was promulgated which penalized offending
owners:

> Ordered that Robert Tredgrove and Francis Hayward be appointed by this Court, with
> the consent of the homage and the tenants present, to drive all the pigs that wander about
> the street to the pound and that they shall have 4d for each hog they do so impound to be
> paid by the owner of the hogs.[10]

A special function of the court was the upkeep of the water supply which had been
installed in the reign of Henry VII. The townspeople had the duty of keeping their
three taps in order and of assessing themselves for the cost. A fourth tap had been
installed for the use of Petworth House. The cleanliness of the water taps was a
frequent concern of the manorial court. For example, Alery Coates was amerced 2d
for washing bullocks' entrails at one of the outlets. Alice Martin connected her own
leaden pipe to one of the taps and was fined 12d and ordered to remove it. Such was
Petworth's public water supply, apart from private wells, until 1782.

A great map was made of the manor in 1610. It shows the lord's parks and his
demesne, some 5000 acres, the 3000 acres farmed by his customary tenants or
copyholders and the 340 acres of commons. It also shows every field, close and
croft, with its measurements and the name of the tenant. Lord Leconfield's searches
indicated that in the years between the two surveys of 1557 and 1610 the outwood of
200 acres had been enclosed into the park and Middlekorne Wood had been made a
common pasture. This and the erection of a fence along the northern boundary of
Home Park was the cause of a long dispute between the Earl and his tenants. The
tenants were not satisfied that the alternative pannage granted to them was adequate
compensation and there was violent opposition. The ninth Earl wrote to Sir John
Pickering, the lord keeper, about the incident after the copyholders had taken the
case to the court of Chancery:

> [19 July 1592] They [the tenants] have oftsoons renewed their secret and riotous pulling
> down in the night season by themselves and accomplices my pales and enclosures, as well
> as those lands in question before the Chancery (whereof my father and self have had quiet
> possession by the space of sixteen years or thereabouts) as of my own freeholds and
> demesne no whit touched by the said controversy.[11]

Commissioners were appointed to examine the issues and resolve the matter. In
the event, the Earl proved conciliatory and a declaration addressed to him by a
substantial number of his tenants suggests that a satisfactory settlement was
reached.

With such a wealth of detail at his disposal – court rolls, maps and surveys – Lord

Leconfield was able to make substantial comments on the Petworth copyholds and their tenants. There is also much information in the manorial records about rents and leases, a subject which will be addressed in some detail later, as well as the town of Petworth itself and the estate iron-workings. The Manor of Petworth and its customs have been quoted at some length because it is such a good example. However, it must be emphasized that no two manors had identical customs. There were regional variations and these would have been apparent to anyone who left his normal place of residence. A surveyor of the manor of Iwerne Courtney in Dorset in 1553 made this very point:

> Their customs are not so universall as if a man have experyence of the customs and services of any mannor he shall thereby have perfect knowledge of all the rest, or if he be experte of the customes of any one mannor in any one countie that he shall nede of no further enstruccions for all the residewe of the mannors within that countie.[12]

Enclosure and improvement

Enclosure implies change from medieval open fields to the smaller hedged fields of the present-day landscape. It was a process that went on piecemeal from the fourteenth century, with variations from region to region and even within different parts of counties. For example, in Devon the chronology of enclosure begins in the eastern part of the county in the middle of the thirteenth century but does not touch some parts until the seventeenth century. In parts of northern England it did not become widespread until the sixteenth century. A type of enclosure that could arouse passions was the conversion by lords of their demesne lands and, more particularly, the commons and wastes, for sheep farming. This appears to have been the cause of the discontent at Petworth in the late sixteenth century. Another form of enclosure was 'engrossing', or the amalgamation of two or more holdings into one to create larger, more compact units, thereby making agriculture more efficient and profitable. This was often the result of local agreement and entered into amicably.

From about 1550 onwards there was renewed interest in the latter form of enclosure; the incentive was to introduce what is known as convertible husbandry, i.e., the alternation of arable farming and grass; a corn crop followed by sheep or the more traditional arable followed by fallow. Large areas of pastoral England – the Wiltshire Downs, the Chilterns, the Cotswolds, the Yorkshire and Lincolnshire Wolds and parts of Norfolk – were put to the plough for the first time. The changes were far-reaching and affected both agricultural practice and the character of the English landscape. In Wiltshire, Dorset and Hampshire the major achievement in agricultural technique was the development of water meadows. This encouraged a much earlier growth of grass, which provided early feed for the sheep flocks and made it possible to keep larger flocks than would otherwise have been possible. Evidence suggests that landlords played an important part. For example, at Puddletown in Dorset in 1629 when the tenants met to decide about watering their meadows, the manorial court book records that:

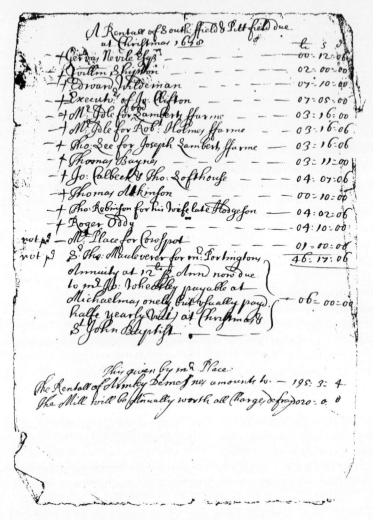

19 A rental of open fields in Armley belonging to the Wentworths of Woolley in Yorkshire.

The honorable Henrie Hastings esquire Lord of the same manor being present with the Tenants of the same and a great debate beinge theare had and questions moved by some of the tenants about wateringe and improvinge thereupon by Full consent yt was ordered in Courte and agreed unto by the tenants in court . . .[13]

As well as convertible husbandry and the floating of water meadows, new types of fodder crops were introduced, especially after 1650. Until this time the main fodder crops were beans, vetches and oats and, in some areas, barley. Root crops were virtually unknown. In the 1650s turnips appeared for the first time as a field crop in Norfolk, Suffolk and Buckinghamshire. Dorset aristocrat, Sir Anthony Ashley of Wimborne St Giles, is credited with the introduction of growing cabbage as a field crop to provide food for stock. New grasses such as clover, sainfoin, lucerne, trefoil and rye-grass came to England from the Low Countries in the mid-seventeenth century. A returning exile, Sir Richard Weston, is believed to have introduced clover and the Walpole family of Norfolk were among the first to make effective use of it.[14]

Some landowners concerned themselves with the problems of drainage and land reclamation. This had been going on piecemeal for centuries but the prospect of increasing food production and providing employment for the growing seventeenth-century population provided the stimulus to invest larger capital sums. By far the biggest undertaking was the drainage of the Fens by the fourth and fifth Earls of Bedford and other landowners between 1600 and 1650. With the backing of legislation and the services of the celebrated Dutch engineer, Cornelius Vermuyden, they financed the drainage of some 400,000 acres of inland peat fens on the Thorney Estate in Cambridgeshire and parts of Huntingdonshire, an area known as the Bedford Levels. Similar work was undertaken in Yorkshire by the Earl of Strafford at Hatfield Chase.[15]

Domestic agricultural production increased sufficiently to cope with a doubling of the English population between 1550 and 1750 and for some historians the agricultural revolution took place in this period rather than the traditional eighteenth and nineteenth centuries. However, it may be safer to argue, as one historian has recently, that the process of agricultural change is too continuous and too varied to enable any one episode in a long history of development to be identified as the agricultural revolution.[16]

In the period 1760 to 1815 there was renewed interest in enclosure due to quickening growth in demand and the sustained rise in prices after about 1760. A novel feature was the use of private Acts of Parliament. Hitherto, all enclosures had been arranged by agreement of sorts between the owners. Where a major landowner owned most or all of the land the difficulties were fewer. In order to obtain more convenient farms, owners large and small had frequently exchanged lands and made inroads into the open fields to serve as additional pasture closes. In this way, as G.E. Mingay has observed, silently and unobtrusively, the open fields and open villages were gradually eroded away. Quite often when an Act of Parliament was obtained in the late eighteenth century, it was simply 'to dispose of the rump of open fields and tidy up the complex of closes'.[17] Occasionally, a landowner did not get things all his own way. Sir Mark Stuart Pleydell of Coleshill saw his parliamentary Bill for private enclosure at Watchfield rejected in 1732. Pleydell's claim for almost one-fifth of the total allotment led to separate counter-petitions from a group of landowners, including Viscount Barrington, all of whom complained that Pleydell was asking for an unfair distribution of land, counter to their own interests. The plan was defeated and Watchfield remained open and commonable until 1792.[18]

From the foregoing it will be apparent that enclosure bills, and to a lesser extent the awards and maps, are to be found in collections of estate papers. Enclosure

·A·N·

A C T

ᵗFOR

Dividing, Allotting, and Inclofing the Open Arable Fields, Meadow and Pafture Grounds, within the Townfhip and Parifh of *Keyingham,* in *Holdernefs,* in the Eaft Riding of the County of *York,* and for making Compenfation for the Tythes thereof, and alfo for the Tythes of certain ancient inclofed Lands, within the faid Townfhip and Parifh.

Ⓗ Ⓔ Ⓡ Ⓔ Ⓐ Ⓢ there are within the Townfhip and Parifh Preamble. of *Keyingham,* in *Holdernefs,* in the Eaft Riding of the County of *York,* certain Open Arable Fields, Meadow and Pafture Grounds, diftinguifhed by the feveral Names of *The Eaft Field, The Weft Field,* and *Kirncroft, The Ings, The Saltmarfh, The Eaft Car,* and *The Weft Car,* confifting of Forty-one Oxgangs or thereabouts, and containing in the Whole by Eftimation One Thoufand Three Hundred and Fifty Acres or thereabouts; and certain Meffuages, Cottages, and ancient inclofed Lands, containing in the whole One Hundred and Thirty Acres or thereabouts:

And whereas there is alfo within the faid Townfhip and Parifh of *Keyingham* a certain Hamlet or Lordfhip called *Keyingham Marfh,* whereof *Edward Conftable,* Efquire, is the Proprietor, confifting of feveral Farms of ancient inclofed Land, containing together in the whole by Eftimation Twelve Hundred Acres or thereabouts; and alfo a certain Hamlet, Lordfhip, or Farm, called *Saltah Grange,* whereof the Corporation of the Sons of the Clergy is Proprietor,

A   containing

20 Inclosure Act for Keyingham in North Humberside. One of many copies of East Riding enclosure awards and acts from c.1735 to c.1820 surviving in the Burton Constable papers.

awards are the findings of the parliamentary commissioners and, together with the accompanying maps, they provide detailed information such as field-names, owners' names and sometimes the boundaries and names of former open fields.

THE LANDED ESTATE: MANAGEMENT AND IMPROVEMENT

Estate maps and surveys

Well-drawn, detailed and accurate estate maps are, in the words of F.G. Emmison, the greatest treasure for the local historian. They range from maps of small estates or even single farms to entire parishes and big estates extending into several parishes. The amount of topographical detail in some estate maps, especially eighteenth-century ones, is quite remarkable:

> Almost certainly all field boundaries, with the name and acreage of each field and wood, the roads and lanes, streams and ponds, greens and unenclosed waste. Every dwelling is shown, miniature drawings usually in block plan but sometimes of the important buildings and farmhouses are given. Colour may be used to show the land use (arable, meadow, pasture, hopfield, quarry etc.) or to distinguish the areas or ownership of farms and smaller holdings. A map of a whole parish normally names the owners and may also give the occupiers. If the map was drawn before the date of an enclosure award, it probably shows the owner's scattered strips . . .[19]

One of the earliest and most comprehensive exercises in mapping and surveying estates was that undertaken at the beginning of the seventeenth century by William Senior. Senior was employed by the first and second Earls of Devonshire from 1600 to 1628. By the end of this period William Cavendish, the second Earl, owned nearly 100,000 acres, approximately 45 per cent of which was in Derbyshire and 26 per cent in Yorkshire. Senior's task was to map and survey the estates. An atlas of his maps is preserved in the Devonshire Collections at Chatsworth. It consists of 65 maps drawn on vellum using a range of colours. They are considered to be relatively accurate and technically very sound for the period. Senior's 1610 map of Hardwick shows the estate soon after the completion of the New Hall by Bess. It shows that there was considerable woodland cover long before the days of landscaped parks and also that there was a very clear division between it and the formal garden in the vicinity of the house. This is what Senior had to say about Hardwick in his survey:[20]

The survey of Hardweeke Belonginge to the right Honorable Lord Cavendish: Taken by William Senior 1609 according to the former accompt

	A.	R.	P.
the Newe and ould halls, their Inner and utter Courtes The gardin and orchard, also the Brewhouse, Stable and other buildings, together with			
the Stable courte	22	1	10
the little cowe pasture	07	1	20
the Swine parke	01	2	25
Robinsons close	39	3	30
Carlaine close	03	3	00
the laine	00	3	10
Bolhill upper closes	21	3	00
Bole hill nether closes	33	0	30
Plumtre closes	14	2	30
Thornie wood closes	4	3	00

Frithes closes	16	1	26
great cowclose	30	3	20
the Lawnd	112	1	10
the Parke	314	1	10
Wast without the Parke gate			
	621	0	11

The most prominent surveyor of the West Riding of Yorkshire in the early eighteenth century was Joseph Dickinson. His excellent maps must have adorned the walls of many a squire's parlour, including the fine, coloured 1711 map by Dickinson of the estate of the Earl of Cardigan in Headingley, Leeds.[21] In common with other surveyors who mapped the estates of wealthy patrons, Dickinson liked to flatter his employer by incorporating decorative features into the maps such as the coloured compass-rose and scale, the full heraldic achievement of the estate owner's arms, and the individually styled cartouche.

Surveys can provide valuable information about individual farms and their tenants, especially when related to estate maps. The ancient manor of Goldsborough in North Yorkshire was purchased by Daniel Lascelles *c.*1750. When he died in 1784 the property went to his brother Edwin, who lived at nearby Harewood House. Goldsborough Hall became well known to the public for a brief period in the 1920s when it was the home of the heir to Harewood, Henry Lascelles, and his wife HRH Princess Mary. The manorial records for Goldsborough do not appear to have survived but eighteenth-century surveys of the manor and estate maps are among the Harewood Papers in Leeds City Archives.

A survey of 1796 gives details of the 10 farms and their leases as well as information about the Hall, the mill and various cottage properties:

> Lofthouse's Farm: Consists of a capital farmhouse with a good barn, stable, and granary, cowhouse, carthouse, pigsties, hovels etc. all brick and tile, substantially built of a uniform construction, commodiously arranged and in complete repair. Lease between Edward, Lord Harewood, and Daniel and Thomas Lofthouse of Goldsborough, all that farm etc. containing 126 acres 2 roods 26 perches with 9 beast gaites and three quarters at a yearly rent of £136. 3 days work. signed with a mark by both Daniel and Thomas Lofthouse.[22]

Rentals and accounts

From the accession of Elizabeth I to the outbreak of the Civil War, England experienced what is termed the Price Revolution. In this period agricultural prices increased faster than manufactured goods and raw materials and may even have trebled. It was a time when landed proprietors had good reason to keep a strict account of income and expenditure. Christopher Wandesford of Kirklington gave the following sound advice to his son:

21 Goldsborough Hall, owned by the Lascelles family from c.1750 to the 1920s.

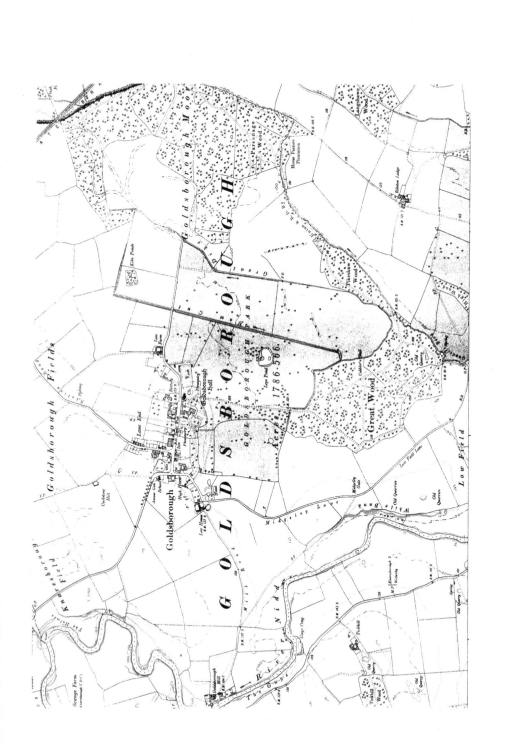

As in other Things so especially a good Order is to be kept in your Rentalls: an exact Accompt of your domesticall and all other Expences; the more plain and particular, the better; and under the more Heads you distribute your Receipts and Disbursements, you will find it more familiar, and less subject to Confusion.[23]

Where rentals and accounts have survived they provide the historian with an opportunity to estimate the relative prosperity of a family. There are considerable difficulties however, as J.R. Wordie found in his work on the Leveson family in the seventeenth century. Not only did the Leveson rentals vary in legibility – some were so badly kept as to be virtually unintelligible – there were other difficulties which made interpretation far from straightforward. His experience taught him that:

EXPENCES *laid out upon the Estate of William Constable Esqr from Mar: 14th 1747 to Decr 31. 1779*

	£
Mansion House and Grounds at Burton Constable. — Farm Houses &c	40034
Labourers Wages	11209
Cherry Cobb Sand	8897
Keyingham Drainage	3779
Sproatley and Burstw. Inclosures	1300
Surveying, Valuing, Fencing, Ditching e Draining, altering e re-setting the Estate when raised in 1775	1200
Hedon Navigation	100
Sproatley Turnpike	260
£	74779

22 Estate expenses of William Constable of Burton Constable 1747–79.

... in the seventeenth century even more than in the eighteenth, rental figures tended to illustrate local policies and standards of estate management far more than any national economic trends and both the standards and policies of landlords varied widely across the country. Fluctuations in the area or population of the property could influence the figures and often the re-grouping of various manors on different rent rolls further complicated the picture. Moreover if good sets of seventeenth century rental and survey figures are rare, sets of arrear figures to accompany them are much rarer and these of course are at least as important as the rental due figures . . .[24]

At the same time, a rental need not necessarily reflect the whole range of a landowner's estate income. This could also include such items as fines, heriots, tithe rents, payments in kind, various obligatory services and other medieval survivals, as well as industrial rents and royalties. In the nineteenth century accounting procedures generally improved, especially on estates where the owner employed a qualified and experienced steward or agent.

Leases and tenancy agreements

In 1812 Edward Lascelles was created first Earl of Harewood and he wasted no time in having some impressive new tenancy agreements printed. One of the first to sign was John Gill of Rigton. Farmer Gill's agreement indicates that he was to pay a yearly rent of £60, contribute to the landlord's property tax, perform two days' boon work, carting and carrying as required, and be prepared to sign any covenants regarding the cultivation and management of his farm.[25] Agreements and covenants were an essential element regulating the affairs of the estate and relations between landlord and tenant. While the Earl was busy entertaining and making Harewood a centre of culture and the arts or spending lavishly in London, his agent Robert Menzies attended to these more mundane matters. For example, an agreement for manure was signed earlier the same year with Farmer Beck:

> An agreement made this twenty eigth day of September, one Thousand eight Hundred and twelve between Robert Menzies on behalf of the Earl of Harewood and William Beck of Beckwithshaw. The said Robert Menzies agrees to permit the said William Beck to carry the crop of corn and grain now standing and growing upon the lands of the said Earl of Harewood now in the occupation of the said William Beck part of which is reaped, from the premises of the aforesaid Earl, upon condition that the said William Beck shall bring back to the lands of the said Earl before mentioned, on or before the 1st day of May now next ensuing Thirty Loads of three Horse Cart each of Dung, under the penalty of two pounds per load.[26]

A survey was kept at Harewood which recorded brief details of any changes in rents, tenancies and special circumstances affecting payments. One poor farmer, William Barrett, who had eight children, was given a helping hand to emigrate in 1850. The entry reads:

> This poor man and his family of 8 children who had no prospect of being able to go on

Dr.   John Crowder with The

1803.

£. s. d.

To Amount of Rents received of the Tenants
at Clifton and Rawcliffe for half a year due
Martinmas 1803 as in the Third Column of Page 6 .... 1749 . 15 . 6

To Do. of Tenants occupying the Manor
Premises as in page 7 .... 89 . 16 . 6

To Do. of Huntington due Lady Day .... 309 . 4 . 2

1803 as in page 8 .... 1754 . 16 . 8
To Do. of Naxby & for half a year due
the same time as in page 13 ....

To Do. of Naffpa due the same time
as in page 14 .... 151 . 16 . 10

Rents within the Manor of Huntington due
Candlemas 1802 .... — . 15 . 2

To received of Mr Thomas Lumley for the
aclage of 180 acres of Pasture Land at Sexby
from Lady Day to Michaelmas 1803 .... 260 . — . —

1804
February 1st   Balance due to John Crowder .... 511 . 4 . 3

Feb 8th 1804 Delivered this as a true Account
(Errors excepted) the Balance being
carried to the next Account .... 4627 . 8 . 1

                                        John Crowder

Right Honorable Lord Grantham.   Cr.

1803.   £. s. d.

                    By Amount of Disbursements as in page
21 Viz.   £. s. d.
        Clifton and Rawcliffe .... 166 . 7 . 3
        Manor Premises .... 50 . 5 . 2
        Huntington .... 9 . 11 . 9
        Naxby & .... 1223 . 17 . 1
        Naffpa .... 4 . 6 . 2
                                    1444 . 7 . 5

August 29th By Remittance to Major Bolero Washington
£ on Account .... 2900 . — . —

By Sundries paid for Lord Grantham as
by Account delivered .... 83 . — . 8

By a years Salary due to John Crowder
1st February .... 200 . — . —

                                    4627 . 8 . 1

here have by the kind assistance of his Lordship been enabled to emigrate to Port Natal. His Lordship forgave the arrears of £55, being nearly 2 years rent and gave him besides £50, Lady Harewood also gave him £20 and other members of the family also subscribed.[27]

In general, it would seem that landlords prior to 1750 did not use lease covenants as a means of persuading their tenants to adopt more progressive methods.[28] Sir Mark Stuart Pleydell, of Coleshill, Berkshire, is an exception in this respect. It would appear that once he had become convinced of the superiority of permanent grass pastures, and the right way to establish them, he went to considerable lengths to convince his tenants that the system and methods that he was advocating would be best for both landlord and tenant.[29] Moreover, this interesting country squire of modest means has left one of the most extensive and informative collections of eighteenth-century estate papers – some 25 volumes, largely in his own hand, have survived, together with hundreds of loose documents.

What was exceptional practice in the mid-eighteenth century became more widely adopted in the nineteenth. At Holkham, for example, there is evidence to show how an intelligent agent, backed by a rich landlord, could influence the conduct of tenant farmers. Here, in the period 1816 to 1842, Francis Blaike, Coke's agent, developed a code of leases. The major provisions fixed the rotations the tenants were to use, under various systems applicable to various soils, and other clauses dealt with insurance, cartage for the landlord, repairs, providing the landlord with a turkey for Christmas and effecting underdraining whenever required. Tenants appear to have taken their covenants seriously and requests to deviate were granted only sparingly.[30]

Taxation

Items relating to the history of taxation frequently turn up in country house archives. This is not surprising bearing in mind that the wealth of the landowner was a major source of revenue. A direct tax, the hearth tax, was imposed in the 1660s and survived, despite its unpopularity, until 1691 when it was replaced by the land tax and window tax. Land Tax bore heavily upon some estates in the first quarter of the eighteenth century. At Holkham, for example, in the period 1707 to 1718 £10,292 was paid, or allowed to tenants, for taxes, a figure amounting to 13.3 per cent of the gross income for those years of £84,938. In the years 1708 to 1710 the land tax, at its usual wartime level of 4 shillings in the pound, took away 17.3 per cent of the gross rents due from the farms in Norfolk.[31] Significantly, it was a member of the Norfolk landed gentry, Whig politician Robert Walpole, who in the 1720s and 1730s worked with some success to reduce the incidence of direct taxation.

---

23 Estate accounts of Lord Grantham, showing income from rents and expenses, 1804.

I John Gill — — —
of *Rigton* — — — — — — in the County of
York, do hereby agree to rent and take of *The Right Hon. Edward Earl of
Harewood*, from *Lady Day* now next ensuing, from year to year, all that
Farm, Buildings, Land and Premises, the particulars of which are hereunto
annexed, at, and for the yearly rent of *Sixty Pounds* — — — .
— — — — — — clear of all deductions or outgoings whatever,
except landlord's property tax, payable half yearly, at *Pentecost* and *Martinmas*,
preceding the end, or expiration of the half year on which such rent shall become due,
and I also agree to perform, by way of boon=service in each year, *Two*
days work, with a waggon or cart, and three horses, in leading coals, or such other
materials for the use of the Earl of Harewood, as he the said Earl, or his Agent
shall direct, without any payment or allowance for the same; and I also agree
to give up the possession at Candlemas or Lady=Day next, of all such lands now
in my occupation as are not mentioned or described in the particulars hereto annexed,
and that I will, when required so to do, execute an agreement with the said Earl
of Harewood, containing such covenants for the cultivation and management of
the said farm and premises herein mentioned, as shall be agreed upon between the said
Earl, and the rest of his Tenants.

Witness my hand this *Nineteenth* Day of
December, one thousand eight hundred and twelve.

Witness hereto,

Robt. Menzies.

John Gill

a r p
43.2.35 Tithe free

24 Tenancy agreement between John Gill of Rigton and Edward, Earl of Harewood,
1812.

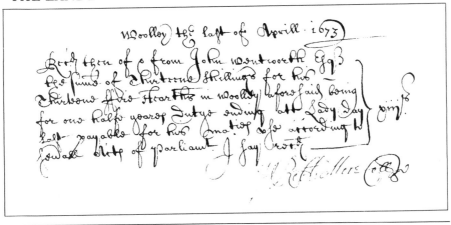

25 Hearth Tax receipt for thirteen hearths at Woolley Hall, 1673.

Godfrey Wentworth Esq
Assessed Taxes viz.

	£	s	d
49 Windows	15	16	9
60£ Rent for House July	0	10	0
4 Servants	0	14	0
1 Chariot	6	0	0
1 Gig	3	5	0
4 Horses	11	0	0
2 Dogs	1	0	0
Armorial bearings	2	0	0
	57	1	9

26 Assessed taxes of Godfrey Wentworth of Woolley Hall c.1790.

In the second half of the eighteenth century new taxes were raised to finance the American War, mainly on luxury items such as carriages, cards and dice. The number and range of assessed taxes on wealth greatly increased as the century came to a close. In 1777 a tax was imposed on male servants. Others followed on horses, dogs, watches and carriages and coats of arms. There was even a tax on hair powder.

But it would seem that landowners were lightly taxed in proportion to their incomes, and tenant farmers were more likely to be hurt by intermittent increases in taxation if their leases required that such taxes should be paid by them without deduction from rents.[32] In addition to centrally administered taxes, landowners also contributed at the local level to the poor rate, constable's levy, church rate and tithe. Correspondence about the latter can often be substantial, especially in cases where the landowner held the advowson.

Home farms and model farms

Marchioness Grey, writing to her married daughter in 1773, pointed out that 'neither here [Wimpole] nor at Wrest have we yet dealt much in the modern improvement of husbandry'. It surprised her that her son-in-law, Lord Polwarth, was beginning to show some interest in the subject. He had apparently been reading Arthur Young and pondering on seed drilling and broadcast sowing and wanted to try his hand at a model farm.[33] There was, of course, widespread interest among landowners in the eighteenth century in agricultural improvement. Some, like Townshend and Coke on their Norfolk estates, have found their way into countless textbooks as pioneers in husbandry and breeding methods. A home farm became a regular institution at Holkham in the 1720s under Thomas Coke, first Earl of Leicester. Evidence suggests that it was a serious and viable enterprise long before the time of the famous landlord, Coke of Holkham (1776–1818), and yet it was during his time that the Park Farm at Holkham was regarded by contemporaries as a model of the best farming practice.

There was equally significant work in progress on other estates. For example, the third Earl of Egremont converted 800,000 acres of Petworth into a model farm. This former parkland, described in the 1557 survey as parks for deer and conies, now became a place of experimentation in drainage, stock-breeding and cropping. The Earl seems to have been the first to succeed in the growing of rhubarb. At Wentworth the Marquis of Rockingham established two model farms, experimented with lime and manure, brought in new implements and improved his drainage. Francis, the fifth Duke of Bedford, carried out pioneering work on his Woburn estates. A member of the Board of Agriculture and a friend of Arthur Young, its secretary, the Duke enthusiastically tried out new methods of growing crops and raising stock. He is best known for his successes in sheep breeding and the annual sheep-shearing at Woburn became a famous and well-attended event. It took place over five days in June and attracted many distinguished visitors, including the presidents of the Royal Society and the Board of Agriculture. Coke organized a similar event at Holkham to which he invited leading agriculturalists and breeders. In 1804 he was present at the Woburn sheep-shearing and issued an invitation to many of those present to come on to Holkham for his event. According to the *London Chronicle*:

> Many accepted the invitation and hastened across the country, a distance of near 120 miles, by every mode of conveyance which the inns or private families afforded; others went round by London, for the convenience of the mails and stagecoaches; and by

Sunday Mr. Coke's hospitable mansion at Holkham, and every inn and farmhouse in the neighbourhood, were filled with visitors.[34]

But, on the whole, historians have tended to play down the aristocratic contribution to agrarian progress. Mingay, Perkin and Bush, for example, have all taken the view that the main concern of landlords was with rents and estate management and that in matters of husbandry techniques most took a conservative attitude and showed little interest. In short, they opted out, leaving risk-taking to their tenants. J.V. Beckett, on the other hand, argues that the overall picture is much more positive, pointing out that an estate was an inheritance and consequently the current owner could not escape responsibility for its improvement, development and conservation.[35] Interesting though the debate is, our primary concern is to reveal something of the evidence.

The landowner as estate manager

The first Baron Ashburnham was extremely successful in supervising his own estates. Many of the hundreds of letters he wrote in the late seventeenth and early eighteenth centuries to his agent in Wales and bailiffs in Bedfordshire and Sussex have survived. They are a clear indication of his interest in farming techniques and his desire to encourage innovation. Ashburnham wrote to his bailiff on such matters as manuring, the best dates for ploughing, the marketing of grain and the importance of not sitting back idly and delaying autumn farming operations. He urged his bailiff to:

> remember to carry up Dung, Mould, Lyme, Marle etc. for the upper Hopp ground now the weather is fitting and putt not off the good day with delays . . . Carriage now is the word and ought to be the Deed, Winter will come, Lazinesse, Lying and excuses beginn to be out of fashion and ever were with wise and honest people, and the future may not be in our power. Earlye in the morning is the time, the Day is short, and would be well employ'd . . . If servants and dayes men would perform as i say, and as justice and reason require, all would go well on every side.[36]

The fourth Duke of Bedford kept a pocket book in which he noted down his observations and thoughts on essential work to be done on the Woburn estate:

> One of the plows Grace plows with is too light for that strong ground . . .
> Speak to Paisy to mend up all the Barrs by ye road side and Brown to make the Banks so steep that no horses can get up them. All the Barrs to be kept shut while I am away . . .
> With what horses the mares shall be covered . . .
> That part of the warren which was Oats last summer and Turnips this, to be fed of the next with deer and then immediately have it plowed and mucked with the best mold from Drakelow pond, and be constant harrowing to be laid down as smooth as possible and then pretty early in the season to be laid down with Barley (and hayseeds with some trefoil) and natural Grass seeds. NB. a small quantity of pigeon's dung to be sowed with

the Barley and if there should be any holes that can't be laid level . . . Brown to help with the Spade.[37]

William Constable received some enthusiastic advice from his friend, J. Scrope, of Danby in North Yorkshire, regarding the use of the horse hoe and cultivator:

> *2 Nov 1764.* Next spring I propose to have my kitchen garden in one of my fields and I don't in the least doubt of having all things in as great perfection as they possibly can be had in a garden, and keep the ground cleaner and finer than any gardines can pretend to be by hand weeding. The advantages of the Horse Hoe and cultivator are such that I think nothing can come up to it . . .

Scrope pointed out that he had briefed Constable's man about progressive methods and went on to offer advice on cabbages:

> I have had some discourse with your man, the bearer. He seems a sensible man and very desirous of improving. He has seen all my ploughs, instruments belonging to my farm and seems well pleased with my cabbages . . . Your man complains of yours cracking already, by which I imagine you will have not got seed of the right kind. Accept a pound of which I'll answer for their standing good till the middle of April, if right managed. Have I not sent you full directions for the first sowing to the last eating? If I have not, be so kind as to let me know and you shall have it with pleasure . . .[38]

Stewards and agents

Not many landowners had the necessary skills, time or inclination to deal with the day-to-day running of the home farm and managing the estate. Indeed, some were absentees for long periods, travelling abroad or attending Parliament or staying with friends and relatives. Inevitably, therefore, many came to rely on professional estate managers and agents. As a Roman Catholic, Sir Marmaduke Constable of Everingham preferred to spend much time abroad and from 1726 relied upon his chaplain to supervise his estates, manorial and business affairs. The following letters indicate the heavy responsibility the chaplain had to bear:

> [Constable to Potts 26 April 1732] I must answer many of your letters in this one. It is impossible at this great distance to give particular orders to everything that may arrive at home: all I have to desire of you is only to give such intendence over my affairs as your prudence will direct . . . Go into Lincolnshire and view my affairs there with Champney and what you think proper give orders for it. Let me know how my new hedges come on there. What ever work is done let it be paid punctually, and wait for no orders from me . . . Let all the trees planted be taken care of, and my nurseries at any charge. Let my tenants know if they prejudice my trees either in their Garths or town gate, my positive orders are that they shall be turned off as if they were insolent. If anything is wanting for the better regulation of the town, see it be enacted by the next Court by Thos. Brown.

The chaplain had little enthusiasm for the job and it is clear that the tenants were taking advantage of the situation:

[Potts to Constable 5 May 1741] You stand in great need of a Steward for some of your tenants do what they please; Robert Dean's servant has not only cut down oak boughs at the side of the Park, but also cut several other saplings in the Intack plantation, thick enough for hedge stakes, and put them to that use, after the time for cutting wood so these will never spring again . . . The tenant that is upon George Harrison's farm will not make up the part of his fence against Blackburn. Garth . . . His two swine trespass in the Intack, he lets all his houses go to ruin and there is little thatch upon his barn . . . Neither he nor Robert Dean have paid anything of their Lady Day rents 1740, so at Michaelmas

---

Burton Conſtable, 1ſt Dec. 1792.

Gentlemen !

I Beg you will peruſe the incloſed papers with due attention. They relate to buſineſs of the greateſt concern to yourſelves and me. I mean the new arrangements which I ſhall propoſe on the farms, which you now hold under me.

It is now 18 years ſince the eſtates (to which I ſucceeded by the will of my late reſpectable Uncle) received any conſiderable riſe ; and during that period, the price of every commodity, ſent to market, has prodigiouſly increaſed.

Beſides, ſuch is the preſent flouriſhing ſtate of this kingdom in every reſpect, and ſuch the probability of its continuing to increaſe in wealth and proſperity, that it appears fair and juſt, that the preſent rents of my eſtates ſhould be conſiderably advanced.

I do not wiſh or intend to aggrieve and oppreſs you. When I think I ought to receive thoſe rents, which my tenants *can* and *ſhould* pay ; I alſo am ſenſible, that *you* ought to receive from the eſtates thoſe advantages, which will enable you to live with eaſe and rational comfort.

In order to aſcertain the value of my eſtates for the purpoſes above-mentioned, I have given my confidence to Mr. Hodſkinſon, a gentleman who has been recommended to me by many of my friends, for his thorough knowledge of his profeſſion, his long experience, his humanity, juſtice and honor.

I need not mention Mr. Raines to you, Gentlemen ! who have been longer acquainted than myſelf, with his humanity and benevolence, his knowledge and honor. He alſo has a right to my confidence.

If any thing in theſe papers ſhould appear obſcure or difficult, I beg you will ſend your obſervations in writing to Mr. Raines, at Burton Conſtable, and they ſhall be attended to.

In order to bring the whole buſineſs to a concluſion, Mr. Hodſkinſon will return to Burton Conſtable in the ſpring.

Believe me, Gentlemen ! At the ſame time that I think it my duty to be juſt to myſelf, I know that I am bound alſo to conduct myſelf in your regard with lenity, humanity and benevolence.

My ardent wiſh, my only ambition, muſt ever be to become your *friend* and to deſerve your eſteem, your regard and attachment.

---

27 Circular letter from Edward Constable of Burton Constable to his tenants regarding rents and improvements, 1792.

next they will be two years in arrears. I am persuaded that . . . there can be no prospect of getting clear with him but by distraining all his goods and crop at Michaelmas next . . . he is a trickey fellow . . .[39]

Few estates were as badly managed as this, and by the second half of the eighteenth century many landowners were employing one or more efficient and knowledgeable, full-time officials. John Hardy was 25 in 1773 when he replaced his father as steward and agent to Walter Stanhope. It was a job that he was to hold for the next 30 years. He had grown up on the estate and had an interest in law. Shortly after his appointment the estate was greatly enlarged through inheritance and marriage and Walter Spencer-Stanhope's lifestyle meant that he was absent from the estate for long periods on the Grand Tour and as MP for Carlisle. Hardy had to perform a variety of roles in this period, buying and selling land, fixing agreements, advising on tax and investment and on the exploitation of mineral resources.[40]

Managing the biggest estates, those in the region of 100,000 acres, required the services of expert administrators. D. Spring has outlined the careers of a number of barrister-auditors who distinguished themselves as advisers to great landowners in the nineteenth century. One of this group, James Loch, served the Duke of Sutherland, the Earl of Ellesmere (Lord Francis Egerton), the Howards of Castle Howard and other great families. His name seems to have become a household word in the highest circles of the aristocracy. Spring's analysis of the letters of James Loch to Lord Francis Egerton in the period 1837 to 1846 shows how this talented Scotsman oversaw the administration of a diverse estate comprising canals, mines and farms, each of which constituted a separate department with its own agent.[41] The Dukes of Bedford had an estate of about 80,000 acres which comprised three country estates and a London one. Woburn, the family seat in Bedfordshire of 33,488 acres, was the biggest; Thorney in the Fens had 23,652 acres and the West Country estate, which included Tavistock and a copper and arsenic mine, comprised some 20,377 acres. Each estate had a well-paid professional land agent and the Duke's auditor presided over the whole from a central office in London. Under the seventh Duke (1839–61) the auditor was Christopher Haedy who was in charge of all estate business and local agents reported directly to him. The penny-pinching seventh Duke kept up a voluminous correspondence with his auditor and together they succeeded in producing a better system of reporting estate business (annual reports were produced from 1839) and generally reducing expenditure.[42] As one might expect, the agent, an intermediary between the landowner and his tenants, could hardly be popular with both. A letter from Francis Constable to his agent William Iveson expressed disapproval at the state of one of the farms which had been vacated:

Wycliffe Hall, 3 December 1811. Sir, the catalogue of depredations at Little Humber Farm is shocking to a great degree. I should never have thought that young Robinson would have been so inconsiderate. For if he did not like to live in the house he ought to have taken care that his hired [labourers] should not have made a grannary and carrot loft of the premises . . . Some fires should have been made occasionally, the windows opened also in fine weather, and the whole kept dry and fit to be inhabited. I do not wish to be hard on the Robinsons but in justice to myself and to the advantage of the successor, young Robinson should be bound to put the place in question in as good a state as he found it.[43]

Tenants were mostly bound by covenant to observe an agreed pattern of husbandry. If doubt existed it was wise to consult the agent. Thomas Thorpe, a tenant on the Constable estate at Halsham, wrote to William Iveson in October 1803. The letter is full of dialect and grammatical errors, and the propositions are somewhat unclear:

> Sir, I made up my mind if agreable to you to plow both my own cars and keep parted for convenience of netting when rape or tornups one for fedarston closs. And the udare to enlarge my tilleg to take two crops of a[?] then fallay and lay two dozon of lime per acar and the udare pice next year fallay and two dozon of lime and niver to take more then thre crops to a fallay.
>
> If you pleas we will see how cars ancers befoor I lay high land when I lay any land down I will sow ten pound wight clover and five pound trafefoyle on evarry acrare. I will plant cwekwood on that pice we take of a first care and that little pice to rape closs and dow all at my own expenc only give me wood for stowps and rales please to geet all staked howt as soon as conveneant . . .
>
> PS. The grane I porpors sowing oats after rape or tonups then beens dreled in then wheat then fallay.[44]

A well-run estate required able people for key positions at all levels. First-class gamekeepers and head gardeners were much sought after. A recommendation might come directly from a neighbour: in 1881 Henry Boynton of Burton Agnes wrote to his friend, Sir Tatton Sykes at Sledmere, about a gamekeeper:

> Dear Sir Tatton, Are you in need of a really good head gamekeeper? I have a man now in want of a situation, he is a thoroughly experienced person in all branches of his profession . . . He lived with me three years ago as under keeper and since then has had a small place. He is 30 years of age, very strong, tall and very active, sober and a particularly good shot; he is single at present! His name is George Myas; should you want a really good servant, I can most strongly recommend him.[45]

A surviving account sent to Godfrey Wentworth by his solicitor in 1863 indicates how keepers had to be present in court when cases were heard for trespass and poaching, etc.:[46]

1862
Sept 22 Attending Mr. Siggs respecting poaching and trespass and court house. 6s.8d.
Sept 24 Attending gamekeeper and before Justice on warrant against Fairclough, committed 3 mths.   £1.1.0d.

1863
Sept 23 Attended keeper before Justices against Wilkinson and 3 others for night poaching. All convicted.   £1.1.0d.
Sept 30 Attending your 2 keepers Ward and Roberts and before Justices on 2 summons for assault against them. Convicted.   £1.1.0d.

GAME.

WHEREAS the **GAME** on the **MANOR**
of   has of
late Years been very much destroyed by
Poachers, unqualified Persons, and others:

NOTICE IS HEREBY GIVEN,

That all Persons who shall be found Trespassing in future, will be prosecuted to the
utmost **Rigor** of the **Law.**

SLEDMERE, 20th August, 1812.

C. PEACOCK, Printer, Courant-Office, York.

---

28 Notice of warning to would-be poachers on the Sykes's family Sledmere estate, 1812.

Rents, profits and depression

General statements about the profitability of estates in the nineteenth century are
not easy to make. For many there were good profits to be had in the boom years 1850
to 1870 but for some there were anxious times in the 1820s and 1830s and more
particularly in the 1880s and 1890s. Parliamentary papers are a rich source for the
study of nineteenth-century agriculture, and committees reported on the periods of
distress mentioned above.[47] Estate papers may indicate how landlords and tenants
responded to the challenge of the times. The problem of untenanted farms and
reduced income was the subject of a letter from Godfrey Wentworth of Woolley
Hall to his ageing father in 1833:

> Dear Father, On Friday next I am going to pay in to Leathams Bank for you. I am sorry to
> say, only a small part of your half yearly income namely £700. The deficit I think you may
> readily account for, when by the newspapers and from every individual you meet, you
> must be aware of the terrible harvest we had last year in the north and the still continued
> depression of the agricultural interests. I think I mentioned to you in my last letter that I
> have had two farms thrown on my hands one of which I have let at a low rent, the other I
> cannot let at any rent. Sir E. Dodsworth has 6 farms on his own hands, Fawkes has

January 1, 1789.

R E N T · D A Y S

A T

BURTON CONSTABLE.

MICHAELMAS.

Firſt. The firſt MONDAY in JANUARY.

Second. SHROVE MONDAY.

LADY-DAY.

Firſt. The firſt MONDAY after MIDSUMMER FAIR at BEVERLEY.

Second. The firſt MONDAY after BARTHOLOMEW FAIR at ALDBROUGH.

ROBERT FOSTER.

JOHN RAINES.

PRINTED BY G. PRINCE, PRINTER OF THE HULL PACKET.

29 Notice of rent days at Burton Constable estate, North Humberside.

reduced his rents 10 per cent. Stanhope the same and Beaumont the same and I, like the rest, must do the same . . .[48]

In the mid-1880s Sir Frederick Augustus Talbot Clifford-Constable wrote to his steward on the subject of his reduced income:

I am much disappointed to find that further reductions in my already diminished Rent Roll are asked for and apparently advised by you as necessary, and I see nothing but ruin staring me in the face. I had far better sell the East Riding Estate altogether than carry it on with great anxiety, as I much fear I am doing, at considerable loss . . . I must again insist that no further repairs of an extensive character are entered into without my sanction. They appear to be by no means appreciated by the tenants . . . I feel as if I were rapidly on the road to ruin . . .[49]

Although Sir Frederick was exaggerating the extent of his problems, agricultural depression was eroding his estate income. It fell by more than £5500 between 1873 and 1883. Despite this, the Constables were understanding of the problems faced by their tenants in these difficult times. Rentals and accounts may indicate declining income and rising expenditure, as is true in the case of Sir Tatton Sykes's compact 30,000 acre estate in the 1880s. A letter written to Sir Tatton by one of his tenants in 1880 is a clear expression of the difficulties of a Yorkshire Wolds' farmer:

[East Heslerton 4 October 1880] I received your letter on the 30th September stating that you would lower the Rent to 21 shillings per acre which I thank you for. But that is not sufficient according to the times and the bad seasons. Everything one grows now on a farm seems to be cut up in price by the foreigners to a very great extent. It is not only one thing but everything. And wool alone that is a verry precious matter that effects a farm like this one to have to sell it now at abut one shilling per stone. Wheat at the present time is making from ten shillings to fifteen less than it was last year per quarter and no prospect of it advancing but very likely to come to a shilling a stone. I have duly considered the matter over since I received your letter and likewise before. As I told you when I was with you £700 per year for it, game included, and then dearer at that amount than it would have been ten years ago at 25 shillings per acre.

The writer, Farmer Simpson, went on to point out the need for some urgent work to be done on the farm and saw it as a chance to bargain over the rent:

The farm is altogether in a poor state and the Fences down below are in an awfull state. As I told you all the land on the wold wanted limeing and the Carr land as well. If you will take the amount I bid I will try to alter the land and by your assistance in quickwood posts and rails I will try to alter the fences to. And I think when you have considered the matter over yourself and the past bad seasons you will think I have bid you a great rent for it . . .[50]

The Sledmere estate accounts for 1882 recorded a loss of £793 through tenants becoming insolvent. But despite these difficult times, the Sledmere inheritance remained intact.

Chapter Four

THE COUNTRY HOUSE AND
THE INDUSTRIAL REVOLUTION

Historians have long been intrigued by the part played by the great landowners in the Industrial Revolution and have sought to explain it. This depth of interest is understandable. Bearing in mind how much land in England was owned by the aristocracy (about two-thirds in 1700 and three-quarters in 1800), and their virtual domination of the political system, there can be no doubt that the great landowners were crucially placed to influence the pace and direction of economic change in the century that saw the beginning of the Industrial Revolution. Although historians are in general agreement that the aristocracy played a significant part in the transition to an industrial and urban economy, they differ in their explanations of the nature and extent of that involvement.

M.L.Bush maintains that the aristocratic role was restricted to helping to construct a 'conducive infrastructure'. By this he means that the aristocracy promoted transport facilities and urban growth and made available a plentiful supply of capital, cheap food and minerals. Their encouragement of mining and urban development was especially important because both of these were almost entirely dependent upon aristocratic backing. But he draws the line here. The entrepreneurial role of the landowner was a limited one, and as far as industrial production was concerned the landowner stood aloof.[1] But did the aristocrat distance himself so completely from entrepreneurial activity? While conceding that they were not leading industrialists, J.V. Beckett argues that landowners played a vital role on behalf of business interests in Parliament, partly because entrepreneurs failed to get themselves into Westminster in any numbers before the mid-nineteenth century. Although their prime responsibility was with their own wholly owned estate resources, this did not mean that they took no interest in developments elsewhere.[2]

In a similar vein, J.R. Wordie has argued that the landlord's contribution was deeper and more subtle than that of simply encouraging the exploitation of minerals and giving support to developments in communications. He points out that it is often forgotten that England's Industrial Revolution was launched, not with steam power, but with horse and human power, and that it began in the countryside. These links between early industry and land remained close and direct. Land supplied many raw materials essential to those industries. Moreover, the landed and ruling classes produced in England an economic, political and social climate which was highly conducive to the development of industry and highly advantageous to the merchant and industrialist.[3]

The landowners' involvement in mining and industry through the four and a half centuries covered by this book can be conveniently considered as having roughly three stages:

1 From the mid-sixteenth century to the end of the seventeenth century entrepreneurs were all members of the landed classes. Economic development in this period, especially from 1540 to the outbreak of the Civil War, was impressive and the evidence points to aristocrats giving a positive lead, especially in mining and heavy industry.

2 By the eighteenth century and well into the classical period of the Industrial Revolution (1760–1830) a more distinct and purely entrepreneurial class began to emerge. Families such as the Foleys and Crowleys, Darleys and Wedgewoods came to the fore. At the same time, the landowner, far from turning his back on economic activity, worked closely with this new breed of professionals. It was a period characterized by collaboration.

3 By the early nineteenth century the landed classes were beginning to disengage themselves from industry and to leave the field to the entrepreneurial middle classes. The reasons for abandoning direct management in preference for a rentier status were frequently influenced by the increasing capital investment required, the inability to find managers and a reluctance or inability to reconcile the aristocratic and entrepreneurial ideals.[4]

There were of course exceptions to be found in each of these stages. Some landowners were leasing their mineral wealth in the sixteenth and seventeenth centuries and others can be found to have been directly managing it at the end of the nineteenth century. Without seeking to resolve the issue of aristocratic involvement, the remainder of this chapter will identify examples of it in the exploitation of mineral resources, developments in transport and communications and urbanization and sources which shed light upon it.

Mineral wealth

One of the most remarkable aspects of economic development in the period 1540 to 1750 was the great increase in coal production. Output increased from around 170,000 tons in the 1550s to between 6 and 7 million tons two centuries later. Many landowners in the North-East, the Midlands, Yorkshire and South Wales took a positive attitude to the mining and development of their mineral assets. In the West Midlands, for example, the Earls of Dudley, the Lyttletons of Hagley and the Holts of Aston owned about one-third of the manors in the area and, through a policy of gradually replacing traditional copyhold leases with leasehold, they encouraged both agricultural and small-scale industrial enterprise.[5] In the sixteenth and seventeenth centuries coal was chiefly in demand for domestic fuel but, as critical shortages developed in the supply of wood for industries requiring it for fuel, notably metal-smelting, interest focused upon the possibilities of using coal as an alternative. A technical breakthrough came with Abraham Darby's discovery of coke-smelting in 1709. Where coal and iron deposits were in close proximity, a number of landowners invested capital in the development of both industries.

In the 1540s the iron industry was chiefly located in the Weald, the Forest of Dean and Cleveland. In 1542 there were eight blast-furnaces operating in the

30 Cartouche from the plan of the collieries of Tyne and Wear dedicated to the Earl of Northumberland, 1787.

Weald and by 1574 the number had risen to over 50. The expansion was, in large measure, due to the active involvement of the gentry and nobility. Landowners such as the Duke of Norfolk, Lord Abergavenny, the Sidneys, the Ashburnhams and the Robertses owned and operated furnaces and forges from the early sixteenth century. They took advantage of a revolutionary new technique, the charcoal blast-furnace, introduced by foreign workers in the reign of Henry VIII. On the Earl of Northumberland's manor of Petworth there was a forge and a furnace. In 1578 the workings were leased for 18 years at a rent of £100:

1. One forge or hammer and all the houses and outhouses thereunto, set, standing and being in the park commonly called the Great Park of Petworth.

2. One furnace . . . adjoining unto a certain piece of land of the Earl commonly called the Freethe.
3. All the cottages, buildings, hovels, sheds and lodges now occupied by the workmen of the furnace and forge or by the tenants of the ironworks.
4. All ponds, banks, sluices, floodgates, paths and ways usual for carts and carriages.
5. All waters and water courses, workmen's houses and garden plots.
6. All coal and mine places used or belonging to the works.[6]

An important reason for the expansion of the iron industry in the Weald in the sixteenth and seventeenth centuries was the demand for ordnance, but by the mid-seventeenth century the industry suffered from the increase in iron imports from abroad and greater competition from charcoal furnaces elsewhere in Britain.

The Fullers of Brightling Park, a gentry family, did well from government contracts until the end of the seventeenth century. They sold over 786 tons of cannon to the government between 1693 and 1698 for which they received £14,411.[7] A large collection of archive material survives from the early eighteenth century for the Fuller estate, providing a detailed picture of the ironworkings. A Furnace Book (1703–40) gives details of the amounts of mine carried, coals, sows, cast iron weighed in and out of the forge as well as payments made. A letter book contains copies of John Fuller's extensive correspondence and a journal, ledger and cash book provide much additional information including, in the case of the latter, insights into his accumulation of wealth. The evidence reveals a close connection between the organization of the ironworks and the estate. Many of the Fullers' smaller tenants were employed in carrying wood and coals to the forge and doing agricultural work as well. Some specialized in gun-making; others were involved in digging and carrying mine and veins. Gun-making was perhaps the most important activity, although large quantities of other articles were made, such as furnaces, skillets, frying pans, kettles, as well as sows and pig-iron. Guns were transported to Lewes or Banbridge on the Tunbridge Navigation.[8] The Wealden industry survived into the eighteenth century but the centre of gravity had long since shifted into South Wales, Shropshire, Staffordshire and Derbyshire. Two other major producing areas were South Yorkshire and the Tyne and Wear. In the Midlands the leading landed families involved in iron-making were the Pagets, the Dudleys and the Talbots. George Talbot, sixth Earl of Shrewsbury, had mining interests which straddled the Pennines from Shropshire and Staffordshire to Derbyshire and Yorkshire. He probably put his first South Yorkshire furnaces into blast during the winter of 1573 to 1574 with the aid of a team of workmen descended from French immigrants who had settled in the Weald.[9] William Dickenson, the Earl of Shrewsbury's bailiff responsible for the financial business of the Sheffield, Derbyshire, Worksop and Staffordshire estates, wrote up his accounts in large volumes. An early example of coal-mining royalties is shown in this extract:

> Stubley. the Collears say that they have for gayteinge of Coales in ye eye of ye pytt the one halfe of Coales and my lord ye other halfe, and when they dryve owte of ye eye, beinge called the hoylings they have ij partes and my lord the thirde part and they sayed yt some weekes yt wolde be worth to bothe the workmen, either of them xxd a weeke.[10]

31 Section of map of the County of Stafford by William Yates, showing Beaudesert Park and coal pits, 1775.

According to Dr Plot, the seventeeth-century historian of Staffordshire, Lord Paget of Beaudesert had a coat of arms carved out of the excellent coal mined on his estate at Cannock Chase, and displayed it in the gallery. Coal-mining requires considerable capital expenditure as the accounts of Lord Paget show for the years 1622 to 1623:

> The price of 1,558 dozen of coals sold in Cannock wood being parcel of 1,694 dozen gotten there in the time of this account whereof 5 dozen spent at Beaudesert house and 131 dozen remain on the bank yet unsold which coals sold a 4s 0d per dozen amounteth to £311 12s 0d.
> Paid for getting coals in Cannock wood   £166 15s 3d.
> Driving heads and sinking there   £33 9s 7d.

Paid for getting coals in Beaudesert park   £178 1s 0d.
Disbursement about the sough there   £20 12s 3d.[11]

In Nottinghamshire, the Willoughbys of Wollaton were unrivalled in the scale of their coal-mining and iron-manufacturing operations. The following extracts from a letter from Sylvester Smith, a servant of Sir Francis Willoughby, to John Bentley, his agent, is concerned with skilled workmen and their wages:

> I have sent a hammerman to his worship for new mill forge and such a man as his lordship may boldly trust, but I cannot agree with him for his wages by reason he expecteth 10s.0d upon the ton and I offer but 8s.0d. so as the matter is referred to yourself and his worship to determine . . . As for a finer, I have heard there is one hired by Mr. Zouche whose name is John Wilson, a man accounted both honest and an indifferent good workman. I have been to have spoken with him to see if he will be content to become Sir Francis's servant, which if he would I meant not to seek any further but as yet I cannot meet with him for that he is gone into Wales to seek workmen . . .[12]

The following letter in the Spencer-Stanhope papers, regarding a furnace at Barnby near Doncaster, is particularly interesting in so far as it deals with the cost of repairs and the problems of water supply and indicates a desire to abandon the use of charcoal:

> Frodsham, Chester 6 Oct 1779. Sir . . . as you say you will let your Furnace at Barnby upon fair and moderate terms. I will endeavour to point out what Repairs . . . are absolutely necessary for your Deliberation . . . I want to work it upon the principle of Mr Walker's of Rotherham work theirs, this with Pitcoal instead of charcoal . . . on acct. of the Scarcity and Dearness of Cordwood, are worked so; and if the Pitcoal on your Estate shows chance to sink there will be a consumption of Seven Thousand Tons annually; that raised near Glasshouse seems to be very suitable for the purpose. When furnaces are worked on this Plan they are constantly going Winter and Summer; on acct. of the great Scarcity of Water in Summer it will be necessary to build a Fire Engine to lift the Water from the Bottom of the Wheel into the Pond, to work it over and over again . . . there is at present a great Demand for Cannon Balls and I should wish to get to work as soon as possible . . . Sir, your most Obedt Servt. Francis Dorset.

Estimate of Repairs			
A new Wheel, Troughs etc.	£50	0	0
Cleaning the Cut below the Wheel	31	10	0
A new Hearth	31	10	0
Widening & enlarging the Furnace for Coak	21	0	0
4 New Cilenders for Bellows, Gearing etc	200	0	0
Floodgates and Washer	10	0	0
A Fire Engine to lift water into the pond	400	0	0
	£744	0	0[13]

By 1750 scarcely any estate of any size within 40 miles of Newcastle did not derive a substantial income from mineral workings.[14] In eighteenth-century Cumberland the Lowther family took the leading role in coal-mining, which had in the

WHITRIGGS MINES.

HIS GRACE THE DUKE OF BUCCLEUCH'S ROYALTY.

Summary of disposal of Iron Ore for the Month of **March** *1863*

Date. 1863	Means of Disposal.	Ulverstone Canal.			Lindal Station.		
Mar. 2	181 Carts				84	4	2
3	69 "				73	15	1
4	65 "				69	19	1
5	58 "				62	17	2
6	63 "				73	10	3
7	55 "				60	18	2
9	60 "				65	4	3
10	116 "				17	9	3
11	178 "				83	5	3
12	63 "				70	11	1
13	60 "				67	9	~
14	48 "				53	15	3
16	182 "				88	7	3
17	77 "				81	16	2
18	64 "				71	8	1
19	73 "				81	6	3
20	62 "				69	2	2
21	65 "	(Uld. by Carts.) — no charge given	13	5	.	70	1	1
23	53 "	(D.o	21	19	.	56	15	3
24	56 "	(D.o	11	9	.	61	2	3
25	84 "					92	8	.	1
26	81 "				90	19	3
27	80 "				90	13	2
28	65 "				74	6	2
30	98 "				108	11	1
31	79 "				90	.	3
	1735 Carts	46	13	.	1910	2	1

---

32 Royalty return for Whitriggs Iron Mine, Cumbria, owned by the Duke of Buccleuch, 1863.

---

seventeenth century been dominated by the Cliffords. In Yorkshire a number of aristocrats were actively exploiting their mineral resources from the sixteenth century onwards, notably the Savilles, the Spencers and the Wentworths.

The Wentworths of Woolley leased their coal-mines. An indenture between William Wentworth and John Foster, husbandman of the Township of Woolley, dated 19 January 1706, granted Foster all the coal-mines in Brimshaw, two corn mills and Woolley Mill and Appleday Mill in the Township of Notton, at a rent of £62 a year plus 80 loads of coals and 25 capons for a period of seven years.[15] A century later Geoffrey Wentworth agreed to a 21-year lease of 'all that colliery, mine, bed, vein or seam of coal called Princes Bed to be found in and under certain closes, lands and grounds situated at Woolley in the Parish of Royston . . .', in all some 252 acres, to John Dodgson Charlesworth, gentleman, at a rent of £100 a year. In addition, Charlesworth was to supply the landowner and his heirs and assigns weekly with as much coal as they required for the house at Woolley, at a price not exceeding 3s 9d per ton.[16]

The long experience of Yorkshire aristocrats in exploiting their mineral wealth prompted others to seek their advice on matters of pricing and leasing. A.M. Bold of Cheshire sought the following advice from William Wentworth:

> *Bold, July 30th 1765.* Dear Sir, Mr Patten having been treating with me for some coal mines I have in Sutton, was here the other day with Tomkinson who drew up proposals for the lease of them, which I herewith send to you and should esteem myself greatly obliged to you to favour me with your opinion – whether you think they are such as I ought to comply with . . .[17]

Similarly, J.A. Stephenson of Lympsham Crop, Somerset, sought advice regarding the value of seven acres of coal on a property belonging to him at Rawmarsh near Rotherham which he wanted to dispose of to Lord Fitzwilliam. He received the following reply:

> *Middleton 13 Sept 1832.* Sir, Yesterday I went over to Rawmarsh to examine the situation of the Plot of Coal you intend to dispose of to Ld. Fitzwilliam and from the information I then collected I am of opinion that you are entitled to £28 an Acre for the Seam called the 9 feet Seam. Its thickness under the 7 Acre field will probably be found not to exceed 7 ft . . . By leave from L.F.'s agent Mr Cooper I descended the Engine Pit at the present working which sunk upon the levels which cut across your property in the Village of Rawmarsh – they dropped within a few yards of your Boundary, and with regard to the sum L.F. should give you for leave to drive those levels thro' your property I am inclined to think that you ought not to require more than £160 for that privilege. I am Sir, Your Humble Servant, Thos N. Embleton.[18]

The great Leveson-Gower estate in Staffordshire and Shropshire comprised three major properties: Lilleshall, Trentham and Wolverhampton. All three were rich in coal, ironstone, limestone and other minerals. In the 1760s Earl Gower assumed the direct exploitation of the Lilleshall mines in Shropshire by forming Earl Gower and Company. It was a partnership in which the Earl held a 50 per cent share. Lord Gower's entrepreneurial role and the story of the company have recently been told in some detail. An important feature of the business was the meticulous accounting system and the close integration of a farming unit into the mining operations. In short, it provides a perfect illustration of the very close links which existed between land and industry in the early days of the Industrial Revolution.[19]

One of the most outstanding examples of a great estate rich in mineral resources is Wentworth Woodhouse in South Yorkshire. In the eighteenth century the second Marquis of Rockingham took a personal interest in the working of his collieries and the kilns for lime, bricks and tiles. His notes included comments on the possibility of extracting oil from coal, on the costs incurred in raising coal and the transport charges involved in moving coal from his own Parkgate colliery to London. The collieries on the Wentworth estate were let on the basis of so much per man employed in the mine, a figure which varied between £7 15s and £21 per man according to the level of production. In 1759 the Marquis's seven collieries produced profit of £1094 and the two largest concerns employed 16 and 12 men respectively.[20] Under Rockingham's successors, the fourth and fifth Earls Fitzwilliam, the industrial undertakings were taken into direct management by the landowner and from 1795 until well into the 1840s they were supervised by one family – Benjamin Hall, his nephew Joshua Biram and, finally, Biram's son Benjamin. Whereas Hall and Joshua Biram had the title steward, Benjamin was known as Superintendent of the Wentworth Estate and Superintendent of the Collieries. This was a period of considerable expansion of estate coal-mining. Between 1800 and 1856 sales increased fourfold, from 70,000 tons to over 300,000 tons; between 1795 and 1850 the number of miners increased from 79 to over 800 and the number of collieries increased from four to seven. The overall numbers employed on the estate increased in this period from 240 to 1100, indicating an expansion in iron-mining and iron-smelting as well as in agriculture. Graham Mee has suggested that the Wentworth estate in the first half of the nineteenth century represented a microcosm of the Industrial Revolution and that many of its essential features were to be seen in close proximity in the estate village of Elsecar by 1815:

> . . . a visitor to the village of Elsecar would have been able to see, within a few hundred yards of the green, coal pits being worked, iron furnaces being tapped, and coal tar and its chemical by-products being manufactured. There was also an internal rail network serving these enterprises, and a canal which provided the link with regional markets and with supplies of essential materials. From the canal wharf were shipped the basic raw materials of the industrial revolution, coal and iron. Dominating the scene by day would have been a Newcomen pumping engine. By night the sky would have been lit by the blast furnaces. Day and night the atmosphere must have been polluted by the fumes of burning coke piles, the coke ovens, tar stills and furnaces. From the latter flowed the raw material for the rails, plates and other iron products for the collieries and tar works. Near to the pit head were the rows of substantial stone-built, miners' cottages with their adjoining gardens.[21]

The Fitzwilliams did not extract and work their own ironstone, with the exception of the Elsecar ironworks, which they fully controlled from 1827 to 1849.

This intimate involvement of the Earls Fitzwilliam with all aspects of the estate economy generated a rich collection of source material – estate accounts, deeds, wage books, instructions to employees, correspondence between the landowner and local managers, diaries, notebooks and even a charities list. Insights into important questions such as why the Fitzwilliams abandoned the role of rentier for that of entrepreneur are to be found in the diaries, notebooks and abundance of correspondence. The notebooks of Benjamin Biram reveal the problems faced by the manager and the extent of his engineering expertise. The problems of draining a new pit are reflected in an entry in Biram's diary in December 1842. He recorded that 8000 gallons of water were pouring into the pit each hour.[22]

Very few of the accounts of the ironworks have survived and a wages book was reported in the 1930s as being in 'a very imperfect state owing to some person unknown having entered the counting house and torn out a number of leaves'. By contrast, most of the colliery accounts have survived. There is a household general account for each year from 1795 to 1857, with separate accounts for each of the departments for which the stewards were responsible. In addition, there are annual statements for each colliery for all but four years. The fifth Earl's correspondence and diaries show him taking great interest in scientific matters associated with mining, such as the problem of firedamp and testing instruments such as anemometers and barometers. Pre-1807 correspondence between the Earl and his steward was about general estate-management matters – the farms, cropping, the horses and hounds, the gardens and building maintenance. After this date the collieries feature in the letters and there is comment on technical matters about coal winnings and the problems of water in the pits.

Roads

Landowners, as Justices of the Peace and Members of Parliament, were involved in road improvement schemes from the middle of the sixteenth century. Growing concern about the state of highways resulted in JPs being empowered to levy a rate upon neighbouring parishes to pay for the hire of labourers and carts and materials to make repairs. They were also empowered to impose fines on those who abused roads with heavy wagons. In 1663 the first Act of Parliament was passed permitting the levy of tolls on travellers to raise money for the repair of a highway. The measure enabled the JPs in Hertfordshire, Huntingdonshire and Cambridgeshire to levy tolls for the repair of that part of the Great North Road which passed through their counties.

Only seven Acts were passed authorizing turnpike trusts before 1700, but in the eighteenth century a great many roads were developed as a result of legislation. Landowners were commonly to be found as trustees of turnpike trusts, and estate archives frequently contain copies of Turnpike Acts which affected roads in the vicinity of an estate. The Acts were periodically revised to widen their scope or to make them more effective. For example, in the Wentworth Woolley papers, there is a revised version of a Turnpike Act originally drafted in 1747, the fourteenth year of George II's reign, for repairing the road from Doncaster through the parish of Penistone in the county of York to Salter's Brook in the county of Chester and also from Rotherham to Hartcliffe Hill in the parish of Penistone. The trustees included some of the region's major landowners – Sir George Dalton Bt., Rt. Hon. William Lord Galway in the Kingdom of Ireland, Sir Lister Kaye Bt., Sir Lionel Pilkington Bt., Sir George Savile Bt., and Thomas Wentworth.[23] As trustees, the landowners were expected to attend meetings of the trust, and the minutes of these meetings often reveal which of the trustees, merchants or landowners, were the most active. From time to time, objections were voiced by landowners or their agents, usually when their monopoly of a particular market was being threatened. The Duke of Kingston's steward on his Buckinghamshire estate linked the problem of arrears in rent in 1763 to the impact turnpike roads were having on dairy farming:

> The Lands at Hanslop are let very dear, as not worth so much as formerly, by reason of the Improvements made at a greater distance from London, and the Turnpike roads opening a conveniency of the London Markets; the Tenants are all grown poor, their Lands not duly stockt, and the Duke has thereupon under consideration a considerable abatement of their Rents.[24]

On those estates where poor communications hindered the development of mineral wealth there was a strong incentive to improve the neighbourhood roads. Sir Thomas Robinson found the roads around Wentworth in bad shape when he visited the estate in 1734. He described his experience in a letter to Lord Carlisle:

> *6 June 1734* . . . As it is impossible in one place or country to have everything, I must acquaint your Lordship, if the axle-trees of your coach are not very strong, you will find it difficult to get thro' the country, the roads being intolerable, by the vast number of iron-stone pits, coal pits, and woods in the country. I have never yet been out, but I have met carts and waggons overthrown, for there have been such plentiful rains of late in this country, that the roads are almost as bad as in winter.[25]

The exploitation and transportation of mineral resources could produce a conflict of interests. At Colton in Staffordshire in the mid-seventeenth century a row developed over the use of a road and bridge. Lord Paget's claim that it was a common highway and as such could be used by his ironworks was contested by Sir William Gresley and local farmers. They insisted that he had no right of way and that carriages from the ironworkings had made the roadways so deep and foul that farmers could not carry their corn out of their fields and meadows without great danger to their own carriages.[26]

River navigation and canals

In the period 1500 to 1700 rivers carried much of England's internal trade and in the second half of the seventeenth century interest in the problems of inland navigation became widespread. Landowners with mineral wealth to exploit and a concern to improve the drainage of their estates readily supported schemes for improvement. In West Yorkshire Lord Irwin and others were attracted to the Aire and Calder Navigation scheme and gave their support to merchants and clothiers in securing the necessary legislation. Several landowners in the region were Fellows of the Royal Society and took a particular interest in engineering projects and hydrography.[27]

The improvement of the Yorkshire Derwent was a matter of some interest to the Wentworths of Wentworth Woodhouse, who owned an estate near Malton. Sir John Wentworth and other interested landowners, Viscount Irwin, Lord Fairfax and Thomas Worsley, were appointed commissioners under the Act of 1702 to mediate between the undertakers and the riparian owners and to ensure that the work was properly executed and landowners' interests not prejudiced. The navigation made an important contribution to the agricultural and mineral profits of the owners, the Wentworths, and their descendants, the Rockinghams and Fitzwilliams.[28]

There was some aristocratic opposition to improving river navigation where raising the level threatened meadow land, weirs and watermills and where a local monopoly of markets might be threatened. It was on these grounds that a Bill for the navigation of the River Weaver was opposed by large landowners and their tenants and the Wye improvement scheme was opposed by the Earl of Kent, who sensed a threat to the monopoly enjoyed by his ironworks.[29] But compromises were reached. When in 1721 the Hallamshire Cutlers company sought powers to make the River Don navigable as far as Sheffield, for example, they met with opposition from landowners, who feared flooding, and the Duke of Norfolk, who was anxious about the effects on the supply of water to his forges and grinding wheels at Sheffield. A settlement was reached with the Duke whereby the navigation scheme stopped at Tinsley, three miles from the town.[30]

William, Lord Paget took the initiative to improve the navigation of the upper Trent. In 1699 he obtained legislation to make it navigable between Wilden Ferry and Burton. In addition, he received a monopoly of the wharves and warehouses between Trent Bridge and Burton. This was particularly enterprising bearing in mind that he was the leading landowner in the Burton district and interested in the local collieries.[31]

The first canal proper to be built in the British Isles was the Newry Canal in Ireland. Financed out of taxation, it was opened in 1742 to transport coal cheaply to Dublin. By the mid-eighteenth century English landowners eager to exploit the mineral wealth of their estates were among the first to recognize the economic advantages of these new-style waterways. The contribution of Francis Egerton, third Duke of Bridgwater (1736–1803) to the development of the canal system in the 1760s was important. When he assumed control of his estates in 1757 at the age of 21, he determined to exploit the resources of coal under his Lancashire properties. Because the roads in the neighbourhood were in such a poor state of repair, he considered the possibilities of improving communications by water between Worsley and the nearby towns of Manchester and Salford. Twenty years earlier a group of Manchester merchants had secured an Act of Parliament to make Worsley Brook navigable down to the River Irwell but nothing had been done. The young Egerton, with the aid of borrowed capital and the services of two talented engineers, John Gilbert and James Brindley, pressed ahead with a scheme for a canal from Worsley to Manchester. It was completed in 1765. In 1776 a Cheshire

R I V E R   S E V E R N.

T O   T H E

NOBLEMEN AND GENTLEMEN

OWNERS of LAND on the BANKS of the SEVERN.

S I R S,

AS an Application to Parliament is intended for an Act to improve the Navigation of the River *Severn* from *Coalbrook-Dale* to *Worcester*, and as this Subject has for fometime paft engaged the Attention of the Public, and much has been faid and wrote thereon, tending to miflead the Judgment and prejudice the Minds of many, who would otherwife be inclined to promote an Undertaking big with Advantage to the Commerce of a very extenfive Country ; I take the Liberty of addreffing you, from a defire to remove that Mifapprehenfion (which is grounded on a Variety of confufed and vague Affertions), by ftating a few plain and undifguifed Facts ; and as I meet the anonymous Publications of thofe who may differ or affect to differ in Opinion with me, by giving my Name, and thereby pledging my Reputation to prove what I advance, I truft I fhall have Credit with candid Men for ftating the Truth to the beft of my Knowledge and Belief.

As the making a Horfe Towing-path has been much difapproved of, and as that Part of the Improvement is given up by the prefent Petitioners, it is unneceffary to attempt to fhew how much that Matter has been mifunderftood ; I fhall therefore relate

33 Address to landowners inviting their support for legislation to improve the navigation of the River Severn n.d.

branch of the canal was completed from Stretford to Runcorn and an extension from Worsley to Leigh in 1800. Bridgwater had plans to link his canal with the Leeds and Liverpool and this did come to fruition some years after his death. By reason of its geographical position and its connections with other waterways, the economic importance of the Bridgwater Canal was assured. The benefits were felt immediately: the price of coal from the Duke's mines sold in Manchester was halved, dropping from seven pence to threepence halfpenny a hundredweight, and production increased. Coal remained the largest single commodity to be carried on the canal, accounting for a quarter to a third of the tonnage in the year of the Duke's death.[32]

Francis Egerton's example was followed by other landowners, especially in the Midlands and the North where mining was widespread. They were frequently to be found alongside the merchants and businessmen in the planning and financing of canals. The promotion of the Grand Junction Canal (1793) was led by the Marquis of Buckingham (his arms were on the Company Seal), the Duke of Grafton, the Earl of Clarendon, the Earl of Exeter and Earl Spencer. In Yorkshire the Marquess of Rockingham took a keen interest in canals. He had two surveys made in 1769 and 1775 and employed William Jessop to build a canal from the River Don to Greasborough in 1779 to facilitate the movement of his coal. The canal, when completed, was leased to Mr Fenton, the lessee of his Greasborough mine. In 1798 Earl Fitzwilliam continued his uncle's work and opened a branch of the Dearne and Dove Canal, thereby giving Fitzwilliam coal access to wider markets through the growing Yorkshire network of canals and rivers. The Earl commissioned another survey for a canal with a view to improving the output of his Elsecar mines, but it was overtaken by another development. The Don Navigation Company and Aire and Calder Navigation sponsored a major canal project to link the Rivers Calder, Don and Trent and to connect the region's waterways with the River Humber. In North Yorkshire the Earl of Thanet built a canal from Skipton to join the Leeds and Liverpool for the easier transportation of lime and limestone from his estates.

There was widespread interest among landowners in canal promotion. In 1788 a pamphlet was issued advocating a scheme for extending the navigation of the rivers Kennet and Avon and the advantages a canal would bring to Wiltshire landowners:

> The price of carriage of coals and all other articles will be greatly reduced: estates of gentlemen and farmers will be improved at much easier expense by the introduction of free-stone, timber, brick, tile and other building materials; lime, peat-ashes, and manure of all sorts. They will find new markets for the produce of their farms and estates: corn, malt, cheese and other productions, will meet with a ready and cheap conveyance to the great marts.[33]

The third Earl of Egremont was an enthusiast for canals in Sussex. He promoted the Rother and the London–Portsmouth and played a leading part in promoting the Portsmouth and Arundel canal. One could provide many more examples. Wherever a landowner has participated in canal development, the family archives may have accumulated maps, plans, surveys, reports, leases, accounts, correspondence and various legal documents. Occasionally, the evidence will reflect conflicts

4th Call £5 p Share   Wakefield, 8th Sept: 1798

Sir

    The Subscribers for making and supporting a Navigable Canal from the River Calder, near Heath, to pass by Barnsley to Barnby-Bridge, in the West-Riding of the County of York, having generally consented to augment their respective Subscriptions so far as to raise the further Sum of £22,000. wanted to complete the Undertaking; I beg leave to inform you, that I am ordered by the said Subscribers to make a Call of *Five* — Pounds a Share upon the Subscription. You are therefore requested to pay that arising upon your *Eight* Shares, being *Forty* — Pounds, on or before *Friday* the *19th* Day of *October next* — at the Old Navigation Counting-House, in this Place.

I am,

Your most humble Servant,

William Rooth   Treasurer.

34 Share subscription call to G.W. Wentworth for the Barnsley Canal Navigation, 1798.

of interest between canal and railway or, as in the case of the second Marquess of Bute, between canal and dock interests. Throughout the 1840s the Marquess was antagonistic towards the Glamorgan Canal Company, which posed a threat to the success of his Cardiff dock. A letter written to the Marquess by the Chairman of the Canal Company in 1847 captures the flavour of the conflict:

> The question between us is not whether we are entitled to any specific quantity of land or not . . . [but] whether you can so cripple us . . . at our shipping port at Cardiff that you can obtain the whole trade of the port through your superior and costly exit to the sea!! This, my lord, is the real question and all the covering of the suits of ejectment and equity . . . cannot hide the real question between us. My lord, I venture further to tell you, not

only as the Chairman of the Canal Company but as an individual freighter of the port of Cardiff – that you cannot succeed in obtaining the whole trade of the port of Cardiff by force.[34]

Railways

Until the 1960s the prevailing image of the landowner in railway history was that of the villain. In a much-quoted article in the *Journal of Transport History*, J.T. Ward set out to redress the balance. While acknowledging that there were plenty of examples of landowners resisting railway development for a variety of reasons, he drew the attention of historians to the muniment rooms and libraries of the many country houses that were rich in largely untapped material. Each famous case of opposition, he argued, could be matched by examples of landowners' support. Ward went on to demonstrate from these very sources – Lane Fox MSS, Gascoigne MSS, Crewe-Milnes MSS and others – that as far as West Yorkshire is concerned, its landowners played a considerable part in railway history as investors, promoters and directors.[35]

Before an application could be made to Parliament for permission to construct a railway, a survey of the proposed route was made. Copies of these plans and the names of the owners and occupiers of land affected frequently survive in collections of estate papers, along with a variety of other items. In the process leading up to the passing of an Act of Parliament a good deal of evidence was accumulated both supporting and opposing the proposed measure. The Acts of Parliament list all the proprietors of the newly formed companies. These frequently include aristocrats. For example, among the subscribers to the Leeds and Selby Railway, which received Royal Assent on 1 June 1830, were the Earl of Mexborough and R.O. Gascoigne of Parlington Hall. Amenity clauses to protect the gentry are to be found in the legislation. No fixed or permanent engine was to be set up on the Leeds and Selby Railway within 880 yards of the residences of any of the 16 aristocrats of whom the Marchioness of Hertford was the first named.[36] Many landowners seem to have taken advantage of railway development but resisted any proposals that threatened to come too close to the family seat and that might destroy its tranquility; this point was made strongly by R.C. Wilmot in evidence to Parliament in 1862, on behalf of Wentworth of Woolley Hall, opposing the Barnsley Coal Railway Extension Bill:

I reside at Woolley and am Land Agent to Mr Wentworth and others. I have carefully examined the route taken by the proposed extension of the Barnsley Coal Railway. It passes nearly two miles through Mr Wentworth's estates and goes through the village of Notton. Mr Wentworth is the owner of the whole of that Township. His estate consists of upwards of 6000 acres and is very compact and nicely situated. Great improvements have been made by Mr Wentworth who is very fond of agricultural pursuits and takes a great interest in the Cultivation and Management of his estate. He resides altogether at Woolley Park. The proposed line goes through and severs very injuriously the best farms on the Estate, and on which considerable sums have been expended in new buildings and improvements. It goes through the heart of the property as will be seen on reference to the map and severs it in a very disadvantageous manner. Mr Wentworth has already two lines of railway through his estate, the Lancashire and Yorkshire on the West and the Midland on the East and also the Barnsley Canal. Every accommodation is therefore afforded to the Public and Inhabitants. The existing railways also open the coal field on the estate and no further accommodation is required for that. If the proposed Extension were made Mr Wentworth would not allow any pits to be established on it. Any pits on the proposed extension would be a nuisance to Woolley Park and no gentleman wishing to make that mansion his residence could ever with a thought to his own comfort allow pits to be opened upon it. He strongly objects to the line . . .[37]

Urbanization

Of the 261 provincial towns surveyed by a royal commission in 1886, 103 were largely owned by lords. Similarly, a royal commission on market rights and tolls found that, of the 531 urban markets in England and Wales situated outside London, 128 were owned and managed by private persons. This close connection between landed estates and some towns and cities had obvious implications for urban growth and development. The following are some of the places where the landed interest was an agent of change:

Liverpool	the Earls of Sefton and Derby
Newcastle	the Dukes of Northumberland and the Earl of Durham
Seaham Harbour	the Marquis of Londonderry
Manchester	the Mosleys and the Earl of Wilton
Sheffield	the Dukes of Norfolk
Nottingham	the Duke of Newcastle
Stamford	the Marquis of Exeter
Whitehaven	the Lowthers
Eastbourne	the Dukes of Devonshire
Keighley	the Dukes of Devonshire
Cardiff	the Marquesses of Bute
Folkestone	the Earls of Radnor
Skegness	the Earl of Scarborough
Torquay	Lord Haddon

Developments in central London were influenced by estate owners such as the Earls of Bedford and Southampton and the Dukes of Manchester, Portland and Westminster. In the case of some towns, the aristocratic influence was confined to the suburbs. As Professor Beresford has pointed out regarding Leeds, 'No peer was to be found in its rate books; the interests of the Earls of Cardigan were confined to the out-townships while Harewood and Temple Newsam estates lay wholly outside the borough'.[38]

Nineteenth-century trade directories, especially those published in the 1820s and 1830s, often provide interesting comments on the exercise of seigneurial rights.

For example, White's *Directory of the West Riding* (1837) has this to say about the Ramsden connection with Huddersfield:

> [It] is a dependent manor within the Honour of Pontefract, and the chief part of it belongs to Sir John Ramsden, Bart.; for though there are several small freeholders in the township, all the land in and near the town, except a small portion belonging to Mr Firth, is the property of this worthy baronet and from it he derives a princely income; the building sites being let at high rents, and many of them without leases; indeed he has of late years refused to grant building leases, but still the town has continued to increase, and many fine streets and handsome houses have been erected on the unleased land, the inhabitants having the utmost confidence in the honour and liberality of the Ramsden family, who have held the manor since the Reformation . . .

The Ramsdens, as lords of the manor of Huddersfield, obtained the right to hold a weekly market there, which became one of the most important in Yorkshire. Charles II granted the charter in 1672:

> . . . we do grant unto John Ramsden Esq., that he and his heirs may have and hold one market in the town of Huddersfield, on Tuesday in every week for ever, for the buying and selling of all manner of goods and merchandise, and receive the tolls, profits and advantages from thence coming and arising for him and his heirs for ever . . .[39]

The liberality of the Ramsdens to which the directory refers took the form of a commodious Cloth Hall erected by Sir John Ramsden in 1765, the site of the National school and two acres of land attached to the infirmary leased for a small annual rent. The Ramsdens were patrons of the living of the parish church and held a substantial block of pews in the nave. Thomas Baines, writing in the 1870s, had this to say about the influence of the Ramsdens on the development of the town:

> Huddersfield has always been a handsome town, having been well laid out by the Ramsden family, the sole proprietors . . . The new part of the town, north of the old market place, is laid out in wide and handsome streets. It has moreover, many fine buildings. Amongst these are the Railway Station, which gave the first impetus to the recent improvements of the town, and caused the opening up of the new parts; the Lion Arcade, which faces the station from the lower side of St George's Square; the Britannia Buildings in the same square; several of the banks; and perhaps finest of all, the lofty and extensive Ramsden Estate Buildings . . . Of late years, too, a portion of the adjoining Thornhill Estate, on the hillside north-east of the town, having become available, the prosperous men of Huddersfield have built themselves commodious, and, in many cases, beautiful residences, in great variety.[40]

In recent years urban geographers and historians have examined in some detail the influence of the aristocracy on the growth of industrial towns. It would seem that, although the Ramsdens never enjoyed absolute control of Huddersfield, they owned enough to expect the dominant say in any development and, in retrospect, their achievements were less commendable than the Victorian source quoted above suggests. Rapid growth of the town in the later eighteenth century under the influence of Sir John Ramsden was followed by several decades during which the family failed to exercise its powers with regard to building control. According to Jane Springett, when they did reassert themselves, after 1840, the terms were such that builders looked to acquire their land from any owner rather than the Ramsdens. For 30 years they effectively priced working-class families out of the new homes market, and it was only in 1885 that they allowed smaller houses to be built on their land.[41]

In the eighteenth and nineteenth centuries the Dukes of Norfolk increased their wealth by exploiting the mineral wealth of their northern estates and developing their urban properties. Income from the estates in Yorkshire, Derbyshire and Nottingham-shire was used to extend and improve their estates in Surrey and Sussex. Under the twelfth Duke some 12,000 acres on the north and east sides of the town of Sheffield were developed with 99-year leases. Baines's *Directory of the County of York* explained the background to this in an appropriately discreet manner:

A spirit of improvement has for many years been in active exercise in the town of Sheffield. A very large proportion of the freehold property of the town is vested in the Howard family, and had descended under settlements of intail from its ancient lords to that noble house. This circumstance was found to operate considerably to the disadvantage of the town, which, from the extent of its manufactures and commerce, called for a more general diffusion of real property. The Duke of Norfolk was not insensible to this circumstance, nor disinclined to take the measures necessary to cherish that spirit of improvement which on every hand presented itself. An act was accordingly procured in the year 1802, on the presentation of the Duke and his heirs 'for vesting several messuages and hereditaments in Sheffield, and divers detached parts of the settled estates of the Howard family in trustees upon trust to sell and lay out money in the purchase of more convenient estates or otherwise.' This was followed by three other acts having the same object in view. Extensive sales have been made under the provisions of these acts with distinguished liberality towards the tenants and occupiers of lands and houses, and the consequence has been a great accession to the list of freeholders in the town and parish . . .[42]

The Duke sold nearly all his property in Sheffield township, except in the Park, a populous suburb. The latter was developed under the direction of his agent, Michael Ellison, with corn exchange, markets and fairs. Also under Ellison's influence, the Shrewsbury hospital was moved to a better site in 1827 at a cost of £10,183.

The role of the Marquesses of Bute in the development of nineteenth-century Cardiff has been the subject of a number of scholarly writings in recent years. Archives relating to the time of the second Marquess (1814–48) are rich and varied and cover all aspects of estate activity – the movement of rent, the leasing of building land and minerals, the development of the Bute Docks and Bute policy towards the railways. Bute properties were widely separated and in diverse parts of the United Kingdom and the family papers are located in places as far apart as Aberystwyth, Cardiff, Edinburgh and London. The first Marquess (1766–1814) neglected administration but made some important purchases of land at Cardiff and within the coalfield, which strengthened the position of the family in East Glamorgan. The family owned so much of Cardiff in the late eighteenth and early nineteenth centuries that its income from rents exceeded the income of the town corporation. The second Marquess devoted himself to estate management and improvement. He has been described as 'a product of his age, a mixture of evangelical earnestness, aristocratic arrogance and the confident ruthlessness of an early nineteenth century industrialist'.[43] As an estate manager he was tireless and concerned himself with every detail. He wrote lengthy business letters and kept copies of every one of them in letter books. The administration was department-alized. In other words, no one at Cardiff had responsibility for estate affairs as a whole. The Marquess corresponded with his permanent agent, his mineral agent, his dockmaster, his agricultural agent and the agent of the Cardiff estate.

The period of the second Marquessate saw great changes in Glamorgan and its county town, Cardiff. Between 1811 and 1851 the county's population rose from 85,000 to 232,000 and Cardiff's increased from a mere 2457 to 18,351. From the insignificant market town of 1814, by 1848 it had become the largest town in Wales and a great coal port. By the 1820s transport facilities, first provided for the iron trade in the late eighteenth century, had become inadequate for the expanding coal trade. In 1828 the second Marquess commissioned a report on the state of the harbour of Cardiff. It concluded that the existing sea-lock of the Glamorganshire Canal was inadequate and that a new dock was desirable. In 1830 Bute obtained powers to build the dock and it was opened in 1839. The opening ceremony on 8 October was marked by great festivities in the town. It was to remain a family business until 1922. The decision to build the dock was linked with the development of the Bute coalfield and the prospect that it would encourage building development on the Cardiff estate. The mutual dependence of the dock and mineral estate is shown most clearly in the clause in the Bute mineral lease that required all coal to be shipped from the Bute docks. But the opening of the dock did not tempt the Marquess into taking over the direct management of his coal mines. He declared himself 'satisfied to submit to the certain loss of letting a colliery at a lower royalty than it is worth, than to be exposed to the unknown amount of loss by bad debts, besides the uncertainty of trade'.[44]

Evidence for the presence of the great estate in nineteenth-century towns and cities survives in a great many street and place names. In Sheffield Norfolk Street is a permanent reminder of the Dukes of Norfolk; in the centre of Huddersfield there are Ramsden Street and John William Street; the Dukes of Devonshire are commemorated in the Keighley Borough coat of arms, in Cavendish Street and the Devonshire Park. But, in the words of John Davies, there can be few cities where the imprint of a single family is as legible as is that of the Bute family at Cardiff:

> Their castle and its park dominate the centre of Cardiff. The statue of the second marquess commands the access to the city's main thoroughfare and the statue of the third guards the entrance to Cathays Park. The names of the Cardiff district of Butetown and the township of Treherbert commemorate the family and its Pembroke ancestors . . . and the names of major features of the city – Ninian Park, Cardiff Arms Park, Bute Park and Sophia Gardens – are memorials to the family . . . The titles of the family – Bute, Dumfries, Windsor, Mountjoy, Crichton and Mountstuart – appear on streets, places, crescents and squares . . . The first wife of the second marquess has a Guildford Street, his second a Sophia Street and a Loudoun Square. Glossop Terrace and Howard Gardens are named after the family of the third marquess's wife and Colum Road, Ninian Road and Lady Margaret's Terrace after her children . . .[45]

Chapter Five

THE LANDOWNER IN SOCIETY: LEADERSHIP AND LEISURE

Informal local influence

However strong the landowner's sense of social superiority, he and his family rarely saw themselves as separate from the local community. They were its natural leaders, whose role was to bind it together. They took for granted the ideal of social unity and of a hierarchically organized community, in which deference would be shown to its leaders. All this simply reflected the dominance of the landed classes in rural Britain.

Seen in the most basic economic terms, the country house was vitally important to the local community as a centre of consumption and employment. A glance at the account books and boxes or files of bills that most archives contain makes this clear. Those of Harewood contain a list dated 19 June 1788 of tradesmen's bills paid by Edwin Lascelles[1] which, along with 42 other items, shows:

A Barclay	Waxchandler	33 16 0
R Dove	Bricklayer	44 10 6
H House	Oilman	108 14 6
E Nevinson	Apothecary	53 4 0
D Porter	Chimney Sweeper	4 6 0

Some of the payments in the list were not to local firms, as with 'Haigh & Chippendale Upholsterers 174 2 6', and luxury items were commonly bought from fashionable dealers in London, but the payments to local tradesmen remain considerable. For consumption by a large household, food alone was a sizeable item. Conspicuous consumption was a mark of aristocracy, especially when important guests were entertained. Sir Thomas Robinson of Rokeby, Yorkshire, wrote in a letter of 1731 to Lord Carlisle of entertaining at Houghton:

> During the Duke of Lorraine's being there the consumption both from the larder & the cellar was prodigious. They dined in the hall, which was lighted by 130 wax candles, and the saloon with 50: the whole expense in that article being computed at fifteen pounds a night.[2]

The bill paid by Edwin Lascelles also calls attention to the employment opportunities offered by the house and its estate. In Charles Greville's *Memoirs*, such opportunities are indicated in his comments of 16 September 1846 on Woburn:

> Such magnificence in House, Park, and gardens, such building all over the estate, farmhouses fit for gentlemen and intended for men of education and knowledge, vast

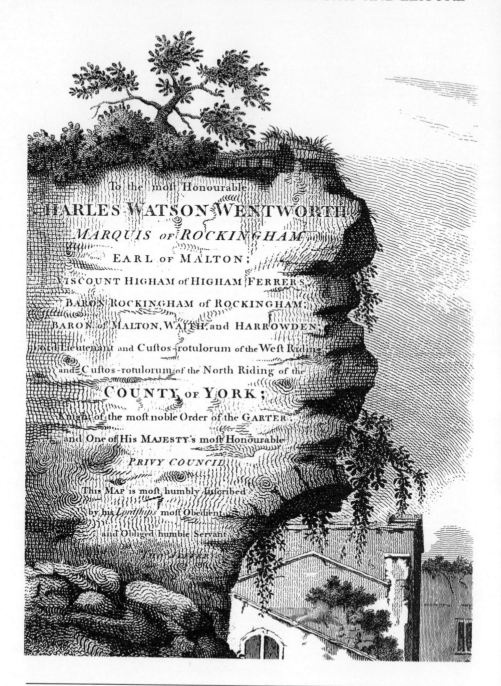

35 Dedication of Thomas Jeffery's map of Yorkshire, 1775, to the Marquess of Rockingham as the county's leading figure.

workshops where everything is done that is required for the property, carpenters, ironmongers, painters, and glazers [*sic*], 300 artificers are in the employment of the Duke, and paid every Saturday night . . .[3]

Not only were there the household servants, grooms, gardeners, gamekeepers and the like, but the building and maintenance of the house and grounds required specialists like those mentioned by Greville, along with supporting labour. Most of these would be drawn from the locality. It has been calculated that some six per cent of men in rural parishes were so employed. Further, where a landowner developed mining interests, he could become a major employer. Because of the expansion of the mining industry in the eighteenth and nineteenth centuries, by 1858 the Elsecar and Parkgate collieries of Earl Fitzwilliam employed 1000 men.

The Fitzwilliams were regarded as good employers, particularly in comparison with many of their fellow but non-aristocratic mine-owners. According to the report of the local mines' inspector of 1845, most of their miners were well housed, received free coal, 3s per week when ill and 2s 6d if injured in the pit and unable to work, and:

. . . every year just before Christmas . . . a handsome piece of beef and a present in money is given to each of the labouring people . . . and on the 3rd February . . . a piece of bacon.[4]

Landowners were generally seen as good employers but, like the Fitzwilliams, they were paternalists, controlling their employees autocratically and expecting deference. Thus, the Whig libertarianism of the Fitzwilliams did not prevent them from sharing in the general landowning opposition to trade unions and was, in fact, consistent with it. The successful formation of a national Agricultural Labourers Union in 1873 was one of the signs that the landowners' days of dominance were almost over.

Aristocratic paternalism in relation to the local community had always been expressed through a hospitality that went beyond the entertaining of social equals to include, on certain occasions, the community at large. In the early eighteenth century Sir James Lowther kept lists of the local merchants and traders he invited to dinner on his annual visits to West Cumberland:

An Account of those that dine with me at Whitehaven which I keep to avoid giving offence least I should omit those that are proper to dine with me. I keep this account because if I should omit to invite any people of note in the town they would take it ill.[5]

Family rites of passage were seen as significant for the community as a whole, so that communal activities were laid on for births, the coming-of-age of an heir, marriages and funerals. Thus, the coming-of-age of Henry, Viscount Lascelles, on 6 October 1845 was celebrated, after the relatively exclusive meeting of the Earl's fox hounds, by a series of 'sports and pastimes', details of which were advertised by poster.[6] The day also celebrated the marriage of the Viscount in July as well as his actual coming-of-age in June, the celebration having been delayed because of the death from typhus in June of two of his brothers.

The celebrations at Charlecote Park of the marriage of Tina Campbell to Spencer

LIST OF THE

SPORTS

AND

PASTIMES

WITH THE

PRIZES

To be awarded to the Successful Competitors

On Thursday, November 6th, 1845,

To celebrate the Coming of Age of

LORD VISCOUNT LASCELLES,

After the Meeting of the Earl of Harewood's Fox Hounds, at the North Front of Harewood House, at half-past Ten in the Morning.

Climbing Soaped Poles.
1st Prize,—The Ox's Heart, and Five Shillings.
2nd Prize,—A Leg of Mutton, and Trimmings.
3rd Prize,—A Goose and Giblets.

Jingling Match, or Bell Race.
BY MEN.
Two Shillings and Sixpence, each Match.—Jingler, One Shilling every five minutes.

FIRST FOOT RACE.
Confined to Parties residing upon Lord Harewood's Property.
200 Yards.
1st Prize,—A Silver Watch.
2nd Prize,—A Scotch Snuff Box.

DIVING FOR SILVER IN FLOUR.
The Hands to be tied behind—the Silver to be taken out with the Mouth.

BOBBING FOR APPLES IN WATER.
Boy getting out Four in shortest time with his Mouth.
Two Shillings and Sixpence.

A DONKEY RACE.
Open to all Yorkshire.—Half a Mile.
1st Prize,—Ten Shillings.
2nd Prize,—Two Shillings and Sixpence.

THE DINNER HOUR.
At Half-past Two, the Sports to be resumed.

SMALL BALLOONS ASCENT, WITH PARACHUTE.

SECOND FOOT RACE.
Open to all Yorkshire.—150 Yards.
1st Prize,—Two Sovereigns.
2nd Prize, Ten Shillings.
Four Candidates at least must start.

SMOKING, BY MEN.
Half an Ounce each in shortest time—Pint of Beer after second Pipe.
1st Prize,—One Pound of Tobacco.
2nd Prize, Quarter of a Pound Tobacco.

WHEELBARROW RACES.
Blindfolded.—The Winner to have Five Shillings.

DONKEY STEEPLE CHASE. HALF A MILE.
1st Prize, Ten Shillings.
2nd Prize,—Two Shillings and Sixpence.

JINGLING MATCH, OR BELL RACE.
By Boys.—1s. 6d. each Match. Jingler, sixpence every five minutes.

FOOT HURDLE CHASE.--BY MEN.--HALF A MILE.
1st Prize,—Ten Shillings.
2nd Prize,—Three Shillings. Six at least to start.

FOOT-BALL PLAYING.
By Men.—Six Men aside, with their arms tied, and without shoes, the Winners to have Ten Shillings.

Four Men blindfolded to whip a Ball out of a hole with cart whips.
1st Prize,—A Whip and 3 Shillings.
The Unsuccessful Candidates to retain their Whips.

FOOT-BALL MATCH.
By Boys.—Six Aside. With their Arms tied, and without shoes. The Winners to receive five shillings.

THIRD FOOT RACE.
For Boys under sixteen years of age. Race, 100 Yards.
1st Prize,—Five Shillings.
2nd Prize,—Two Shillings.

The whole of the Sports will be under the Direction of

Signor ALDIBIRONTIPHOSCHOFORNIOCHRONONHOTONTHOLOGOS,

ASSISTED BY

DON DIEGO DIOBLASCOKILLOCUROEVERYWHEREO,

And other Professors of Fun and Frolic.

T. HARRISON, PRINTER, 55, BRIGGATE, LEEDS.

36 Poster announcing the coming-of-age of Henry, Viscount Lascelles, 1845.

Lucy on 5 July 1865 were recorded by Lady Mary Lucy, Spencer's mother, in her journal:

> People lined the road all the way from Warwick to Charlecote, from the village to the entrance gates. Hundreds were assembled to hurrah with all their might . . . All the tenantry, their wives, sons and daughters lined the road to the old Gateway . . . A booth 120 feet long was erected in the park at Charlecote, where dinner was laid on for all the tenants . . . All the poor on the estate were feasted with as much as they could eat and drink. 600 lb weight of meat was consumed, 200 cwt of plum pudding, and upwards of 400 gallons of old ale, brewed at Charlecote, was drunk. There was a large tent for the wives and daughters of the tenants who met together to have tea and cake, and wine etc. All the women and village children had tea and plum cake, of which they cut 200 lbs weight. Then followed all sorts of music and dancing until it grew dark when the revels were brought to a close by a grand display of fireworks.[7]

Such events were reported in some detail in the local press, as was the funeral of the 90-year-old Sir Tatton Sykes at Sledmere in March 1863. It was attended by 'the nobility gentry and tradesmen of the district' as well as the household and family, while the pallbearers were 'twelve aged labourers all of whom have lived upon the estate all their lives'. Phrase after phrase in the obituary in the *Malton Messenger* of Saturday 28 March expressed appropriate sentiments:

> On every hand his charity was felt, and in every place his presence was hailed with delight; his cheerful countenance and amiable disposition was open to all, and he would converse as freely with the peasant as with the lord . . . He was the very type of a country gentleman of the olden time, and he died doing his duty to man, in that exalted station of life in which he was placed . . .[8]

Royal events like the jubilees of Queen Victoria were widely celebrated with dinners and dances to which household and estate staff, tenants and other local people were usually invited. The way in which all these activities were designed to achieve both social cohesion and deference is made clear by the exclusions that could be practised: a pamphlet listing the prizes to be awarded to tenants of Sir Charles Domvile's estate at Sawtry in Ireland in 1859 concluded, 'Any tenant, with whom Sir Charles Domvile feels reason to be dissatisfied, will neither be allowed to compete nor invited to be present at the Estate Show.'[9]

If the leadership of the local community imposed the obligation to maintain its unity, it was also seen as involving the duty to assist the less well off. Thus, there were landowners who built schools, parish churches and cottages and, in the nineteenth century, provided their labourers with allotments or encouraged them in self-help. Financial support for and involvement in the management of local institutions were seen as appropriate obligations. Landowners were particularly active after the revival of Anglicanism under the stimulus of the Evangelical Revival and the Oxford Movement and in response to the threat from below that was shown in the agitation for the 1832 Reform Bill. Thus, when Dacre Banks Hill-top School, North Yorkshire, was transferred to the newly constituted district School Board in 1874, the local squire, Sir Henry Ingilby of Ripley, was involved. The Ingilbys had long been managers of the school, and on 5 May the clerk to the Board requested Sir Henry's formal consent to the transfer and continued:

> Also the Board would consider it a munificent gift if you would make over to them for the use of the master the cottage at Dacre Banks usually occupied by the teachers of the Hilltop school . . . The Board likewise learn from the Clergyman of Dacre Banks that you are willing to pay to any parties authorized to receive it the sum of £200 for purposes of education at Dacre B.[*sic*] . . .[10]

Sir Henry's endowment was eventually used to purchase £225 of India Stock.

Of course, such actions need to be seen in a broader context. The overall extent of such generosity has been estimated at from four to seven per cent of income for the leading families and one to two per cent for the gentry. Moreover, charity could be motivated by the need to display publicly the paternalistic role of the landowner, while along with the socially concerned were others interested in their estates simply as a source of income. Further, the public-spirited actions of individuals could be contradicted by the decisions made by landowners in the institutions that they controlled, as when the House of Lords displayed apathy to the provision of allotments and, in the 1840s, vetoed a Bill to compensate tenants for improvements that awaited statutory backing until 1875.

Indeed, it is easy to exaggerate the local influence of the landed classes; it had its limits. Most obviously, it operated at its best only in 'closed' villages, i.e., villages dominated by one or two landowners, where landlord leadership was seldom challenged in either secular or religious matters. In 'open' villages landowning was more widely distributed, without dominant holdings. There, landlord influence was limited; a frequent comment in the returns of the Archdeaconry of Oxford in 1854 is, 'landed property very much divided. Dissent much among them.' On average, 79 per cent of parishes with subdivided property in Kent, Lindsey, Leicestershire and Northamptonshire contained at least one Dissenting chapel in 1851, while only 21 per cent of those in concentrated ownership did so.[11] Landlords showed little interest in the housing or welfare of their tenants or employees in open villages, while in closed villages they might refuse land for a Nonconformist chapel or even exclude Nonconformists from their tenantry. As to the extent of the two village types, in nineteenth-century Leicestershire there were 174 open and 134 closed villages, though their incidence varied from county to county and parish to parish, with closed villages being more usual in the south and open in the north of England.

Influence over the religious life of the parish had long been held by those landowners who possessed an advowson, as the Ingilby family did at Ripley. In 1759 Sir John Ingilby offered the living at Ripley to Samuel Kirshaw, Vicar of Leeds, whose grandfather had formerly held it. Kirshaw sought the best possible terms for himself in his reply, dated 5 November:

> . . . Patronages undoubtedly are very important Trusts & a good Man will be cautious how He uses them; and ye Residence of Ministers is generally in some great Degree requisite to the best Advantage of the People. But perhaps there may be Cases wherein ye partial Residence of ye Minister, together wth the constant Residence of a Curate well

approved, may be more acceptable to the People on Account of Connexions they may have wth, or opinion they may have of, such Minister, & therefore more likely to be more beneficial to them, than ye perpetual Residence of a Minister not so circumstanced wth respect to the People . . .

He went on to recommend that he should reside in the parish for part of the year, employing a curate for the rest, recommending his cousin, Richard Hey, 'Fellow of Sidney College & resident there, & one of a most excellent Character for Temper, Morals, & Learning'. Sir John was agreeable.[12]

National and local government

The dominance of the landed classes in the political life of the nation throughout the period under study is reflected in their surviving papers. At the national level, those of any minister of the Crown will almost certainly contain official documents and a good deal of political correspondence. Thus, to give only two of many possible examples, the papers of William Cecil, Lord Burghley (the Salisbury MSS), have been widely used in the study of the reign of Elizabeth I, and those of Henry Pelham, Duke of Newcastle (the Newcastle MSS), for the eighteenth century. Sir Lewis Namier made use of some 40 collections for his classic study of eighteenth-century government, *The Structure of Politics at the Accession of George III*. Further, the archives of those who were not leading politicians are likely to contain documents arising from a parliamentary election, a contentious local issue or involvement in a matter of patronage.

Thus, the Strafford Papers contain several attractive public notices put out by the rival contenders in the election for the county of Yorkshire in 1734, including the announcement of their candidature by the Tories Rowland Winn and Cholmley Turner, as follows:

Sir George Savile having declined standing Candidate for this County at the ensuing Election for Members of Parliament; at the desire of a great Number of Gentlemen, Clergy and Freeholders met here . . . We offer you our Services, assuring you that we are hearty in the Interest of our Country, and will do all that is in our power to preserve our happy Constitution in Church, and State as by Law Established; and desire you to favour us with your Votes, and Interest, and the Obligation shall ever be acknowledged . . .[13]

As controllers and chief beneficiaries of 'our happy Constitution in Church, and State', the landed classes firmly supported it, though critics emerged from time to time. Thus, correspondence concerning the activities of the Yorkshire Association, which, in the early 1780s, set out to limit government influence through the granting of sinecures and other offices, can be found in the papers of Lord Rockingham in the Wentworth Woodhouse MSS. The Revd Christopher Wyvil's letter to the York press explained the general aims of the Association as follows:

. . . to petition the House of Commons to appoint a Committee to inquire into the State of the Civil List, in order that all exorbitant Salaries, sinecure places and unmerited pensions may be reduced and abolished. But least this Petition should be Slighted as a

> former one was, they wish to support it, by entring into an Association to elect such
> Candidates only at the next General Election as will engage to Promote the object of the
> Petition . . .

Close to the letter may be found the draft of one from Rockingham, endorsing
the objects of the Association.[14]

Another supporter of the Association, Sir Thomas Gascoigne of Parlington, came
from a Catholic background, but joined the Church of England in 1780 in order to
qualify for election to the Commons and was promptly returned for the pocket
borough of Thirsk. A critic of government policy towards the North American
colonies in revolt, he erected a triumphal arch at Parlington in support of their
independence at the end of the war. While the house at Parlington no longer survives,
the arch still stands, with its inscription 'Liberty in N. America triumphant
MDCCLXXXIII'. An early design for it can be found in the Gascoigne Papers.[15]

Much more common than individual protest is the considerable evidence of the
patronage that oiled the workings of the constitution before the development of a
professional civil service recruited by public examination. It is no surprise to find
many examples in the correspondence of the most famous string-puller of the
eighteenth century, Thomas Pelham, Duke of Newcastle, like the letter from his
friend Charles Lennox, Duke of Richmond, of 16 October 1742, saying:

> Since I saw your Grace this morning I have another letter from the Archdeacon, in which
> he presses for a peremptory promis of the Chancellorship when vacant, so I must beg of
> you when you see the Bishop to gett this promis of him . . .[16]

Correspondence of the office-holding first and second Lords Grantham of Newby
Park, Yorkshire, is to be found in the Vyner Papers. For example, there is a letter
from Lord Shelburne, Secretary of State for the southern department, offering a
post to a nephew of Lord Grantham, Thomas Robinson, as compensation for the
loss of office by Lord Grantham himself.[17]

As with the leading national political figures, the archives of the senior local
official, the Lord Lieutenant, will contain both official papers and political
correspondence. His role, as the chief county executive, required all the wealth and
prestige of a major landowner, commonly a leading peer. His formal powers
included responsibility for raising the militia when civil disturbance or war
threatened and the recommendation of deputy lieutenants and Justices of the
Peace, but it was no sinecure, requiring constant activity in both politics and
administration. As representative of the sovereign, he was technically above politics
but was in fact expected to give loyal support to the government of the day and had
immense electoral influence. In times of crisis his vigilance was crucial, making him
the obvious person to inform of suspicions of disloyalty. Thus, at the height of the
1745 Jacobite rebellion, Lord Irwin, as Lord Lieutenant for the East Riding of
Yorkshire, received the following anonymous letter:

> Whoever is well affected to his country will make search for arms concealed in the house
> or somewhere about it of Stephen Tempest of Braughton near Skipton a Papist, for the
> Person who writes this to the Ld Irwin has had sufficient information that arms are there

Lᵈ Irwin / Whoever is well affected to his country will make search for arms concealed in the house or some where about it, of Stephen Tempest of Broughton near Skipton a Papist, for the Person who writes this to the Lᵈ Irwin has had sufficient information that arms are there concealed, & he is willing that his name should be so too therefore he only subscribes himself

his Country's Friend.

Let diligent search be made as well under ground as above, with a sufficient number of trusty people. August 22.⁴⁵

Secrecy, Diligence and Expedition

37 Anonymous letter to Lord Irwin suggesting the search of the home of a suspected Jacobite, 1745.

concealed, & he is willing that his name should be so too, therefore he only subscribes himself

> his Country's Friend

Let diligent search be made as well under ground as above, with a sufficient number of trusty people.

August 22d 45

> Secrecy, diligence and expedition[18]

A Lord Lieutenant's own disloyalty could, on occasion, bring dismissal, as happened to Earl Fitzwilliam for his protest over the action of the Manchester authorities at Peterloo.

Next in order of precedence came the sheriff. In the sixteenth and early seventeenth centuries he still held real power, particularly at election times, when his intervention might turn the scales one way or the other, but the duties of office were time-consuming and expensive, so that as its power declined it lost its appeal. By the eighteenth century it was an office that was accepted readily only by new and

Copy of a Letter from Penrith, *to the* Poſt-Maſter *of* Brough. Saturday, November 23d 1745. *Three in the Afternoon.*

SIR,

WE are now clear of the Highland Army; by an Exact Account taken at *Eamont-bridge*, which they could not avoid paſſing, their whole Force is not above Five Thouſand: They have thirteen Pieces of Artillery, two Cohorns and another ſmall Piece. The Diameter of moſt of their Pieces not above three Inches. Their Baggage and all gone forwards for *Kendall*, except ſome few Carriages which they are ſending back to *Carliſle*. They have left at that place a Guard, not exceeding 120 Men. Little inconſiderable Partys of Straglers are coming all this Morning; in ſhort, their Forces inſtead of being formidable are poor ſhabby Fellows moſt of them. All their Heads with their Prince are gone forward, their Chiefs are the Dukes of *Perth* and *Athol*; Lords *Kilmarnock, Nairn, Pitſligoe, Dundee, Ogilvy, Geo. Murry, Secretary Murry* and *Glenbucket.*

38 Copy of a letter received by Lord Irwin as Lord Lieutenant about the progress of the Jacobite army, 1745.

wealthy landowners eager for recognition, but avoided by others. Ralph Docksey wrote plainly about his reluctance to accept office to Thomas Coke, MP for Derbyshire and Vice-Chamberlain, on 10 November 1707:

> I hear I am one of the three nominated to be sheriff for this County which much surprises me, being very unfit to bear such an office . . . my estate being at best worth but about £300 a year, £200 of it settled on my wife; and the other £100 a year, there is a debt of £1,000 owing to Sir Nathaniel Curzon, so that the bearing of that office will, at this time, be the undoing of me, I having a numerous family, my wife being big of the thirteenth. This is to desire the favour of your interest to get me off . . .[19]

The war-horses of county justice and administration were the Justices of the Peace. Their official papers are usually located in quarter-sessions papers, though some may be found in estate archives, as may the private notebooks that they were encouraged to keep. Tudor governments made great use of this office, loading the JPs with new responsibilities. Their key role was to maintain law and order, but they also acquired a wide range of administrative duties, helping to regulate wages and prices, maintaining highways and bridges, administering the Poor Laws, licensing alehouses and establishing apprenticeships. Thus, an Act of 1576 empowered any two JPs to take measures for the maintenance of an illegitimate child, preferably by the reputed father, so that the cost should not fall on the parish, and for the punishment of the mother and father; the Salisbury Papers contain the records of such a case, judged at Hatfield on 4 April 1588:

It is . . . orderid and adjudged by us Henrie Coningsbie, knight, and William Took, esqr, two Justices of the Peace . . . that the said Vincente Brandon, the reputed father . . . shall contribute and paie towards the kepinge of the said childe xiid everie weeke from the tyme of the birthe duringe the space of seven yeares, and the mother to discharge the reste duringe the said tyme . . . And furthermore we do order and adjudge that the said Elizabeth Walshe, mother of the said childe, shall on Mondaie the viiith of this moneth of Aprill, sitt in the stockes in the churche yard of Hatfelde . . . shall publiquelie confesse her fault and aske for the forgiveness of God and of the congregation, and . . . [be] severelie whipped and so redilivered to the stocks againe . . .[20]

The political importance of the role of the JPs was recognized in the exclusion from their ranks of both Catholics and Dissenters, initially by government pressure and later by legislation, and in the property qualification required, especially in the eighteenth century when it was raised from £20 to £100. The bench was therefore dominated by the gentry, except that, for reasons that are not very clear, in the very century that is seen as their golden age, the eighteenth, they showed some reluctance to accept office. Consequently, from the middle of the century until the 1830s clerics were frequently appointed to the bench. They had never been wholly absent from it, but during these years were appointed in significant numbers. Thus a list of the 55 West Riding magistrates at the end of 1812 contains 17 clerics.[21] The gentry began to accept office more readily from the 1830s, though in industrial areas the ranks of the magistracy were increasingly strengthened by the inclusion of professionals, merchants and manufacturers.

As in the Tudor era, the nineteenth century saw the significant extension of their duties. For example, the oversight of prisons and asylums was added. However, in the absence of an effective police force in the early years of the century, they were frequently preoccupied by their fundamental duty to maintain law and order. During the Luddite disturbances of 1812 to 1814, the defence of mills and mill-owners fell to the JPs and the military, and in the West Riding Joseph Radcliffe of Milnsbridge House, Huddersfield, acted so vigorously against the Luddites that threats and warnings like the following came his way:

Mr Radcliffe Dear Sir
This cumes from a frend
I feined my self to be and got into the seckrets of the Ludites and knowing the dredfull Plots that is going forwards I send this to you There is dredfull Prapration Goen forwards for Great Destrucktion
It is Reported you Back Thos Atkinson it was ordered a wile a go for your place and Bradley Mill to be Burnt one Night But I Pled it of with great to do
When that time Cumes foal[?] nor Horses will Be of aney use there will be a Great Destruction you must not Cumpell Watching & Warding you Must side with the Luds if you Live
I should a spoak Personley to you But durst Not if this was Known it is Deth to me
From Mr Love Good[22]

Radcliffe survived such threats, receiving a baronetcy in recognition of his work. However, even though the role of JP remained vital in local administration and justice, the landowners' dominance of the office declined. The Municipal Reform Act of 1835 and the County Councils Act of 1888 were significant steps along the way, as is discussed more fully elsewhere.[23]

Social life

The popular image of a series of elegant and gracious activities within the house and a vigorous life of hunting and shooting outdoors derives in large measure from the abundance of sources from the eighteenth and nineteenth centuries. Bills and accounts, correspondence, travellers' descriptions, journals, press reports and even census returns and advertisements may all provide appropriate evidence.

For the sixteenth and seventeenth centuries the evidence is much more limited and, in the main, is drawn from the nobility, so that it may be appropriate here to cite evidence concerning the gentry. Household regulations and accounts are the main sources. These can be frustrating in that the former may represent ideals or theory rather than practice, while accounts offer only the bare bones of household activities, leaving a great deal to imagination or surmise.

Wollaton's 'orders . . . to be observed by Sir Francis Willoughby's servants', which are probably from 1572, are well known for the courtly commands of the usher, 'Give place, my masters' and 'Speak softly, my masters', though less so for their context:

> . . . the usher . . . is to have regard of every person that comes into the hall, to the end that if they be of the better sort . . . they may be entertained accordingly. If of the meaner sort, then to know the cause of their coming . . . to the end they may be dispatched and answer'd of their business, provided always that no stranger be suffered to pass without offering him to drink, and that no rascall or unseemly person be suffer'd to tarry there . . .
>
> . . . [when] the meat is ready to be served, he is with a loud voice to command gentlemen and yeomen to repair to the dresser. At the nether end of the hall he is to meet the service, saying with a loud voice, 'Give place, my masters' . . . and so to goe before the same service untill he come to the upper end of the hall, carrying a little fine rod in his hand . . . He is to appoint some one yeomen . . . in the winter time to carry the torch before service in the night time
>
> All disorders in the hall are by the usher to be reformed, and if there shall be any stubborn persons, he is to expell them out of the hall, and to command all men at dinner and supper time (if any great noise shall be) to keep silence, saying with a loud voice, 'Speak softly, my masters'.[24]

This evidence of the persistence of medieval ceremonial in a gentleman's household well into the sixteenth century no longer survives as an original document, for, along with other archival material, it was copied by Cassandra Willoughby when she was compiling a history of the Willoughby's of Wollaton in the early eighteenth century, and only her copy remains.

The nature of the meals eaten on such occasions is described in the household books of a gentleman of similar status to Sir Francis Willoughby, Sir William Fairfax of Gilling Castle, North Yorkshire, whose house-steward's daily, weekly and yearly expenditure on provisions and the bill of fare for dinner and supper on every day of the year for over a decade, from 1571 to 1582, have survived. The fare varied according to the nature of the day and to rank or status. On 'an ordinary flesh day' in 1580 dinner and supper consisted of:

DYNNER	SUPPER
To my Master	
Boyld meates	Mutton in pottage
Beif boyld	Boild meates
Beif roste	Beif slysed
Pige roste	Mutton roste
Venison backe	Chickins roste
Chickins	Venison pastrie
Boardes end	
Boild meates	Boild meates
Beif boild	Beif slysed
Beif roste	Mutton roste
To the Officers	
Boild meates	Boild meates
Beif boiled and roste	Beif slysed
	Mutton roste
Hall	
Beif boild . . .	Boiled meates . . .
	Mutton roste . . .[25]

On fast days the dishes were no fewer in number, but were all fish, though more latitude seems to have been shown in the keeping of fast days when only the young men of the family were at home than when Lady Fairfax was with them. Guests were almost always present, mainly gentry neighbours, but when they were of exalted rank the bill of fare was most extravagant. Household accounts may fill out rather more of the social life of such households. At Wollaton the following are scattered through the accounts for 1573:[26]

The firste of January, in reward to the musyssyons for playing at my Mr.
   his chamber dore   iis.
[12 Jan] in reward to the weates of Nottingham for playing before my
   Mr. and the rest of the justysses   iis.
To my Mr . . . to playe at dyce with   vis.
To Mr Blythe [15 Jan], that he paid to vi m[en] that played before my
   Mr. an enterlede   iiis.iiiid.
[26 Nov] To a vergenall player   iiid.
To my Lord Tawbote his players   xxs.

THE LANDOWNER IN SOCIETY: LEADERSHIP AND LEISURE

Two seventeenth-century diaries, one of a great and the other of a minor landowner, reveal simple, pious lifestyles. Lady Anne Clifford, a northern heiress and wife of the third Earl of Dorset, described her life at Knole in March 1617, when the Earl was in London:

> Upon the 5th Couch puppied in the morning. The 8th I made an end of reading Exodus with Mr Ran. After supper I played at Glecko with the Steward as I often do after dinner and supper.
> Upon the 9th Mr Ran said service in the Chapel but made no sermon. In the afternoon I went abroad in the garden and said my prayers in the Standing. I was not well at night so I ate a posset and went to bed.
> The 11th we perceived the Child had two great teeth come out so that in all she had now 18. I went in the afternoon and said my prayers in the Standing in the garden and spent my time in reading and working as I used to do. The time grew tedious so as I used to go to bed at about 8 o'clock and did lie a-bed till 8 the next morning.[27]

This diary reads like an account drawn up long after the events it describes, but that of Henry Ferrers, the Worcestershire antiquary, seems to be a record written more or less daily. It survives for 1 to 30 November 1622 and 1 February to 24 March 1629 when Ferrers was in his late seventies.

> [17 February 1629, Shrove Tuesday] . . . my folkes rosted the hen that I had of Soly to supper, & brought it in first to me. I did eate twoo or three bittes, because it was the last nyghte of flesh eating, & sent it them agayne into the kitchen for ther supper, being all of which they had that I know of . . . [but earlier in the day] John Gibson played uppon his taber, in the kichen, & he & his wyfe gave my folkes milk & flour to make them fritters & pancakes, & they brought me som, & I did eate a fritter & a pancake well strewed [?] with sugar . . .
> [12 March 1629] I said som prayers after I was in bed, but being oppressed with sleepe I scarce tell how many I said, or whether I made an end of them as I should have don
> [Undated] Two poor folkes begging belowe, I went down to them they were worstershire folkes, one called Mansell and the other Haslewood [?], the later shaking of an ague, ther was nothing in the house to give them nor single money, wherfore I sent the widowe Harrison to the grene with vid. & they went with her, & she gave them iid. & brought a twopeny loafe & two pence agayne.[28]

During the eighteenth century social life in the country house acquired an informality and flexibility that contrasted with the earlier more formal regimes, though relative formality lingered on in the early decades of the century. Thus, when the Irish peeress Lady da Cunha, youngest sister of the second Viscount Kenmare of Kenmare House, Killarney, wrote home from England in 1717, she described her stay at Lord Waldegrave's of Navestock, Essex:

> . . . during the whole time I was there, which was from Monday to Monday, I had not a moment's time: for as soon as breakfast was over a pool of 'bagamon' was begun, I was one of the five that played, which party lasted till dinner. And after dinner I played at penny ombre with the two ladies till supper, which was between nine and ten, and after we went to bed, so you see I had no spare time . . .[29]

(71)

> Tuesday, Aug. 10.th
> We returned to Newby. (I had
> walk'd almost down to the Kitchen
> =Garden.)
> The East-India Company have
> heard over-land, that Peace
> is at length concluded with
> Tippoo Saib.
>
> Wednesday, Aug. 11th Fine Weather — Walk'd to the
> Cascade at night. I wrote to Mrs J. Yorke.
> Friday, I wrote to Mrs Yorke.
> Saturday Aug. 14th
> Din'd at Mr. Weddell's walk'd over his Gallery
> of Antiques & Flower-Garden á second time.
> The Dining-room & the Vestibule are painted
> since last Year. — Mr. Weddell shew'd us
> some pretty Designs of Mrs & Miss Hoare,
> & some Copies of her doing after others.
> Mr. Dundas has actually brought in
> Bill for restoring all the forfeited
> estates in Scotland, & it is going

---

39 Entries from the journal of Lady Amabel Yorke, 1784.

But an older-fashioned regime of earlier meals and elements of Catholic piety marked the day at Ingatestone, Essex, where Lady da Cunha stayed with Lady Petre. She described the daily round in a letter of 26 October 1717:

> . . . Their hours are a little odd to me but in a little time I shall bring myself to 'em. They rise very early, as indeed I do considering what a lazy person I am, for I'm in the tribune a little before nine, which is the hour at which mass is said. After prayers we all eat our breakfasts together and at eleven oclock we separate. At one oclock we go to dinner and sup at seven. As to the supping part I'm not yet come to it, for I generally sup at ten in my

own chamber. All the family retires at nine oclock and are abed by ten . . . In short no convent can be more regular than this house.[30]

Country house owners welcomed visitors, especially those of their own social class, and visiting was made much easier with the improved transport of the eighteenth century. It was thus possible to occupy part of the year in visiting distant relatives, and impressions might be recorded in a journal, as was the case with Lady Amabel Yorke of Wrest Park, Bedfordshire, whose multi-volumed journal is to be found in the Vyner Collection in Leeds. In the eighth volume, she provides brief, almost daily, comments on her visit to Newby Park, North Yorkshire, during July and August 1784. During one week of August she writes:

Sunday August 8th. Young Mr George Pelham came. I took a view after church from the Chinese building. Lord and Lady Grantham visited and Mr & Mrs Wood.

Monday August 9th. Lady Grantham went to Milo Hill. I took a few views, walked about the fountain and in the garden. Walk'd in the park at night.

Tuesday August 10th. We returned to Newby (I had walk'd almost down to the kitchen garden). The East India Company have heard overland that peace is at length concluded with Tippoo Saib.

Wednesday August 11th. Fine weather; walk'd to the Cascade at night. I wrote to Mrs Yorke.

Saturday August 14th. Din'd at Mr Weddell's; walk'd over his gallery of antiques and flower garden a second time. The dining room and the vestibule are painted since last year. Mrs Weddell shew'd us some pretty designs of Mr & Mrs Hoare, and some copies of her doing after others.[31]

When she stayed at Marchmont House, Berwickshire, the home of her father-in-law, Lord Marchmont, she described days spent eating, gossiping, walking and, in the evening, playing games. But these were the relatively uneventful days spent at Marchmont House itself; most of her time was passed in a whirl of visits elsewhere, often involving two-hour drives over mediocre Lowland roads. The highlight was Kelso races, with its three days of public breakfasts, races at noon and public dinners and balls at night.[32]

Bills and receipts can offer glimpses into the life of the country house. Those from fashionable shops are usually headed in ornate copperplate alongside pictorial symbols, like the receipt for lavender water and almond powder bought by Lady Irwin in 1765 from James Smyth and Nephew of New Bond Street that can be found in the Temple Newsam papers, worlds apart from the scrap of paper that acknowledges the receipt by John Williams of 10s 6d from Lady Strafford for killing bugs at Wentworth Castle in 1741.[33] The Strafford family papers also provide an entertaining insight into the everyday life of a nobleman's house when the master was away and the only visitor a young relative who whiled away his time writing a letter to his brother in the form of a 'dull rhyme'.

At Morn to my good Lady I go down,
Who at Eleven has huddled on her Gown;
We sit an Hour sometimes over Coffee,

40 Confectioner's bill to Charles, son of eighth Lord Irwin, 1760.

> And sometimes trifle with our spoon ore Tea,
> Here's alone our Trifling Variety.
> Then in comes Charles and takes away the things,
> My Lady's Toilet, & Work Beckey brings;
> And Lady Anne does some work or other,
> But Clarendon alone reads your Brother.

And on goes the day (and the doggerel), with chatting, an informal dinner at two o'clock, more reading by the writer, with cards from dusk until a light, informal meal leads on to bed. He concludes:

> By this long scrawl you may easily see,
> How the dull hours pass heavily with me;
> Or I should never thus have past my time,
> In troubling my self, & you with dull Rhime;
> But as it is take it as I intend,
> From your Loving Brother & your Friend.[34]

The writer was not alone in finding life in the country tedious. In contrast, the attractions of town life were considerable, so that the wealthier landowners divided their year between a London season of some four months, a month or so in Bath and another in travel, with the rest of the year at home. The provinces had their own alternatives to London and Bath, like Buxton or York, where Anne Lister of Shibden Hall, Halifax, attended a ball at the Assembly Rooms that owed their design to Lord Burlington. In her journal she recorded:

> *Wednesday 1 March* [1820]
> A little before 7, walked to the Belcombes' to dress & go from thence to the Officers' Ball at the Assembly Rooms. . . The most elegant supper I ever saw. All managed by Mr & Mrs Barber of the Black Swan, who had a confectioner down from London. The tables in the little Assembly room beautifully ornamented. At one end of the little middle table, fronting the sideboard, a large & beautifully done boar's head of brawn. At the other end a large swan swimming on jelly &, in the middle, a beautiful windmill near a yard high. . . According to the list of the company taken by one of the sergeants, there were present 340 people . . . The entrance to the room was through a tent lined with soldiers. The Egyptian Hall looked finely imposing & the whole thing was uncommonly well-managed & went off most uncommonly well. Only 2 or 3 country dances, all the rest quadrilles . . . I came away at 5 . . .

Anne Lister's journal is unusual in that sections of it are in cipher, for, as she hinted in a quotation from Rousseau on 20 August 1823 ('Je sens mon coeur et je connais les hommes. Je ne suis fait comme aucun de ceux j'ais vus; je croix n'etre fait comme aucun de ceux qui existent' – I know my own heart and understand my fellow man. But I am made unlike anyone I have ever met. I dare to say that I am like no one in the whole world), she was in fact lesbian. Her nickname among the people of Halifax was 'Gentleman Jack'. In the ciphered sections, she thus goes beyond the social to the deeply personal, as when she described how she and her lover, 'M', made love when in Scarborough on 14 September 1823:

> Perhaps about 12½, every door & window in the house seemed to rattle, which disturbed us exceedingly . . . Very vivid, fast-succeeding flashes of lightning enlightened the whole room . . . In the midst of all this, we drew close together, made love & had one of the most delightfully long, tender kisses we have ever had. Said she, in the midst of it, 'Oh, don't leave me yet.' This renewed & redoubled my feelings & we slept in each other's arms.

She also offers fascinating comment on her need to keep social inferiors at a distance, as when she was out walking with her father on 22 June 1820:

> . . . near Whitley's, met Mr Jenkinson of the White Lion. To my dismay, my father shook hands with him. Near his ironworks, met Job Brook who, still more to my surprise, accosted my father very familiarly & then clapped him on the back. Shocking! I thought to myself, & will mind how I walk with you again to Halifax . . . Told my uncle & aunt of my father's shaking hands, etc, & how I was shocked. They evidently wondered & were shocked, too.[35]

The distinctive social gathering of the late eighteenth and nineteenth centuries was the house party, which often coincided with some local event like a race meeting or a coming-of-age. While guests were left very much to do as they liked in the early part of the day, particular activities might mark the evening. The great hall of the Victorian house could accommodate a variety of them from charades to billiards, while families with a penchant for more serious theatricals might put on a play. Some houses were even equipped with a theatre. At Burton Constable plays were regularly produced in the early Victorian period. Surviving playbills show members of the family playing leading roles, as in one for the *School for Scandal*, which was performed on 3 April 1850. An annual steeplechase open to all England also accompanied the house party.

A social gathering may even be recorded on a census return, as at Burton Constable in 1851, when the family were accompanied by several visitors:[36]

Thomas A C Constable	Head	m	44 Baronet	Stafford, Tixall
Mary Ann "	Wife	m	46	Devon, Colversleigh
Frederick AJC "	Son	u	22 Gent	Sussex, Brighton
Mary B Chichester	Sister	wid	49 Lady	Stafford, Tixall
Henry A "	Nephew		4	Canada, Toronto
Eliza "	visiter	u	48	Devon, Culversleigh
George "	"	u	50 Major	" "
Percival Ratcliff	"	"	26 Gent	York, Campsall Park
Swinburne F Berkley	"	"	25 Gent	Middlesex, Crawford
Edward F "	"	u	23 "	" "
Charles Middleton	"	"	30 "	York, Storkhill
Stephen O Jay	"	u	28 "	Middlesex
William F Webb	"	u	25 "	Berkshire
Elizabeth Coretil	"	wid	43 Ladys maid	Warwick

Sporting activities

Assemblies or house parties were one side of entertaining, field sports the other, providing a variety of major activities for the landed classes. For some, hunting was an obsession. A famous nineteenth-century Irish master of fox hounds, Robert Watson of Ballydarton, Co. Carlow, thought that he would be reincarnated as a fox; on his death he was buried in a fox's earth and the mourners cried 'Gone away!' As a small boy, Talbot Clifford-Constable shared the family enthusiasm for it in his dutiful letter of 6 January 1837 to his 'dear papa':

> You see I promised to write to you after mamma. My pony is quite well and so are your horses; your hounds have never missed a day without exercise. I hope you will come home very soon to go a hunting . . .[37]

However, other attitudes towards the sport found expression within the landed classes. Those of William Gossip of Thorp Arch were contradictory: he could object to the damage done to his estate by a fox hunt yet enjoy the excitement of seeing a fox hunted by greyhounds. He wrote to his son George on 23 January 1756:

My dear papa,

You see I promised to write to you after mamma. My pony is quite well, and so are your horses; your hounds have never missed a day without exercise. I hope you will come home very soon, to go a hunting. Please tell mamma that I feed the Macaw every day. Give my love to mamma and to aunt Eliza, also to Dowdall, and to Rossiter. —

My dear papa.

I remain

your affectionate son,

Talbot Clifford Constable.

Burton-Constable.

Jan'y a 6th 1837.

41 Letter to his father from Talbot Clifford-Constable, 1837.

. . . There has been a grand fox hunt at Wetherby this week with Mr Jolliffs hounds. They tell me there were 25 or 26 Gentlemen in Scarlet, the livery of that Hunt. But I did not see them. They came not nearer me than Whinney flats which I was not sorry for; I have too much of such company in the Grounds: sometimes 3 different packs of Foxhounds in one week. Viz Mr Lanes, Mr Bowes & Mr Jollifs. The first were here about a fortnight ago; and the servants made sad havock in walks in the wood: which I can't help thinking very hard: but complaint signifie[s] little in such cases. These Gentlemen of the turf generally make a jest of them. On Saturday last Mr Best came over with his Greyhounds to entertain yr Brothers, we ranged the whole morning & could not find one hare: but Pierrott disturbed a brace of foxes solacing themselves in the field toward Walton. The Dogs divided; Prince sticking wisely to the majority made a shift to pull down the Dog Fox. He made a fine defence & gave me more Diversion than I believe he did Mr Best (who was in a violent hurry to save him). I dare say he would be heartily roasted about it at Wetherby . . .[38]

Foxes were vermin, so that no legal barrier ever stood in the way of participation in the hunt, even if dominance by the gentry and, later, the nobility was natural. But from the later fourteenth century the right to kill game was restricted by law, making shooting a minority sport. Socially exclusive, it became a badge of membership of the landed classes. Increasingly severe game laws protected the social monopoly. A printed notice from Sledmere House dated 20 August 1812 might have been found on many other estates as well:

Whereas the game on the manor has of late years been very much destroyed by Poachers, unqualified persons, and others, notice is hereby given, that all persons found Trespassing in future will be prosecuted with the utmost Rigor of the Law.[39]

It was not until the Ground Game Act of 1881 that tenants were able to destroy hares or rabbits on their own land without their landlord's permission.

Gamebooks can record staggering kills, like the totals for 1869 in the Studley Royal book: 920 hares, 1106 partridges, 2903 pheasants, 11 woodcocks, 26 wild fowl and 1229 rabbits.[40] As sources for sporting activities in general, journals and diaries, accounts, paintings and the press may be added to those already cited for field sports. Thus, the household accounts of the Dukes of Rutland contain expenses for horse racing and hunting in the early seventeenth century, like:

[22 March 1603] Paid to Mr Charles Hargill for his Lordshipp ridinge charges layde forthe by hym at the horse race at Lincolne, xxxixli iiis ixd

Delivered, the 10th of April, 1618, to my Lord . . . on huntinge the foxe, 5s; and which I sent his Lordshipp more at nighte per Mr Cole, 15s-xxs.[41]

Paintings of the chase or the races and of favourite horses or dogs take second place only to those of the family in sporting households and have their place elsewhere.

A liking for the cruel popular sports that were made illegal in the nineteenth century was shared by many members of the aristocracy. The Memorandum Book of the Yorkshire squire Sir Walter Calverley records his participation in and betting on cockfighting:

STUDLEY ROYAL.

GAME KILLED.

1869	BY WHOM	Hares	Partridges	Pheasants	Woodcocks	Wild Fowl	Rabbits	TOTAL	REMARKS
Dec 8th	Brought up —	516	1078	1195	4	10	746	3545	✓
	Mr R. & Mr Came & Mrs Parkes &c								
	Lord Grosvenor Lord Grosvenor Mrs &c								
	Lady Grosvenor Mr R. Aynor &c								
9th	Revd. Melville Lady Grosvenor &c	227	10	538	6	5	220	1006	Jas Gill Y-
10	Earl de Grey Lord Grderich Lord								
	Lonsdale Lord Cardley Mr &c								
	Grey Mr Aynor Mr Jurvallé Mr—								
11th 30th	Kumour Mr Mark Mr Phister	175	8	1170	1	11	263	1627	The Keeper &c Y-
Nov.	Keeper		7					7	
31st	Keeper	2	0					8	
	Total of the Season 1869 — 920 x 1108 x 2903½ x 11						26 x 229 x 6190		

Sir Walter Hawkesworth & I made a match for cockings with my Lord Irwyn & Mr Ramsden; were to show one & thirty cocks a side, out of which we had 18 matches, & fought at Leeds, at Mr Nottingham's, on 11 & 12 June, 1700, for one guineay a side a cock, & 10 guineays the main, out of which my Lord Irwyn & partner got 6 battles, & we got 12. I won some money besides the wagers.[42]

Two of these sports enjoyed a considerable, if very different, social significance. The shooting of game was always divisive because it was so clearly exclusive. It displayed aristocratic dominance and privilege at a price, whereas hunting at least involved landowners in the wider local community. Tenants could never doubt that landowners controlled the sport and might be angered when their fields were hunted over, but they could always participate by following the pack on horse or foot. In the eighteenth and early nineteenth centuries cricket possessed a similar significance. What had begun as a folk game had by then been brought under aristocratic patronage, but served to bring the landowner into contact with a broad cross-section of the community. Both hunting and cricket served to unify the locality under landowning leadership.

But, in that this work deals with sources for the historian, it may be well to end this chapter on a different note. Quite by chance, a quarter of the sources quoted in it were written by women. Denied the leading role in the history of the country house by both convention and the English insistence on primogeniture, their role has yet to receive adequate attention from the historian. Individuals like Bess of Hardwick and Lady Anne Clifford have attracted interest, but as a whole they have yet to find their historian. Studies focused on them would probably alter perspectives on the history of the country house.

---

42 Entries in Studley Royal gamebook, 1869.

Chapter Six

DOWNSTAIRS:
SERVANTS IN HOUSE AND ESTATE

The briefest examination of the documentation for below-stairs life in the country house makes plain its central problem: the sources are almost entirely an above-stairs product. The records of the landowner are the source of nearly all that is known of his servants; little is known of their life outside the homes of their masters or before and after they were in service. With much of the evidence that remains it is therefore wise to take a large dose of the historian's traditional scepticism.

Recruitment

When landowners required servants they looked initially to the locality. Suitable young men and women, boys and girls could be drawn from the families of existing servants and from those of neighbouring farmers, craftsmen or labourers. Contacts and word of mouth were the means of communication. But, as the middle classes increasingly saw the employment of servants as vital to their social prestige, servant numbers reached a high level: in the nineteenth century domestic service was the second largest occupation and, for women and girls, the first. More formal methods of recruitment like newspaper advertising therefore developed, while the written reference supplemented oral recommendation. Such changes were also made necessary by transport developments, firstly in the improvement of roads and coaches in the eighteenth century and then by the introduction of the railway in the nineteenth: servants could travel easily to distant posts and masters could therefore look to a wider field. Where references survive, they offer a fascinating source to the historian, even if they suffer from all the limitations of the genre, for few referees could be as honest (or as vivid) as Charles Berkeley, a son of the fourth Lord Berkeley:

> Catherine York is the best cook I have had in twenty years or more that I have kept house. She may have lived here about ten months. I believe her honest, not extravagant in the kitchen; she is very clean. Her temper is like charcoal, which kindles soon, and sparks to the top of the house. She is passionate and ungovernably wilful in her way. We had many quarrels and bore many faults for the sake of the table. The final quarrel was, my wife, according to custom, sent her maid to see the other maids' candles out. Catherine York bolted her door, and denied her entrance. I do not charge her with drinking but with being as impetuous as if she did drink. I was afraid we might be burnt in our beds.[1]

DOWNSTAIRS: SERVANTS IN HOUSE AND ESTATE

When the agent of Lord Strafford of Wentworth Castle was seeking a footman for his master, he wrote to John Jordan at Harborough. The reply, dated 9 August 1734, offers, incidentally, a good deal of information about servant life at the time:

> . . . I shall be very glad to serve his Lordship: as to my grandfathers cosent there is no ocation for it. I am only a hired servant from year to year and as to my Carrectter if his Lordship pleases to enquire after when he comes this way as to drinking whoreing or anny such thing though I should not speak of it myself Thank God I am very free from it and I never was guilty of it in my life: I would willingly stay in my place Till after our fair wich is the 8th of october for the proffit of the fair is as much as a quarter of a years vails: and my grandfather cannot provide himself with a servant till then it being that time oth year that people proviod themselfs with servants. I will learn to shave as soon as I can: as to the guinea you speak of it is a commen custum and [if] my Lord alows of it I shall not be against it . . .[2]

Certain foreign servants were valued for the prestige they brought to a household, most notably the French chef and lady's maid. Some French chefs fled the Revolution to find posts with the English aristocracy, and the French chef and the Italian confectioner were the key figures in the creation of a fashionable dinner in the Victorian and Edwardian eras. The French lady's maid was valued for her knowledge of fashion and coiffure. Black servants were not unusual in the eighteenth century. Most were initially slaves, though they resisted slave status and had largely won their freedom even before the Mansfield judgement of 1772. They were frequently indulged and petted, treated as finely-dressed adornments to a household, arousing both affection and jealousy among their fellow servants. Some were talented, like the two musicians sent from North America by John Wentworth, Governor of New Hampshire, to join the household of his friends, the Rockinghams. He wrote to Lady Rockingham on 1 December 1776:

> By the Tamar Sloop of War, I have this day embarked Two Negro men slaves (named Romulus & Remus) who are good Proficients on the French-Horn, and Remus a remarkable good taste to Music, as his Masters have told me; In hopes that they might be some Amusement in the Country, I have taken the liberty to ask your Ladyship's condescension to honor me with their acceptance. They have been with me from their childhood and are faithful, honest and free from vice . . .[3]

Duties and rules

The general duties of servants in the eighteenth and nineteenth centuries are known from the household manuals that were then published. Mrs Beeton's is, of course, the most widely known. In practice, specific posts reflected the size and condition of particular households. Thus, a handwritten note on 'Hiring Servants & their Particular Business' in the mid-eighteenth-century letters of the Purefoy household at Shalstone, Buckinghamshire, lists the duties of the household's servants, giving those of the cook-maid as:

By the Tamar Sloop of War, I have this day embarked Two Negro men slaves (named Romulus & Remus) who are good Proficients on the French-Horn, and Remus a remarkable good taste to Music, as his Masters have told me; In hopes that they might be some Amusement in the Country, I have taken the liberty to ask your Lady=ships' condescension to honor me with their acceptance. They have been with me from their childhood and are faithful, honest and free from vice.

Permit me again & ever to repeat my highest thankfulness to your Ladyship & Lord Rockingham, and my anxious wishes for your ladyships recovery & perfect Health and my Lords', and that My most dutiful Respects may be accepted, from

Your Ladyships'

most obliged and truely devoted, ever dutiful humble Servant;

J. Wentworth.

43 Governor Wentworth of New Hampshire sends two talented black slaves to England, 1776.

Cowick-hall near Doncaster 8ber 30.

Sir,

I am very sorry to trouble you with this letter, but as you & your Lady are yt. only persons that can give me satisfactory information upon the subject of my enquiry, I hope you will excuse this application. a person has offer'd herself to Lady Downe for a housekeeper, who lately lived with you in that capacity; her name I don't recollect, her age is about five & thirty. we are unwilling to take a servant without a very good character from yt. last family, in which she lived, & Lady Downe would therefore take it as a very great favor, if Mrs. Sykes would be so good as to send her opinion of this woman; with regard to her temper honesty & sobriety; & also her skill in yt. direction and management of a Dairy; which knowledge is more essential, than any qualification of a profess'd housekeeper; likewise curing Hams would be a valuable accomplishment. Lady Downe joins with me in presenting her comp's & excuses to Mrs. Sykes, & I am Sir with yt. greatest respect your most obedt. servt.

Downe

an answer is desired by
the return of yt. post

44 An enquiry about a potential housekeeper, 1763.

To roast & boil butcher's meat & all manner of fowls
To clean all the rooms below stairs
To make the servants beds & to clean all the garrets
To clean the great and little stairs
To scour the pewter and brass
Or to do anything she is ordered
If she has never had the smallpox to sign a paper to leave the service if she has them.

An undertaking for the latter is preserved in the family papers.[4]

The combination of the duties of cook and maid was not unusual in small or medium-sized houses, while a gardener or groom might be required to wait at table at a particular meal or on specific occasions. William Gossip of Thorp Arch sought help in obtaining such a gardener who could, on occasion, wait at table; on 1 March 1755, he wrote to George Mitchell, a Scot who had formerly worked for him:

> I have been obliged at last to part with my old Gardiner, so am in present want. If you know of one that will be proper for me I shall be obliged to you if you will recommend him. You know I must have one that understands forest work as well as kitchin garden & pruning wall trees & be sober and tractable & to wait at table on Sundays & when I have company . . .[5]

But only a landowner as hard-headed as Sir Walter Calverley of Esholt could have driven through the contract that he recorded in his Memorandum Book on 28 August 1704:

> Agreed with Joseph Mawde to serve me one year from this day, for which he is to have £5, and 20s. to buy him a frock with for brewing, & a livery, vizt, coat, waistcoat, breeches, hat & stockings: & his imployment is to be, to look to all the stables, horses, & mares, both in the house & pastures, & to keep the fold clean, & also the pheasant garden & little garden within the pales in the fold, & to see the trees to be therein nailed any time on occasion, & also to keep the court before the hall door clean, & grass places in good order, & also to brew the master all his drink, to keep the jack in order, to take care of the calash & drive it, to keep the boat carefully locked, cleaned, and dressed, to wait at the table when occasion, &, if he does not his best, but neglects these things, to have no wages.[6]

Many country houses added general orders or rules to the duties of each particular servant. The nineteenth-century versions may still be observed, inscribed on varnished boards in the servants' quarters. Copies of the orders of Sir Charles Domvile for his estate workers at Sawtry, Dublin, in the second half of the nineteenth century, can be found in longhand in a notebook in the Irish National Library:

1st. Whoever is not at the Steward's house when the bell rings to pay 2d fine.
2nd. Whoever does not bring home his tools at night to pay 6d fine.
3rd. Whoever cleans up Gravel or Bed without a Wheelbarrow to pay 6d. fine.
4th. Any Cottager who does not clean the space appointed to pay 1s. fine.
5th. For not wearing the full Labourer's Dress to pay 1s. fine.
6th. All Labourers are to consider themselves as Police on the Demesne.

7th. Any one using a Horse is to be very careful, and on no account to be rough with it.

The humane solicitude for the horses is striking coming from a landowner who expected his staff to be not merely dutiful and obedient, but also totally at his disposal, as is stated unequivocally in the conclusion to a printed booklet of rules for his estate labourers from 1864:

His whole time being mine, he is not to leave home without permission, as each man is liable to be called in at night, in case of fire, etc.[7]

These rules were harsh by contrast with others, strict though the norm was, possibly because of the military background of Sir Charles Domvile.

The servant hierarchy

During the period covered in this book the nature of the staff of a country house changed considerably. A list of servants in a sixteenth-century house is quite different from one of the nineteenth century. Such lists are commonly found in accounts or wages books; one in the account books kept at Belvoir for the Duke of Rutland gives an idea of the staff of a great house in the year with which this study opens, 1540. The list may be tedious, for it shows wages being paid to a staff of considerable size, but it is informative and therefore worth struggling through.

It begins with the senior staff: the controller, two gentlewomen waiters, two chaplains, physicians, apothecaries, surgeons, secretaries, five gentlemen waiters and the clerk of the kitchen. Also working within the house were three school masters, two nurses, two yeomen ushers, two yeomen waiters, two grooms of the chamber, the barber, the usher, the almoner, three yeomen of the wardrobe, two minstrels and the porter, while in or linked to the kitchen were the caterer, the cellarer, two pantry servants, two buttery servants, two bakers, two brewers, the yeoman cook, four grooms of the kitchen, the larderman and the sculleryman. Stable, estate and other workers external to the house were three stablemen, the pursuivant, the gardener, two hunters, the keeper of the haybarns, slaughtermen, the smith, four women launderers, the miller, two masons, two joiners, two glaziers, the slater, the carpenter, the keeper of the warren, the poundcaster and keeper of the pounds, the master scourer and the waterbridge man. Gentlemen ushers were included in the list but no payments to them recorded, presumably because none was employed when the list was drawn up.[8]

Such neo-medieval households were vast. When it was on the move from seat to seat, it proclaimed in conspicuous display its master's status. For reasons of economy, households tended to decrease in size from the early seventeenth century. In the eighteenth and nineteenth centuries a large house would normally be staffed by no more than 25 to 50 household servants, with as few as ten in a small one. A house that was famous for its entertaining, like Petworth with a staff of 135 in 1834, was exceptional. Outside staff like gardeners, keepers and estate workers grew in number in the nineteenth century but, otherwise, numbers remained much the same until the 1880s and beyond.

DOWNSTAIRS: SERVANTS IN HOUSE AND ESTATE

Long before that time the dominance of men that is apparent at Belvoir had ended. Until the late seventeenth and early eighteenth centuries men occupied all but a small number of posts particularly appropriate to women, like the personal servants of the lady of the house, but from that time women were taken on as part of a general attempt to reduce running costs, for they were cheaper to employ than men. Eventually, the housekeeper, as the senior woman, was usually junior in status (and, of course, pay) only to the senior man, the steward, and within the house women were often in the majority.

Further, the servants were homogeneous neither socially nor economically. Upper servants, occupying administrative and supervisory posts, were of very different background and status to those whose work was largely manual and unskilled. Seven waiters at Belvoir were gentlemen or gentlewomen, distinguished as such from those categorized as yeomen, for service by members of lesser landed houses was seen as providing both a practical education and a way to preferment for a man and to a suitable marriage for a woman. Thus, Bess of Hardwick, the daughter of a minor Derbyshire landowner, began her adult life as an upper servant of Sir John and Lady Zouche of Codnor Castle, Derbyshire, and may have met her first husband when he was serving in the same household. Such servants saw themselves as having more in common with their masters than with those, like the sculleryman, who were at the other end of the servant hierarchy. So did their masters, as is apparent in household orders like those issued at Hatfield in 1635 'touching expenses at £800 to be lessened':

> 1. That for my Lord's honour and service his Lordship's own table be furnished with more rather than with less plenty and variety than heretofore, and that according to the use in [my] Lord's father's time; as they shall find cause one or two dishes of the first course and one dish of the second course may be removed after it is taken off my Lord's unto the Steward's table, so much as shall sufficiently furnish it . . .
>
> 3. That the Clerk be sure to provide store of ordinary and cheapest provisions for the inferior servants in the Hall, in case company increaseth, and those provisions to be served at the lower end; and the provisions from my Lord's table at the upper . . .[9]

Such distinctions were still present in the nineteenth century, when, from 1841 to 1891 the most accessible lists of servants are provided by the decennial census enumerators' returns. They also provide, from 1851, a clear indication of the birthplace of each servant, thereby suggesting something of the wider geographical field for servant recruitment brought about by the railways. The 1851 returns recorded the following servants at Burton Constable:[10]

Female Servants

Elizabeth Styche	Servant	Wid	53	Housekeeper	Durham, Gilesgate
Antoine Reny	"	u	40	Ladys Maid	France, Paris
Martha Walton	"	u	35	Housemaid	York, West Newton
Elizabeth Rossiter	"	u	40	Ladysmaid	Devon, Princeton
Ann Liddle	"	u	25	Housemaid	Lincoln, Barton
Margaret Cowell	"	u	25	Housemaid	Lancs, L. Crosby
Elizabeth Harker	"	u	20	Housemaid	York, Ellerby

Martha Hoe	"	u	62	Asst. Hs. Md.	York, Welton
Lydia Little	"	u	33	Laundry Md.	Notts, Chilwell
Ann Earsden	"	m	22	Laundry Md.	North'nd, Felton
Phoebe Crow	"	u	32	Stillroom Md.	Norfolk, Syston
Elizabeth Jackson	"	wid	49	Dairymaid	York, Ottringham
Elizabeth Higham	"	m	50	Nurse	York, Ottringham
Ellen Hay	"	u	37	Kitchenmaid	York, Welwick
Elizabeth Mead	"	u	23	Kitchenmaid	Middlesex
Elizabeth Purden	"	u	22	Kitchenmaid	Yorks, Sancton
Emma Jackson	Visiter	u	23	Ladysmaid	Devon, Washfield

Male Servants

Peter Purden	Servant	u	32	Footman	Yorks, Ellerby
James Watson	"	u	22	Valet	Yorks, Broughton
Edwin Tomlinson	"	u	20	Footman	Stafford, Tixal
Thomas Tomlinson	Visiter	m	57	Gamekeeper	Stafford, Sanden
William Hodgson	Servant	u	19	Extra Valet	York, West Newton
Charles Bridault	"	u	34	Cook	France
Charles Fairbank	"	u	33	Usher	York, Flinton
James Derbyshire	"	u	17	Footman	Lancs, L. Crosby
William Towe	"	u	15	Footman	York, Ellerby
Robert Swails	"	u	22	Groom	York, Austwick
John Laycock	"	u	21	Groom	Northants, Brix'th
Michael Hudson	"	u	27	Postillion	Yorks, W. Newton
John Harrison	"	m	53	Horsebreaker	Yorks, Ottringham
Frederick Lenard	"	m	49	Helper	Stafford
William Lashcock	"	u	35	Helper	Newcastle
Arthur Drake	"	u	26	Helper	Bucks, Ab'don
Edward Harrison	"	u	19	Helper	York, Ryhill
John Marshall	"	u	19	Helper	Lincoln, Lg. Sutton
William Blashill	"	u	10	Helper	York, Ellerby
Lewis Forfitt	"	u	15	Kennelman	Dorset
George Joanes	Visiter	u	23	Groom	Bucks, Marlow
John Brigham	"	u	27	Groom	York, Water

Taken together, the lists of servants from Belvoir and Burton Constable indicate the elements of both stability and change in the staffing of a country house discussed above. They remain valid, in spite of the obvious differences in size and status between a ducal household and the home of a wealthy baronet (and the omission of most estate workers from the census at Burton Constable). At Burton Constable the increased employment of women is apparent, particularly in the more menial tasks within the house. Distinct in status from those who performed such tasks are the handful of upper servants like housekeeper and lady's maid, though by the end of the seventeenth century it was rare for them to be drawn from the gentry. Men and women of education and ability were always needed to serve in the country house, but from that time they were more likely to be the offspring of small farmers or clergymen than of gentlemen. But while the social span from which servants were recruited had narrowed, they still formed a hierarchy. In large households the upper servants ate apart, waited on by their subordinates, while in smaller households they would sit at the head of the table, sometimes enforcing on the lesser fry the same rule of silence unless spoken to that was taken for granted by those who waited at the master's table.

Success as a servant rested as much on a nice understanding of social distinctions as on work well done, and the distinctions within the servant ranks were probably as important as those between masters and servants. At times they produced friction, as may be seen in a relatively unusual source, a petition. Seventeen servants at Welbeck Abbey petitioned the Duke of Portland on 12 December 1769 as follows:

> We Your Graces Servants whose names are here inclos'd, beg leave to petition for Ale; not for ourselves particular, but for the Servants of Your Grace's friends, which we have been frequently refus'd by Mr Martin, Your Grace's Butler, without giving any reason for the same, but saying I am Master and you shall have none . . .[11]

The Duke himself could not have been more peremptory.

Conditions and welfare

To a significant extent, a servant's lot depended on the nature of his or her master or mistress and, for the lower servants, that of the upper servants under whom they served. On the positive side, in the patriarchal tradition some landowners exercised considerable care on the welfare of their staff. The household accounts of the Russells at Woburn in the seventeenth century show numerous payments for medical attention to them, like:

> *December 26 1670* . . . the sum of forty shillings for the cure of Frank, the footman, of a gunshot wound in his toe . . .
> *October 1676.* Item the curing of a boy that belongs to the stables thrust through the hand with a fork, my lord's pleasure.

For the helper.	Imprimis letting blood	1s.0d.
	Item a purging aporem	2s.6d.
	Item for other necessaries and dressings, my lord's pleasure.	
November 21 1678	Item Richard Berry plasters for the bite of a horse.[12]	

Upper servants frequently received pensions, and long-serving servants were certainly given consideration by their masters, who might provide for them in their wills, like the fourth Earl of Chesterfield, whose will included the following:

> I give to all my menial or household servants that shall have lived with me five years or upwards at the time of my death, whom I consider as unfortunate friends, my equals in Nature, and my inferiors only by the difference of our positions, two years wages above

DOWNSTAIRS: SERVANTS IN HOUSE AND ESTATE

what is due to them at my death, and mourning; and to all my other menial servants one year's wages and mourning.[13]

These terms were generous to all his servants, long-serving or otherwise, but the sentiments of the will were more remarkable. Perhaps only a witty cynic like Chesterfield could break out of the assumptions of his age and social group to see servants as equals, even if only 'in Nature'. Assumptions that the structure of existing society was ordained widened and strengthened a gap that wealth, living standards, taste and culture had certainly established by the early eighteenth century, ensuring the distancing of servants from their masters that had begun with the development of the backstairs in the seventeenth century. Their function in enabling servants to go about their duties without infringing on their master's privacy is neatly indicated by a brief notice that can still be seen on a wall of Burton Constable:

All Servants are Requested not to Cross the Stair-Case Hall. But to pass up this Staircase [i.e., the backstairs, indicated by a pointing hand]. N.B. Except those who have to go to the NORTH WING

The invention of the bell-rope enabled the separation to be expressed still more clearly in the planning of a house. The servants' wing could be located away from the main block, while a green baize door frequently divided family and servants symbolically. Rules about not being seen and not speaking unless first spoken to reinforced the gap.

House plans may reveal both the working areas and sleeping quarters of the servants, though the architect's intention may not have been wholly reflected in practice. Practice, however, is apparent in inventories and, to some extent, in sale catalogues, so that these sources can also be used to throw some light on living and working conditions. As might be expected, the nature of sleeping accommodation reflected the status of its occupants. In an inventory of Temple Newsam,[14] drawn up in 1734, the housekeeper's room is better furnished than the cook's, and the cook's than the adjacent kitchen man's. The housekeeper's room and the one adjoining contained:

1 Feather Bed, 1 Bolster, 2 Pillows, 3 Blankets, 1 Quilt, 1 Little Table Bed, 1 Bolster, 1 Pillow, 3 Blankets, 1 Quilt, 1 Large Press, 2 Lesser Presses, 2 Chests, 1 Pair of Drawers, 2 Trunks, 1 Box, 7 Cain Chairs, 2 Bass bottom'd Chairs, At the Door, A Table, A Range.

The cook's room held only '1 Feather Bed, A Bolster, 2 Pillows & Blankets etc, 4 Cane Chairs, 1 Plain Chair, 1 Table & dressing Glass', while the kitchen man had to make do with '1 Feather Bed, 1 Bolster, 3 Blankets & 1 Rug, 1 Small Dressing Glass'. Stable staff usually slept over the stables, with furnishings that were even more basic, as in the provision for the coachman at Wentworth Castle shown in an inventory of 1748.[15] His room over the stables contained only 'Three blue & White Check'd Beds, two feather Beds two Bolsters, three Blankets & one Double D[itt]o, two Ruggs, one flock Bed & Bolster, 2 very old Blankets, 2 very old Ruggs'.

Each of these houses was to receive a major internal facelift only a few years after the inventories were made, Wentworth Castle by the addition of another wing and

THE MANSION, GRIMSTON PARK.

PLAN OF GROUND FLOOR

Scale of Feet

Temple Newsam by significant internal alterations. More fashionable interiors resulted, and what is striking about the inventories is that when they were drawn up only the bedrooms of the master and mistress and the Yellow Damask Bed Chamber that was the bedroom of a 'state' suite at Wentworth Castle were furnished with much greater sophistication than those of the upper servants. From the inventory alone it is not easy to distinguish between rooms intended for their use and those intended for sons and daughters, relatives or (with the one exception at Wentworth Castle) guests; even though, in the grandest houses, like Hatfield, several splendid guest rooms reflected the status of the important visitors who used them. Further, all the servant bedrooms itemized in the inventories contained at least one feather bed. Thus, servant sleeping accommodation in houses like these was not necessarily as spartan as it might on first sight appear, and was no doubt as good, if not better, than that of the homes from which the servants came.

Upper servants, like the steward and the housekeeper, were provided with their own offices as well as bedrooms. Far from opulent, often furnished with cast-off household tables, chairs and cupboards, they nevertheless reflected the standing of these officials. But the bleakness of the usual servants' hall, the gathering place for the lower servants or, in small houses, the whole staff, indicates the low status of its occupants. At Temple Newsam there were two halls in 1734, old and new. 'The Old Servants' Hall & Passage' contained 'A Large Round Table, 1 Long Settle, 3 Hair Cloths, belonging the Parlours, A Long white Table, A Squab', while the new hall held '3 Long Tables, 3 Forms, 1 Cupboard, A Range etc'. It is worth noting that almost every room in the house contained a fireplace, making its absence in the old hall striking, but the possibility of warmth from the fire was about the only merit of the servants' hall at Wentworth Castle in 1748, for which the inventory simply lists 'Two Long Tables, 3 Old Benches, Iron Grate and pooker'.

Remuneration

Information about wages is not usually difficult to find, for most country house archives contain wages books or other notebooks in which wage payments are recorded. Sometimes they give little more than lists of names and payments, like the Burton Constable Wages Book for 1840 to 1847. The following payments are noted for 21 January 1840 by Mr Ceroti, the major-domo:[16]

	Received from Mr Ceroti		for half year wages
Peter Purdon	"	£9	"
A. Eney	"	£10	"
Mary Booker	"	£3.4.2	"
John Styche	"	£10.10	"
Martha Walton	"	£6	"

45 Ground-floor plan of Grimston Park, 1872, showing the servants' wing.

Mary Dobson	"	£8.8.0.	"
John Sherwin	"	£18.7.6.	"
Thomas Young	"	£10.8.4.	"
Charles Whitehead	"	£3	"
Mary Marcroft	"	£16	"
Elizabeth Styche	"	£12.10.0	"
Edward Lowing	"	£9.9.0	"
Henry Styche	"	£34.2.6	"
William Butler	"	£2.18.2	"
William Wilson	"	£5.11.3	"
Thomas Bilton	"	£26.5.0	"
Myself	"	£20	"

Somewhat more useful are lists that indicate the role of each servant, like the note kept in his diary for 1752 by Richard Sykes of Sledmere,[17] in which he lists what appear to be annual wages:

MATTHEW GOTHORPE, my coachman, wages £10.10 due March 10th

EDWARD GUTHRIE, my gardiner at Sledmere, wages £12.12. He to wash himself, due January 4th

MATTHEW WEATHERILL, my butler, wages £6.6 due August 19th

MARY BROCKLESBY, my housekeeper at Sledmere, wages £6.6 due May Day

ELIZABETH MITCHELL, my housekeeper at Hull, wages £6 due Ladyday

THOMAS PORTER, my groom, wages £5.5 due Ladyday

ROBERT SMITH, my postilion, wages £3.3 due August 31st

MARY MITCHELL, chamber maid, wages £3.3 due May Day

ANN WALLIS, my cook maid at Sledmere, wages £3.3 due March 1st

MARY JEAVES, my cook maid at Hull, wages £3.3 due Michaelmas

ROBERT COLLINGS, wages £2.12.6 due September 4th.

Finding such material may not be difficult, but interpreting it is another matter, quite apart from the problems involved in the study of wage rates in general. Initially, a clear distinction between two different types of servants' wages needs to be made, namely, board wages, which left the recipient to make his or her own arrangements for food, and the more usual wages paid to the servant for whom food was provided. Board wages were paid when a family was away from home, during the London season, for example, though in some houses, like Woburn in the nineteenth century, they were the norm. Further, whatever the nominal wage might be, it was frequently supplemented by occupational perks as well as the provision of food and accommodation for most indoor servants. A steward who rendered especially notable service might be given substantial gifts, and gifts for all might be distributed at Christmas or other special occasions. Clothing was commonly supplied, especially where, as for footmen, a distinctive uniform was required, while a valet usually received his master's cast-off clothes. Where the supply situation was competitive, housekeepers and cooks could charge commission to shopkeepers with whom they dealt. They could also eat all too well at the family's expense and the housekeeper would be tipped by visitors who came to look

46 Wages of farm workers at Woolley Hall, 1684.

round the house. Footmen delivering messages or gifts expected tips, as did the staff in general from guests, who could well have to give out appropriate sums to the entire indoor staff who awaited their departure in the entrance hall. Such was the expense for guests in the eighteenth century that organized resistance to the giving of vails (as tips were then called) developed. It began in Scotland in the late 1750s and apparently achieved success within some 20 years, at least in cutting out what were felt to be the worst excesses, for tipping never died out.

Clearly, nominal wages should not be seen as the total emoluments of all servants, even if evidence of the extras is not easy to come by and it is impossible to judge their extent. The servants most favourably placed for receiving tips were often assumed to double their salaries, and examples can certainly be found of servants who acquired more wealth than their wages could easily have enabled them to build up. Thus, the will of Mary Webster, the thrifty housekeeper of the Yorke family at Erddig, North Wales, who died in 1875, surprised fellow servants and family alike. The surprise was recorded in the doggerel customarily accorded to faithful servants by the Yorkes:

> And at the reading of the Will
> In Bank (we do not mean a Hill,)
> Were more than thirteen hundred pounds
> 'Gainst rainy day!

Even more remarkable was the case of James Phillips, who spent his whole working life as a gardener at the house, becoming head gardener in 1841 at a salary of £35 a year:

> This faithful steward, just and true
> Died here, in eighteen eighty two,
> At the full age of fifty eight,
> Like 'shock of corn,' mayhap of wheat;
> When 'as bare grain' his body sank
> Were nigh four thousand pounds in Bank.[18]

If, on the other hand, it seems likely that the most junior of the lower servants would receive little in tips, this was not always the case. As hall-boy to the local squire, William Lanceley described how, on his arrival at the hall in 1870:

> I was then told in a confidential way that if I looked after the visiting ladies'-maids, cleaned their boots nicely and got the luggage up quickly . . . I should pick up a nice little bit of tips, which proved correct.[19]

Duties that brought a servant into regular personal contact with family, guests or friends offered the best hope of tips, but the lower servants who received little or nothing in the way of extras earned wages which, by any calculation, were low.

Leisure

One of the handful of servant voices that has survived for the period covered by this book is, in fact, Lanceley's. Few though these voices are, they provide interesting evidence of servant leisure. It was set in a very different context from leisure today, where fixed hours of work and guaranteed holidays are largely agreed and independent of the employer's whim. Both the obligations of the employee and the claims of the employer are limited. But, until the present century, the occupation of servant was carried on within the looser norms of pre-industrial society, where occupations involving personal service were clearly in the master's control. 'His whole time being mine' was how Sir Charles Domvile defined the relationship between himself and an estate labourer,[20] and, if this is an extreme statement of the master's attitude, it is nevertheless a pithy expression of the fact that the servant was employed to minister to his master's convenience without regard to his own.

The complete absence of leisure that this could involve was perhaps most obvious when the house was a centre of activity during the shooting or hunting season, the local races or for a social gathering like the nineteenth-century house party. In the 1870s William Lanceley worked as footman to a master:

> . . . who revelled in hunting six days a week and would have hunted seven had there been a Meet, a sentiment he often expressed. This made it very hard for me, as I had hunting kit as well as footman's duty to do. The clock in the village church steeple struck twelve most nights before I left the brushing-room.

He instantly adds, 'but still I liked the place', and follows with a description of life in the same employment when in London, where opportunities for leisure were frequent:

> My duties in London were light, and two or three times a week I was given 2s.6d. to go to the theatre, the next morning having to give a description of the plays seen, which generally amused the lady, who was an habitual theatre-goer . . .[21]

Other surviving servant sources also comment on leisure activities. The autobiography of a sixteenth-century music master, Thomas Whythorne, mentions how, after he joined the household of Lord Ambrose Dudley in the 1550s, the servants 'received diverse favours & courteous entertainments with friendly cheer' from the housekeeper (who saw Whythorne as a future husband) and her master at a nearby gentleman's home.[22] The *Memoirs of an eighteenth century footman* by John Macdonald, which was first published in 1790, describes social occasions in London, including a supper and ball attended by 30 men and 22 women as guests of a servant turned publican:

> I was one of the company, which was very genteel, from noblemen and gentlemen's houses. The evening was spent very agreeably by the company at country dances, cards and drinking. Supper was at eleven o'clock. After supper the company came into the drawing-room and began again.[23]

Admittedly, all these comments come from upper servants or personal servants who might be expected to show a certain independence or to be treated more favourably than their menial brethren. Long hours, beginning for most before the family awoke and ending only when they had gone to bed, were usual, though not necessarily without leisure. Lanceley described the situation when he was a teenage hall-boy:

> My duties . . . started at six o'clock. A.M. . . . first light the servants' hall fire, clean the young ladies' boots, the butler's, housekeeper's, cook's, and ladies' maids, often twenty pairs together, trim the lamps (I had thirty-five to look after) . . . by 7.30; then lay up the hall breakfast, get it in, and clear up afterwards . . . My day's work followed on . . . [to] bedtime after a day's work of sixteen hours; yet I seldom felt tired as the work was so varied and the food of the best, and we generally got a little leisure in the afternoons . . .[24]

All servants benefited from the communal celebrations that took place as a result of paternalistic traditions of hospitality. As has been seen in an earlier chapter,[25] family rites of passage and national occasions like the jubilees of Queen Victoria were likely to involve the whole household in feasting, sports and merrymaking. Further, it is possible to argue that particular servants might share their master's pleasure when, for example, they accompanied him as footmen on the hunting field or, as valets, travelled to London or abroad. But, in all these cases, a vital ingredient of true leisure is missing: the choices were made for the servant by his master. When a servant shared his master's leisure he was still a subordinate and still on duty, as he was in periods of idleness within the house, where he was always on call. Times of genuine leisure were fitful and rare.

The servant problem

Complaints about servants were common, shrill even, in the eighteenth century and the second half of the nineteenth, when they were aired in the press and correspondence. Dissatisfied employers described them as lazy, disobedient, incompetent, impudent, dishonest, mercenary, drunken and sexually promiscuous. Some of these comments can, in effect, be found in the orders and rules of the sixteenth- and seventeenth-century country houses. Anthony, second Viscount Montague of Cowdray, in his *Booke of Orders & Rules* of 1595, commanded his steward:

> that in civil sort he do reprimand and correct the negligent and disordered persons and reform them by his grave admonition and vigilant eye over them, the riotous, the contentious, and quarrellous persons of any degree, the revengers of their own injuries, the privy mutineers, the frequenters of tabling, carding and dicing in corners and at untimely hours and seasons, the conveyors of meat and other matter out of my house, the haunters of alehouses and suspicious places by day or by night; the absentees from their charge, and lodging abroad without leave, and they that have leave of absence that do not return home at their time limited without lawful let.[26]

If the misbehaviour that the steward was commanded to prevent was not all occasioned by servants, they clearly played their part. Like the later factory owners the masters of the great houses tried to impose order and discipline on a sizeable labour force, but they lacked the discipline of the machine and the relative ease of supervision provided by the open floors of the factory. Even families that claimed to enjoy good relations with their servants had their difficulties, like the mid-eighteenth-century Purefoy family of Shalstone. Henry Purefoy had occasion to write to his London agent, Peter Moulson, in 1753:

> I should be glad to accept [your invitation] & should endeavour to make a suitable return, but at present my coachman is run away from me for fear of a great belly a girl lays to him, & our cookmaid was forced to go to Oxford Assize to be evidence against a felon there, & when she came home she said she was married, & our gardiner has married my mother's maid, & we have had a very valuable mare lamed with a fork . . . so our little family is in a state of confusion at present . . .[27]

Constant problems arose because most servants were young but unmarried. Married servants were not welcome, particularly for internal situations, if only because accommodation was not designed for them and because marriage involved a loyalty to a family other than the master's. But a household in which several single men and women lived together with little possibility of outside friendships put sexual restraint to a severe test, made all the harder by the not uncommon view of young gentlemen and even the master of the house that servants were fair game sexually. Outside friendships were not easy to maintain when leisure was so limited and unpredictable and when leaving the house was difficult. Exit from the house was controlled not just to ensure that duties were done but to discourage divided loyalties. The latter was the concern of Susanna Whatman in laying down the relevant rule for her servants at her house at Vinters, near Maidstone:

> A servant is not to go out without asking leave. Neither is she to expect to leave every Sunday that it is her turn to go to Church. Such a custom would be the means of laying the servants under constant and frequent obligations to their friends and acquaintances, and make the leave of going out no favour at all . . .[28]

'Admirers' of young women were therefore dangerous in a number of ways. Advice on how to deal with one such troublesome young man was sought by William Gossip of Thorp Arch, Yorkshire, from J. Wilmer, his brother-in-law and lawyer (probably in May 1754):

> My uneasiness & disturbances from servts must I think never have an end. The [impudent] fellow John Smith I turn'd away still skulks & hovers about here, nor can I get quit of him. Tho I believe his leading motive is Lust, yet his amours are conducted in such a manner as may reasonably give me apprehensions of another sort. Tho' I have discharged him the house, yet I have reason to believe he is generally about it as soon as dark. Last night abt 10 I surprized him and his Paramour very lovingly together in one of my Out Stables, & imprudently in my first heat gave him a stroke with the stick that supported me . . . He immediately seized me & endeavoured to wrest the stick out of my hands . . . However he never struck me tho' he once collar'd me & was all the while very sassey & provoking with his Tonge. Told me that he came there to speak to one of my servts & wd come in spite of me . . . Now Sr I wd beg your advice in what manner I must act to remove this troublesome fellow from me . . . The first step I have taken is to pack of his Madam this morning which was highly necessary: for she has been tampering with the housekeeper (but in vain) to connive at being introduced into the house at nights after we were in bed . . .[29]

Gossip saw John Smith as a troublemaker, which no doubt he was, but his dismissal of the female servant was merely the conventional response to the discovery of this kind of situation. His behaviour was prudential as well as 'moral', for an illegitimate child would have been an unwelcome burden on the local poor rate as well as a stigma on the house, so that pregnant female servants were usually dismissed to take their problem elsewhere. Drunkenness also brought dismissal, but it, too, was in part a reflection of conditions in the house, in that alcohol was usually readily available. Most servants received either a generous daily allowance of beer, or, for upper servants in great houses, wine, or a financial allowance in lieu.

Via some unusual sources, the North Wales house, Erddig, poses the 'servant problem' acutely. The warm relationships that seem to have been enjoyed between the Yorke family of Erddig and their staff have in fact formed the subject of a book.[30] Portraits of servants, at first paintings, and, later, photographs, were made, while the masters of the house clearly took delight in writing encomiums of their favourites: as portraits and accompanying inscriptions, these line the walls of the servants' hall. There are, for example, portraits of an unnamed black coachboy from the 1730s (unusual in that he is painted in isolation instead of as an adjunct to a scene), of Jane Ebbrell, a mid-eighteenth-century spider-brusher (housemaid), and of Thomas Rogers, a carpenter, painted in 1830. The doggerel is what it is, but genuine affection occasionally shines through, as in the final stanza of 48 on Sarah Davies, maid and ultimately nurse in the nineteenth century, known as 'Lalla' by the Yorkes:

> This faithful friend of years gone by
> We hold in estimation high;
> Her joy lay in her loving care,
> In sorrow too she had her share;
> She learnt and labour'd, not in vain,
> Her honest livelihood [*sic*] to gain,
> And did her duty in the state
> Where Heav'n assign'd her humble fate.

Of course, as the closing lines make plain, distinctions in role and status were taken for granted. Letters of Philip Yorke in the 1770s take a strongly authoritarian line towards workmen. As he wrote to his agent, John Caesar:

> I am ever jealous of my Workmen; I must insist on your asserting that authority, which is necessary, to restrain any Licentiousness in them, and to make them do their duty towards me . . . for mankind are ever to be corrected rather by a distant, and resolute behaviour, than by Intimacy and too much mildness, and easy nature . . . Workmen are the same in all countries, and will pick your pocket equally, without Remorse . . .[31]

These are sentiments that most landowners would have taken for granted: they were present in the late-sixteenth-century *Booke of Orders & Rules* quoted above.[32] But their very rigidity might help to explain the problems which arose between the Yorkes and some of their servants. When their agent, John Caesar, so declined as to be markedly unreliable in the late 1760s, his young son, Jacky, acted as his deputy, unpaid apparently for many years. Within the Yorke family there was some discussion about whether or not it was wise to make use of the young man in this way without some financial reward. At all events, he began to falsify the accounts during the three years in which he finally filled the post of steward. He was eventually dismissed at the beginning of 1787. Philip Yorke wrote to him:

> . . . I am very sorry to say I can see no marks of innocency, and mere mistakes of Figures, and omissions of charge in your accounts, tho Repetitions of this sort would disable you as a Steward; the Fluctuations of many of the year's totals could not be so continually varying by errors of that kind only, but must have had their source in traffick, very injurious to me and disgraceful to yourself . . . Perhaps on the whole your salary was not too much, but the manner of raising it, had a very bad aspect. I desire you will as soon as possible appoint Mr Jones to meet you at Erthig and that you will deliver into his hands all my Keys and Papers . . .[33]

Perhaps the Yorkes suffered from their agent's dishonesty not because of authoritarian attitudes but because, in this instance, they trusted him sufficiently to give him genuine responsibility instead of supervising his activities closely.

After his long-serving father, Jacky Caesar was a grave disappointment. Servants like Caesar senior were valued and accorded moral worth, as the general use of the epithet 'faithful' to describe them indicates. Thus the Yorke portraits and verses are probably best seen as a rather extravagant expression of the normal appreciation of 'good' servants rather than evidence of close relationships with them. What remains striking about the relationships is the lack of evidence that, above and beyond the performance of particular duties, the Yorkes looked for subservience. With their strong hierarchical assumptions, most masters did. When Sir William Wentworth wrote down advice for his son, the future minister of Charles I, he put it like this: 'For SERVANTES be verie carefull to keepe only those that be borne of good & honest frends and be well willing, humble, diligentt and honest'.[34] In a more sophisticated age Augustus Hervey commented on his host, Lord Temple of Stowe, in a letter of 12 October 1765 to his lordship's brother, George Grenville:

> I never saw so large a house so well conducted, servants that have no embarras, no noise, but all attention and respect; 'tis a miracle how they have formed them so, and rubbed off the dirt and familiarity from the foreigners and inattention and ill-breeding from the English ones; I wish the master of a certain great family had the art of conducting his as well, then we should see order restored instead of confusion, respect instead of flattery and efficiency in the place of inability.[35]

What was expected of a servant was understood and neatly expressed by Revd Timothy Thomas, who, as chaplain to the second Earl of Oxford, accompanied him on a tour through Scotland and the northern counties in 1725. He kept the journal of the tour. After visiting Durham, he wrote:

> The whole situation of the place is somewhat romantic, but to me seems not unpleasant, being altogether upon hills which have a descent to the river. Others of better judgement [meaning his master] condemn this site, to whose opinion I always submit my own, to my great advantage and instruction.[36]

To his great advantage it was, for he was soon to succeed the scholarly Humphrey Wanley as the Earl's librarian, but by no means all servants were acute or willing enough to comply so readily with their masters' wishes. Henry, ninth Earl of Northumberland, the 'Wizard Earl', warned his son not to pitch his expectations too high. 'I have them more reasonable than either wife, brother or friend: [but] you must not expect to find gods of them for knowledge, or saints for life'.[37] The critical difference in handling servants to their satisfaction as well as their master's was between those who saw their servants as persons and dealt with them considerately, and those who regarded them as inferior creatures, necessary but without significance. The social system fostered the latter.

However, this does not mean that all that was needed to solve the servant problem was for masters to behave more considerately, but rather that such behaviour would have compensated to some extent for the one-sided nature of domestic service. Long hours, low wages, low status and lack of freedom may have been offset in some measure by the accommodation, food and companionship of service in the country house. But it seems likely that only the self-esteem of those who gained great satisfaction from identifying with the aristocratic families they served may have protected the country house from the extremes of servant discontent.

Chapter Seven

CHANGING FORTUNES: DECLINE AND RENEWAL

The decline of large landowners

Many factors have influenced the development of country house estates and most were underwritten by the pressure to maintain the status of the landowner and his family. Similarly, the decline of the country house was the result of a variety of changes many of which served to undermine this status. These factors will be outlined in the following chapter.

The social and political developments of the nineteenth century, the processes of industrialization and urbanization brought obvious advantages to many landowners and, as we have seen, were to a large extent actively assisted by their own self-interest. The large estates contributed to the improvements in agricultural practice and recognized the need for more reliable forms of transport for people and produce. In some significant cases, like that of the Duke of Bridgwater, they led the way. Many landowners, who could supply coal or other minerals from their land for the new industries, invested in the development of mines, docks and railways. But this connection brought with it long-term problems for many estates. Iron mines scarred the landscape and reduced the value of agricultural land once the lives of the pits were over.

The sixth Duke of Bedford was far from typical in refusing to allow the ironstone found on his Midland estates to be mined because it would disfigure the countryside.[1] The development of coal-seams under the parkland to the very foundations of the house, as happened in so many parts of the Yorkshire and Nottinghamshire coalfields, ultimately brought about the destruction, in several cases, of the house itself. Several houses had to be demolished because they were structurally unsound as a result of mining activity. Methley Hall, Kippax Park and Swillington Hall are three examples in Yorkshire.

Other houses were abandoned to their fate, like Thoresby Hall, Nottinghamshire, which was purchased by the National Coal Board as recently as 1977 to open a new seam of coal at nearly 3000 feet below the estate. In this case, though, a reprieve came with the changes in rules for the conduct of mining underneath areas where liability for subsidence damage could be high and, as a result, the property was sold in 1988 to become a hotel. Yet the Earl Manvers can have had no such end in mind when he started to build the hall in 1864, spending a total of £171,015 4s 3d by the time the books were closed in 1876.[2]

Similarly, the process of urbanization was assisted by those landowners with land in strategic places. In the 1870s the ninth Earl of Scarborough turned to the developments of the seaside town of Skegness as a non-agricultural source of income at a time when his farms were becoming more difficult to let. Hand in hand with railway development, this was a fashionable investment which led to the emergence of towns like Eastbourne fostered by the Duke of Devonshire. But as Beastall has demonstrated, with reference to valuations of the Skegness estate of 1875 and 1895 to 1896, the investment did not necessarily protect the landlords' income during these years.[3]

At the outset, such landowners did not plan to destroy their own estates. They merely wanted to profit from the assets discovered on them, developing a resource that had probably been known to exist for centuries. Such resources were sufficient to enable some to offset the decline in income that resulted from the agricultural depression of the period 1872 to 1895. They also helped to cushion them against the introduction of death duties in 1896.

There were, of course, many more country house owners whose estates did not benefit from such assets, who were almost totally dependent on the agricultural economy and had to find other ways of preserving their incomes. Some were in a position to develop their links with the City of London and, as Thompson has demonstrated by analysing the diaries and account books of the second and third Earls of Verulam, improve their incomes by investment on the stock market and accepting company directorships.[4] Others, like the Duke of Bedford with 119 acres of land in London, in Bloomsbury, St Pancras and St Martins, could bolster their incomes with ground rents. In particular, the sixth Duke was able to develop his Covent Garden Market into the chief produce market in the kingdom, employing his own staff to let the stalls as well as collecting the tolls on produce sold and keeping the peace.[5]

Those with only agricultural land were in a more difficult position and forced to retrench. Like many others, Spencer Lucy of Charlecote had his income reduced, in his case by more than half, in 1879. Depression combined with poor harvests forced his tenants to give up their farms or to ask for a reduction in rent. In the 1890s his son, Henry, was reduced to selling the family collection of paintings to maintain the estate.[6] Families might even contemplate the sale of their libraries and muniments, thus destroying at a stroke the cohesion of their family and estate archives by taking advantage of the popular antiquarianism of the nineteenth century.

In 1885 the seventh Earl of Jersey sold some of the Osterley Park manuscripts at Sotheby's. One of the major sales in 1899 was to be that of the papers of the first three Earls of Hardwicke which were withdrawn at Sothebys and purchased by the British Museum to ensure that the archive was kept together. Amongst the material were 20 volumes relating to the family estates in Cambridgeshire, Gloucestershire, Hertfordshire and elsewhere. Such a fate was, perhaps, preferable to the destruction that could take place on a change of ownership. When Spencer Lucy died in 1889 at Charlecote, his wife went back to Scotland, let the house and ordered the agent to burn the family papers. A massive bonfire consisting of inventories, letters, medieval charters and title-deeds spanning four centuries was held in the courtyard.[7] Others were unfortunately forced to sell the very basis of their power, the land itself.

CATALOGUE

• OF THE

MAGNIFICENT CONTENTS

OF

ALTON TOWERS,

THE PRINCELY SEAT

OF

THE EARLS OF SHREWSBURY,

WHICH (BY ORDER OF THE EXECUTORS OF THE LATE

RIGHT HON. BERTRAM ARTHUR, EARL OF SHREWSBURY)

Will be Sold by Auction, by

MESSRS. CHRISTIE & MANSON,

AT THE TOWERS,

On MONDAY, JULY 6, 1857,

And Twenty-Nine following Days (Sundays excepted),

AT TWELVE O'CLOCK PRECISELY.

——o——

May be viewed on and after Monday, June 22nd, with Catalogues
only, price 7*s.* 6*d.,* to admit Three Persons, from 9 to 6 o'clock.

NO ADMISSION ON SUNDAYS.

47 Sale particulars for contents of Alton Towers, 1857. The sale lasted 30 days.

Sale of land

The sale of land could be contemplated because of the decline in the influence of the
landowner, ushered in by the processes of urbanization and democratization. Land
had been sold in the past as a natural part of the farming economy, reducing acreage
in one place to consolidate in another. At the turn of the century land was being sold
to preserve fortunes and the traditional stewardship of an estate was abandoned. In

Ireland, after the years of famine and the agitation for home rule, there was an added political encouragement for divestment.

Rural areas lost population to the towns and the bonds of loyalty and deference were loosened. Local administration became increasingly diffused through new bodies, from Boards of Guardians under the New Poor Law in 1834, to School Boards under the 1870 Education Act and Local Boards of Health under a variety of statutory arrangements. There was, of course, still a role for the landowner but he was subject to more direct democratic control. The creation of County Councils in 1888 took much of the responsibility for county administration away from the appointed Justices of the Peace and Lords Lieutenant and passed it to yet another elected body. The expansion of the electorate by the three Reform Acts of 1832, 1867 and 1884 made the exercise of the influence of the landowner steadily more difficult. It remained stronger in rural constituencies but the towns tended increasingly to return the largest employer of labour. The Ballot Act 1872 and the Corrupt Practices Act 1883 made the exercise of undue influence on the voter less feasible. As a result, by 1885 'for the first time the number of commercial men and manufacturers in the House of Commons was greater than the number of landowners'.[8] This process did not produce a Parliament entirely dominated by commercial interests, however, since many businessmen had themselves purchased landed estates. At this time they were content for the landed classes to take the lead in representing them. It was no contradiction, then, that between 1886 and 1916 out of 101 men who held office 41 were landed proprietors with, on the whole, large landed estates.[9] This period has in fact been regarded as 'the Indian summer of the country house'. Fostered by King Edward VII, country house entertaining was at its most fashionable.

In many cases, there were still wealthy bankers and industrialists whose natural ambition was to acquire a country estate to gain acceptance amongst the highest echelons of society. The possession of a large estate could establish the necessary credentials for the granting of a title, but it was no longer an essential prerequisite. It has been estimated that

> 246 new titles were granted between 1886 and 1914. Discounting the royal family and promotions within the peerage there were 200 individuals entering the nobility for the first time. Not more than one half acquired a landed position.[10]

William Waldorf Astor, the American industrialist, purchased Cliveden from the Duke of Westminster in 1893 and was created a Baron in 1916 and Viscount the following year. By this time, he had also purchased Hever Castle in Kent and started on a programme of restoration. A fall in land values did not discourage some large transactions, like the sale of the Norton Hall estate of 7000 acres by the Marquess of Ripon to a Bradford manufacturer.[11] Nor was the depression in agriculture a deterrent for the commercial investor. Viscount Oxenbridge (seventh Baron Monson) sold his estate at Gatton Park in Surrey to Jeremiah Coleman, the 'mustard king', in 1888 and Henry Davenport sold his 4000-acre Maer Hall estate in Staffordshire to a Liverpool shipowner, F.J. Harrison, in 1892.[12] Only wealthy businessmen, like Sir Julius Wernher, could contemplate the annual expenditure

THE GRIMSTON PARK ESTATE,
YORKSHIRE.

PLANS AND PARTICULARS

OF THE

VALUABLE & HIGHLY IMPORTANT FREEHOLD RESIDENTIAL DOMAIN,

CALLED THE

GRIMSTON PARK ESTATE,

NEAR TADCASTER,

IN THE WEST RIDING AND AINSTY OF THE COUNTY OF YORK,

CONTAINING, WITHIN A RING FENCE, AN

AREA OF 2880 ACRES,

INCLUDING

MANSION, PLEASURE GROUNDS, GARDENS, HOME AND DAIRY FARM,

GRIMSTON LODGE,

Together with several HOMESTEADS, LODGES, and other RESIDENCES,

OF THE

ESTIMATED ANNUAL VALUE OF £6677,

THE PERPETUAL ADVOWSON OF KIRKBY WHARFE, VALUE £345 PER ANNUM,

THE IMPROPRIATE TITHES OF ULLESKELF, AMOUNTING TO £98 0s. 7d. PER ANNUM,

THE MANOR OF ULLESKELF,

THE VALUABLE SALMON FISHERY IN THE RIVER WHARFE,

WHICH

WILL BE SOLD BY AUCTION,

IN ONE LOT,

BY

MESSRS. DRIVER,

AT THE MART, TOKENHOUSE YARD, LOTHBURY, LONDON,

ON

TUESDAY, THE 2ND DAY OF JULY, 1872,

AT TWO O'CLOCK IN THE AFTERNOON PRECISELY.

Copies of these Particulars, with Orders to View, may be obtained of T. S. CUNDY, Esq., Hall Orchards, Wetherby; COLONEL GRATTAN, Grimston Lodge, Tadcaster.

MESSRS. BENBOW & SALTWELL,

SOLICITORS, STONE BUILDINGS, LINCOLN'S INN

and of

MESSRS. DRIVER,

SURVEYORS, LAND AGENTS, AND AUCTIONEERS, 4, WHITEHALL, LONDON.

Leeds:
J. F. MASSER AND SONS, LITHOGRAPHERS, BOAR LANE.

of £30,000 to maintain the Luton Hoo estate, on which he would 'only stay rarely for shooting in the autumn and occasionally on Sundays', and maintain a full staff of 54 gardeners, 10 electricians, 20 to 30 servants and a horde of labourers whom the Webbs were unable to count.[13]

The Rothschilds had established such a network of estates in Buckinghamshire during the second half of the nineteenth century that the Vale of Aylesbury was popularly called 'Rothschildshire'. Meyer Rothschild built Mentmore as the centre for an estate of 5000 acres, Anthony enlarged Aston Clinton and Lionel purchased Tring Park for his son Nathan. They were model landlords in the established manner. Ferdinand de Rothschild, who built the 222-roomed Waddesdon Manor between 1874 and 1884, transformed the nearby village by employing 90 per cent of the villagers:

> He provided a village hall and encouraged its use by sponsoring a local orchestra and dramatic society. Elderly residents still remember how the Baron donated instruments for any children who showed musical aptitude, hired costumes from the best agency for performances of Gilbert and Sullivan operettas and then brought his 'fancy friends from London' to watch the rustic thespians. He hired a professional coach to teach Waddesdon lads cricket. The highlight of the year occured on the first Thursday in July which was set aside for 'The Baron's Treat'. There were sports in which the youngsters competed for generous prizes, a fair, and a sumptuous tea. Little wonder the Baron was a popular landlord![14]

As other young members of the family grew to adulthood, they followed this example, with Alfred building a house at Halton near Wendover in the 1880s and Lionel building Exbury with 250 acres of garden around 1918.

Despite the activities of ambitious industrialists and wealthy bankers, the underlying trend was towards sale and divestment of the encumbrance of land by the landed classes. Sales began in the period following the Settled Land Act of 1882, which enabled landowners tied by settlements to sell their estates to life-tenants. The campaign by Lloyd George against the land monopoly introduced the Incremental Value Duty and Undeveloped Land Duty and successfully persuaded many landowners that the time had come to sell. Under the Finance Act 1910, a comprehensive survey of landownership was undertaken, for which the relevant returns have recently been distributed by the Public Record Office to county record offices or, in some cases, libraries. The use of the valuation books in conjunction with the Forms 4- and 37-Land, which were used for the valuation of the land and should be locally held, with the field books, selected for permanent preservation by the PRO (ref. IR 58), should enable studies to be undertaken into the breakup of country house estates. Where the relevant working copies of large-scale Ordnance Survey maps are also locally held, it should be possible to compare the changes in ownership and tenurial and land usage patterns since the tithe surveys of the 1840s.

---

48 Sale particulars for Grimston Park estate, 1872.

25

UNOFFICIAL.

DUTIES ON LAND VALUES.

(Finance (1909-10) Act, 1910.)

REFERENCE : to be quoted in all communications.

RETURN TO BE MADE BY AN OWNER OF LAND OR BY ANY PERSON RECEIVING RENT IN RESPECT OF LAND.

(Penalty for failure to make a due Return, not exceeding £50.)

Reference to the accompanying Sheet of Instructions (Form 2.—Land).

SEE INSTRUC-TION 2.

Particulars extracted from the Rate Books.		This space is not for the use of the person making the Return.
	Parish	
	Number of Poor Rate ...	
	Name of Occupier	
	Description of Property ..	
	Situation of Property	
	Estimated extent	Acres Roods
	Gross Estimated Rental (or Gross Value in Valuation List*)	£
	Rateable Value	£

(* Applicable to the Metropolis only.)

IMPORTANT.—As the Land is to be valued as on 30th April, 1909, the particulars should be furnished, so far as possible, with reference to the circumstances existing on that date.

See Instruction 3.

1. Particulars required by the Commissioners which must be furnished so far as it is in the power of the person making the Return to give them.

See Instruction 4.

(*a*) Parish or Parishes in which the Land is situate.

See Instructions 1 and 5.

(*b*) Name of Occupier ... ...

(*c*) Christian Name and Surname and full postal address of the person making the Return.

See Instruction 9.

(*d*) Nature of Interest of the person making the Return in the Land :—

(1) Whether Freehold, Copyhold, or Leasehold.   1

(2) If Copyhold, name of the Manor ...   2

(3) If Leasehold, (1) term of lease and date of commencement (including, where the lease contains a covenant for renewal, the period for which the lease may be renewed), and   3 (i.)

(ii) name and address of lessor or his successor in title.   3 (ii.)

Form 4—Land.

49 A blank Form 4 -Land.

The value of these sources has yet to be fully evaluated but the potential for the study of individual landowners has been recognized.[15]

Many great estates came on to the market just before and after the First World War, including Houghton, Norfolk; Apethorpe, Northamptonshire; Berrington, Herefordshire; and Millichope, Shropshire. The Duke of Bedford sold the Thorney estate in the fens to his tenants in 1909, nearly half his total acreage. Thompson has shown that between 6 and 8 million acres changed hands in England between 1918 and 1921. 'Such a permanent transfer of land had not been seen since the dissolution of the monasteries in the sixteenth century! Indeed, a transfer on this scale and in such a short space of time had probably not been equalled since the Norman Conquest'.[16] He attributed the scale of transfer to a temporary boom in the market for land rather than a forced sale as a result of taxation and death duties. It was a continuation of a pre-war trend towards the contraction of estates by the sale of outlying parts, thus liberating capital for more profitable purposes. Nevertheless, the sales preceded years of even greater depression in land values and accompanied a period during which large numbers of country houses were put on the market or demolished.

Redundancy and demolition of country houses

In previous centuries there have been many examples of the deliberate destruction of country houses, most prominently Nonsuch by Barbara Villiers in the seventeenth century, when desperate remedies were required to reduce estate expenses. In many cases, only a portion of the house had to be reduced, as at Audley End, Essex, in both the eighteenth and nineteenth centuries. But after the First World War a number of factors contributed to demolition being seen as a generally practical solution to an insoluble problem. There was no longer a sufficient market for large estates, after the short boom. Lloyd George introduced further burdens on the landed interest in the budget of 1919. Death duties were increased to 40 per cent on estates over £200,000 in value, a change that particularly affected those families in which the heirs had been lost in the war. The Mineral Duties Act introduced in 1918 made inroads into the income of those landowners that had benefited from such ownership. The Duke of Northumberland's mineral income was reduced to £23,890 net from £82,451 by the five per cent mineral rights duty and 80 per cent excess mineral rights duty on the amount by which tonnage rents exceeded pre-war levels.

Economic change combined with social change made life more difficult for the owner of a country house. Domestic service became unfashionable. Government commissions pinpointed the problem but the state was powerless to improve the situation. *The Report on the Supply of Female Domestic Servants* of 1923 found that domestic service had failed to keep pace with the great changes in industrial life in England – fixed hours, recognized rates of pay, inspection of factories, better social and recreational facilities. Census figures show that the decline in the numbers of servants started after 1891, when there were nearly 1.5 million men and women, boys and girls employed in private households, but the downward trend was gradual. In 1911 the numbers were over 1.3 million, and in 1921 they were down to just over 1.2 million. During the 1930s high unemployment forced many back into service and pushed the figures back to pre-war levels but the Second World War marked an end. The landowner was placed in a difficult position in attempting to maintain a life-style that was increasingly unfashionable. He could not attract servants without paying ever-increasing wages and could not afford sufficient numbers to maintain the houses at their traditional standard. As a result, for example, the Marquis of Bath, who came into the world surrounded by 43 indoor servants, has today to make do with a live-in married couple.[17] Of course, the improvement in domestic labour-saving appliances has also made a contribution.

Tenants also gained rights that challenged the financial position of the landlord. Although a customary system of 'tenant rights' had developed since the late eighteenth century by which the landowner paid compensation to an outgoing tenant for his unexhausted improvements, it was not until the passing of the Agricultural Holdings Act in 1908 that it became a universal legal right. In many cases, landowners had to reduce rents to encourage good tenants and were thus faced with reduced returns. Increasingly, tenants were keen to purchase their farms and landlords were unable to let their land. Even the last bastion of social privilege, the hunting and killing of wild animals for sporting purposes, had begun to fall. In 1881, by the Ground Game Act, it had become legal for all tenants to kill game trespassing on their farms.

In such a climate the country house became redundant in its traditional role and was no longer seen as embodying social power. For many landowners, the choice had to be made between keeping and maintaining a showplace or concentrating on farming the estate. In cases where alternative smaller houses existed on their estates, fitted for a reduced standard of living and yet economically viable, the larger house was abandoned. Thus, the heir to Clumber, Nottinghamshire, Lord Lincoln, found he was unable to support the house, sold the contents in 1936, demolished it and went to live in a nearby vicarage. Similarly, Frederick Richard Thomas Trench-Gascoigne abandoned the main family residence at Parlington, West Yorkshire, on inheriting the Gascoigne estates in 1905 and moved to nearby Lotherton Hall. Parlington was left to decay until finally being demolished in 1953.

Where the landowner could not contemplate demolition, he was still faced with the cost of maintenance. The solution adopted after the First World War was leasing. There were still tenants willing to take on good sporting estates for a season or more or even on a more permanent basis. Major estates were advertised to let during the 1920s in the pages of *Country Life*. Kedleston Hall, Derbyshire, was available with fishing and 6000 acres of shooting in December 1928, as was Levens Hall, Cumbria, with 1814 acres of shooting, one and a half miles of salmon and trout fishing and a grouse moor of 5200 acres.

But for many landowners who inherited the burden of an unfashionable house, or one which was too large for practical purposes, the only solution was demolition. Some attempted to sell their properties but there were few buyers in the period after the First World War. The evidence of sales particulars at this time is no proof that

By direction of Sir JOHN LINDSAY DASHWOOD, Bart.

BUCKS.

Within ten minutes' walk of West Wycombe Station on the G.W. and G.C. Joint Railways, 2¼ miles from High Wycombe Station and 31½ miles by road from London.

𝔍𝔩𝔩𝔲𝔰𝔱𝔯𝔞𝔱𝔢𝔡 𝔓𝔞𝔯𝔱𝔦𝔠𝔲𝔩𝔞𝔯𝔰, 𝔓𝔩𝔞𝔫 𝔞𝔫𝔡 ℭ𝔬𝔫𝔡𝔦𝔱𝔦𝔬𝔫𝔰 𝔬𝔣 𝔖𝔞𝔩𝔢

OF THE

Very Valuable and Attractive

FREEHOLD COUNTY SEAT

KNOWN AS

West Wycombe Park

Dating from the Early XVIIth Century, and containing Entrance and Central Halls, Magnificent Suite of Reception Rooms, Sixteen Principal Bed Rooms, Four Bath Rooms, Ground Floor Offices and ample Servants' Accommodation.

Stabling.   Garages.   Two Lodges and several Cottages.

FINE UNDULATING PARK.

WOODLANDS, LAKE and HOME FARM.

The whole extending to

Over   338   Acres.

For Sale by Auction by Messrs.

GIDDY & GIDDY

At the London Auction Mart, 155, Queen Victoria Street, E.C. 4,

On WEDNESDAY, 19th JULY, 1922,

At 2.30 precisely
(unless   previously   Sold   by   Private   Treaty).

LAND AGENT - Mr. W. R. BUTLER, 15, High Street, High Wycombe.

SOLICITOR   · Mr. E. VERNOR MILES, 30, Theobald's Road, Bedford Row, W.C. 1; and 15, High Street, High Wycombe.

AUCTIONEERS' OFFICES :—
11a, REGENT STREET, S.W. 1; and Maidenhead and Windsor.

---

50 Title page of sale particulars for West Wycombe Park, 1922. The house and estate were not ultimately sold.

---

properties were in fact sold, as can be seen from the example of West Wycombe Park. They can, nevertheless, be informative about the size and condition of the estate, or that part that was for sale. Merlin Waterson has recorded, in a fascinating series of recollections of country house owners, Helen, Lady Dashwood's reaction to her husband's plans: 'It's the most beautiful house I've ever seen in my life.

MANSION OPENED TO LEEDS PUBLIC.

HISTORIC EVENT.

"A PETRIFIED EPITOME OF ENGLAND."

HOUSE OF TREASURE.

The Minister of Labour (Sir Montague Barlow) yesterday opened to the public the historic mansion and estate of Templenewsam which has recently been acquired by the Corporation of Leeds on very generous terms from the Minister of Education (the Hon. Edward Wood).

Mr. Wood parted with the famous property largely on account of the increasingly heavy burden of taxation, and in order that the old Jacobean mansion might be preserved in perpetuity as a national monument he has handed it over to the city of Leeds. The purchase price to the Corporation was £35,000, and as this was barely the market value of the estate alone, which comprises 913 acres of land, the mansion was virtually a free gift.

Mr. Wood has also presented to the Corporation a valuable collection of pictures and antique furnishings, and now that these have been appropriately distributed about the mansion—together with a number of pictures loaned from the City Art Gallery—Templenewsam has become a magnificent show-place of which the citizens of Leeds may well be proud.

The Corporation has also proceeded to develop the estate for agricultural and recreational purposes. There is now a fine herd of Friesian cattle browsing in the park, and a model dairy farm is to be established on the estate for the supply of milk to various municipal institutions. An eighteen-hole golf course has been laid out, and this will shortly be supplemented by a second similar course, while tennis courts, cricket pitches, football grounds, and bowling-greens are also to be constructed. At the same time, the unique historic interest of the mansion and estate is being preserved, and the Corporation hope to make Templenewsam fulfil the description applied to it by the veteran Viscount Halifax, as "the Hampton Court of the North."

A DISTINGUISHED COMPANY.

At the opening ceremony yesterday Sir Montague Barlow was accompanied by the Lord Mayor and Lady Mayoress of Leeds (Alderman and Mrs. Frank Fountain), together with most of the members of the Corporation and a distinguished company of guests. Alderman Sir Charles Wilson, M.P., (the chairman of the Templenewsam Estate Committee) was present, with Lady Wilson, Mr. John Lambert (the vice-chairman of the committee) and Mrs. Lambert, Sir William Middlebrook, Sir George G. Cockburn, Mr. E. George Arnold (Pro-Chancellor of the University of Leeds) and Mrs. Arnold, Lady Grimthorpe, the Lord Mayor and the Lady Mayoress of Bradford (Alderman and Mrs. Thomas Sowden), the Mayor and Mayoress of Morley (Mr. and Mrs. Joseph Harrop), the Mayor and Mayoress of Pudsey (Mr. and Mrs. Richard Ingham), the Town Clerk of Leeds (Sir Robert Fox), Mr. W. Lunn, M.P., Mrs. Owen Connellan, Mrs. W. Hodgson, Mrs. Robert Armitage, Alderman and Mrs. George Ratcliffe, Sir Edwin and Lady Airey, Mr. and Mrs. T. B. Duncan, and Mr. David Little (the president of the Leeds Chamber of Commerce).

---

51 Cutting from *The Yorkshire Observer*, 20 October 1923.

We're not going to sell *this*.[18] Although the idea of sale was consequently abandoned, the house was reduced in size by half, with the servants' wing of 30 or more bedrooms facing demolition.

One way of disposing of a country house at a time when there was little or no market became possible where the property was adjacent to a centre of population. This was to sell the property at much less than the market value to a local authority.

In this way, Temple Newsam was acquired by the City of Leeds. The *Yorkshire Observer* of 20 October 1923 reported at length on the opening of the mansion to the public by the Minister of Labour, Sir Montagu Barlow, noting that:

> Mr Wood (the Hon Edward Wood) parted with the famous property largely on account of the increasingly heavy burden of taxation, and in order that the old Jacobean mansion might be preserved in perpetuity as a national monument he has handed it over to the city of Leeds. The purchase price to the Corporation was £35,000, and as this was barely the market value of the estate alone, which comprises 913 acres of land, the mansion was virtually a free gift.

In addition to the estate, much of the contents of the house was included in the sale and in 1937 the Ingram family papers were also purchased by the City Council. Similar accommodations were made in other towns between the wars, with the purchase of Wollaton Hall and 800 acres by Nottingham Corporation in 1924 and the Kings Weston estate by Bristol Corporation in 1937.

Where neither leasing nor disposal was possible and the house owner was not prepared to maintain the property, it was abandoned and ultimately demolished. Both Fryston Hall, Castleford, West Yorkshire, and Wheatley Hall, Doncaster, South Yorkshire, were demolished in this way in 1931 and 1938 respectively. Some houses like Sutton Scarsdale, Derbyshire, Kirby Hall, North Yorkshire, and Cassiobury, Hertfordshire, were sold and gutted in the 1920s and their contents were dispersed around the world. Three rooms from Sutton Scarsdale are now in the Philadelphia Museum of Art and a Grinling Gibbons' staircase from Cassiobury is in the Metropolitan Museum of Art in New York.[19] Clemenson has demonstrated that, out of her sample of 500 country houses, 35 were demolished between 1916 and 1945, of which at least ten were as a result of fire and two due to wartime bombing. The researches of Peter Reid have led him to believe that 4000 of such houses have been lost over the last 100 years, the periods of highest destruction being the years 1926 to 1940 and 1946 to 1965.[20] There are no accurate figures on the subject since no official record has been made. Part of the problem, of course, relates to the definition of what constitutes a country house; as Cornforth has acknowledged, '. . . the country house defies neat classification because it is invariably a synthesis of architectural quality, social intention and a way of life based on the ownership of land'. He has, nevertheless, estimated that there have been some 348 'notable' country houses demolished since 1945. Of this total, 21 houses have disappeared in Wales, 71 in Scotland and 256 in England.[21] This estimate contrasts with the more recent calculation that 629 such houses were demolished over the same period.[22]

One comprehensive attempt to record all family seats that are standing or have been demolished has been the series published by Burke's and Savills entitled *Guide to Country Houses*. But, as yet, only three volumes have appeared, covering Ireland; East Anglia; and Herefordshire, Worcestershire, Shropshire and Warwickshire.[23] The editor has estimated the number of those houses in the British Isles as 10,000, 2000 of which are in Ireland. This total breaks down to 80 in Cambridgeshire where 10 have been demolished, 120 in Norfolk where 50 have been lost and 258 in Suffolk where 29 have been demolished. There is a similar variation also in the number of estates where there is continuity of occupation by one family since the seventeenth century. Only the Pemberton family of Trumpington and the Jenyns family of Bottisham are identified in Cambridgeshire, whereas there are still some 20 such families in adjoining Norfolk.

Tracing the lost country house

Such discontinuity creates particular problems for local historians, both in identifying the sites of former houses and parkland and in tracking down any related source material. The first edition six-inch Ordnance Survey maps, where areas of parkland can readily be seen, are the most useful source. Additional details can also be extracted, like the existence of paths, woodlands and lakes, and the overall acreage can be assessed. Comparison with later 25-inch and earlier, pre-Ordnance Survey printed and manuscript maps, particularly tithe maps, where available, can enable changes to be monitored and some features to be more clearly identified. Cross-reference to directories and census returns should identify the owner or occupier. Since leasing country houses was quite common, even in the nineteenth century, care should be taken to ensure that the true owners are found. Only then can the attempt be made to trace any surviving family papers. Institutions exist which can simplify the search for information on lost and surviving country houses. The National Monuments Record and the National Monuments Record for Scotland, both founded in 1941, keep an index to houses and other historical buildings and, while not 100 per cent complete, can be extremely helpful.[24] Originally established 'to make and preserve records of historically important buildings in anticipation of their possible destruction by enemy action', they have developed into a central record of historic and prehistoric sites. They can supply copies of photographs or architectural plans from their files. Similarly, the National Register of Archives can assist local historians to track down relevant estate papers, held throughout England and Wales.[25] Established under the auspices of the Historical Manuscripts Commission in 1945, its task was to collect and disseminate information about manuscript sources for British history outside the public records. The NRA consists of more than 32,500 unpublished lists and catalogues of manuscript collections. The Scottish NRA is based in the Scottish Record Office in Edinburgh.

Wartime occupation 1939–1945

Many country houses were used during the First World War as training camps and convalescent homes. Temple Newsam became a military hospital and Lotherton Hall served as a Voluntary Aid Detachment Hospital from 1914 to 1919. But country houses found a greater variety of roles in the Second World War. As yet, little has been written about this aspect of country house life. It is a particularly suitable subject for local study using oral history techniques, while those with direct experience are still living. One example is this glimpse of the plight of a great estate provided by Mary, Duchess of Buccleuch:

> War came, oddly enough, before one expected it. The army moved into Bowhill, with not a thing put away. The officer's sitting room was where all the Van Dycks were. It was terribly badly used; the army did terrible things to the house, all the proverbial things that troops are supposed to do – hacking down the banisters to make firewood, and throwing darts at the pictures. They couldn't have done more harm, and ended up by nearly burning it down twice. But it survived . . . Boughton was occupied by the British Museum, and so at least they kept the house warm. But we didn't really put things away – they just remained intact. Bowhill was a barracks; Drumlanrig was a school; and the other houses were also barracks. Langholm had to be pulled down after the war – it couldn't be shored up, because it had got such dry rot in it, through the troops being there for four and a half years.[26]

This account sums up many of the uses to which such large houses were put. Few were destroyed by enemy action, although Trafford Park, Lancashire, and Sandling Park, Kent, were damaged beyond repair in bombing raids. Even houses very distant from centres of population felt the impact. Mount Edgcumbe, Cornwall, was gutted in a bombing raid and Chatsworth was shot up. A desk is still displayed there bearing a bullet embedded in its front. But the value of such properties was recognized, as is shown by the large-scale occupation by the armed forces for a variety of military purposes. They ranged from the glamour of the use by Southern Command of the double cube room at Wilton, Wiltshire, as the 'operations' room, to the use of Arbury Hall, Warwickshire, as a base for a prisoner-of-war camp. Many houses were used as convalescent homes, from Preston Hall, Kent, to Stapleford Park, Leicestershire, and others saw service as military hospitals, like Harewood House, West Yorkshire, and Leeds Castle, Kent. All were requisitioned under the Compensation Defence Act of 1939. Few managed to escape occupation, although some, like Felbrigg, Norfolk, lacking a modern electricity supply, could not be adapted for any military or civilian purpose.

Evidence of wartime occupation can be found as local folklore but documentary proof may be difficult to find, even amongst family and estate papers deposited in a local repository. Local newspapers do not help where information of wartime activity is concerned as strict censorship of such news was observed. The difficulties in finding source material for contemporary local history have been well rehearsed in *Twentieth Century Lincolnshire* by Dennis Mills, one of the few attempts to deal with the issues.[27] However, it is easy to overlook the resources of the Public Record Office, Kew, in this area. Numerous classes of records are now accessible relating to the interest of specific Whitehall departments in requisitioning property and the subsequent payments of compensation. Some, however, remain under periods of extended closure, from 50 to 75 years. The most valuable, if incomplete, class is the WORK 50 government property registers. The registers, WORK 50/23–29, are of requisitioned and derequisitioned property and cover Berkshire, Buckingham-shire, Hertfordshire, Oxfordshire, Surrey, Hampshire and the Isle of Wight.[28]

Claims for compensation for wartime occupation could be very high when the consequences were such that a country house had to be demolished. Some, like Lowther Castle and Rigmaden Hall, Cumbria, were never rebuilt as a result of the damage suffered. Occupied houses were not even safe at the end of the war, as the example of Sunderlandwick Hall, Driffield, Humberside, demonstrated. Canadian troops billeted there set fire to the curtains during celebrations for VJ night and the house was burnt down.

Post-war renewal

Two earlier developments came to have increasing significance for the preservation of country houses after 1945. One was the compilation of lists of buildings of special historic and architectural interest under the Town and Country Planning Act 1918. A beginning was made to identify and grade such buildings within local authority areas and was continued and refined under the Acts of 1947 and 1968. Originally the responsibility of the Ministry of Housing and Local Government, these lists are now produced by the Department of the Environment. Grade 1 listing can ensure grant aid for repair work and, to a limited extent, serve to prevent demolition. The lists themselves can be informative sources for the local historian, detailing features of architectural interest and periods of construction.

The other development was the passage of the National Trust Act in 1937. The Trust, originally founded in 1895 to 'act as a Corporation for the holding of lands of natural beauty and sites and houses of historic interest to be preserved intact for the nation's use and enjoyment', was by the 1930s increasingly being seen as the possible saviour of the country house. In 1931 it accepted Montacute, given by Mr E. E. Cook through the Society for the Protection of Ancient Buildings, and, in the same year, the Finance Act exempted land transferred to the Trust from death duties. Lord Lothian, in 1934, asked the Trust to extend its protecting arm in a definite and considered manner to historic country houses. He wanted the exemption from death duties extended to houses and gardens, income tax relief on repairs, maintenance and improvements, derating, and the possibility of bequeathing a house, its contents and estate to the nation in place of death duty.

Widespread support for these ideas encouraged the Trust to seek its second parliamentary Act in 1937. This permitted the Trust, for the first time, to acquire and hold land or investments as a source of income for the maintenance and conservation of property. In return for such a gift, the owner and his or her descendants would be allowed to stay on in the house as tenants. What has become known as the 'Country House Scheme' took some years to get under way. Wightwick Manor was the first country house to be presented to the Trust under the scheme in 1937 and it was not until 1940 that the first great house was received, on the death of Lord Lothian, in the shape of Blickling Hall, Norfolk, together with its contents and an estate of nearly 5000 acres. Other important houses followed during the war: Wallington Hall, Northumberland; Cliveden, Buckinghamshire; Polesden Lacy, Surrey; and Hillerton, Devon. By 1945 the charity owned 17 country houses, all of which were open to the public: and by 1950 36 houses had come into its care. Another significant aspect of the 1937 Act was that local authorities were empowered to give land and buildings to the Trust or to contribute to the acquisition and maintenance of Trust property. As a result, houses like Lyme Park, Cheshire, and Shugborough, Staffordshire, are leased to local authorities.

Concern that Labour government policy would be hostile to the future of country houses was, to some extent, dispelled by the creation in 1946 of the National Land Fund out of the sale of surplus war stores as a 'thank offering for victory'. The fund was to be used for the acquisition and preservation of property of national interest. It enabled the Treasury to reimburse the Inland Revenue for property accepted in lieu of estate duty (now capital transfer tax) and to transfer it to non-profit-making bodies such as the National Trust. Where country houses are concerned, the Treasury has transferred many to the Trust, including Cotehele, Cornwall; Penrhyn Castle, Gwynedd; Hardwick Hall, Derbyshire; Ickworth, Suffolk; and Saltram, Devon. The National Trust for Scotland has also received Brodick. A major difficulty with the system of Treasury transfers lies in the lack of an endowment, which means that some properties, like Heveningham, Suffolk, have not been accepted. A similar fund was established for Ulster in 1949, and was used for the acquisition and endowment of properties transferred to the National Trust in Northern Ireland, including Castlecoole, Ardress House and Castle Ward.

The Labour government also established a Treasury Committee under Sir Ernest Gowers to examine the country house problem. His report, *Houses of Outstanding Historic or Architectural Interest*, was published in 1950 and resulted in legislation in the Historic Buildings and Ancient Monuments Act of 1953. Under this measure the Historic Buildings Councils were set up in England, Wales and Scotland to advise their Secretaries of State about the listing and/or acquisition of buildings of outstanding historic or architectural interest or their contents or adjoining land, and about the awarding of grants and loans towards repair and maintenance, usually in exchange for an agreement by the owner to open his home to the public. As Cornforth has demonstrated, not all the money allocated to the Councils goes to country houses, rather, about one-third is received by them in grants.[29] Nevertheless, they have made a vital contribution to the survival of a great many houses.

From what has been said, it might appear that concern over the fate of country houses was concentrated on the fabric of the buildings rather than on the totality of the house, its contents and parkland, but increasing pressure from many quarters has gradually ensured that an ever greater variety of the contents of houses can be offered in satisfaction of estate duty. Not until the Finance Act of 1973 was the definition of works of art that could be so offered extended to include books and manuscripts and groups of objects of national, scientific or historic interest. Sales by private treaty to public collections have also been encouraged by the reduction of estate duty and capital gains tax. In this way, major family and estate collections, like the Warwick Castle archives, have been preserved intact for the benefit of future generations. However, existing mechanisms were shown to be inadequate to prevent the sale and dispersal of the contents of Mentmore in 1977. As a result, in 1981 the Land Fund was converted into the National Heritage Memorial Fund, which has greater flexibility to assist local authorities and non-profit-making bodies and institutions to purchase property and contents. It has aided the National Trust with the purchase of Canons Ashby, Northamptonshire, and the Chippendale furniture at Nostell Priory, for which £6.1 million was provided.

The National Trust, although the largest conservation society in Britain, only owns just over 100 country houses. Quantification is notoriously difficult but Clemenson has shown that, out of her sample of 500 country houses in 1880, there were still 394, in whole or in part, extant in 1980. Of these, 381 were still occupied or could be; 210 were in private hands and 160 in public or institutional ownership, 32 being held by the National Trust. However, only 30 per cent were in the hands of their original owners, with 41 per cent of great landowners as opposed to 26 per cent of gentry still in occupation.

Those houses that have passed out of the hands of private ownership have predominantly ceased to function as the centre of an estate and, thus, as focus of a local community. They have been adapted for multiple occupation, like Grimston Park, West Yorkshire, or for private occupation as flats or by housing associations like the Mutual Households Association. Other houses, like Stowe, Buckinghamshire, have become educational establishments; Heslington, North Yorkshire, and Stanmer, East Sussex, have become the core of universities. Those that have survived on their estates, if on a reduced scale, have had to adapt to their changing social status and recognize their attraction for the new, mobile leisured classes. Opening the house to the public, as a serious attempt to attract tourists, has been one means to finance the house. The sixth Marquis of Bath at Longleat was the first to enter the stately home business on 1 April 1949 and had spectacular success, attracting 138,000 visitors in the first year. He was slowly followed by other aristocrats, employing new marketing ploys to interest the general public. Lord Montagu opened Beaulieu in 1952 and the Duke of Bedford entered the business in 1953. They all shared a common realization that they could attract more visitors to the spectacle and glamour of the country house with good public relations. Many of such houses had always been accessible to the determined visitor: Beaulieu had been open since the 1890s to the general public. What changed after the war was the recognition that there was a new public, perhaps uninformed about the history of the house and its architecture, which came simply to be entertained. As the Duke of Bedford acknowledged:

> I wanted to make people enjoy themselves, give them service and value for money and make sure they would come back again. If this enabled me to live in my ancestral home, then everyone would be satisfied.[30]

By 1980 well over 1300 historic buildings had been opened to the public and visiting them has become one of the most popular leisure activities. Visitors are attracted by a vast range of alternative features, from safari parks to bird gardens and motor museums. Guidebooks of today concentrate on the family, the architecture and furnishings of the house, perhaps including some references to the problems of housekeeping and maintenance. The visitor can, all too easily, be left totally unaware of the significant historical role of such houses in the urban and rural communities of which they are a part. It remains for the local historian to investigate family and estate records and reveal that significance.

NOTES

Abbreviations:

BL = British Library, Manuscripts department; HMC = Royal Commission on Historical Manuscripts; HROB = Humberside Record Office, Beverley; PRO = Public Record Office; WYAS = West Yorkshire Archive Service.

Introduction

1 For example, J.M. Robinson, *The English Country Estate*, National Trust, 1988.
2 J.M. Robinson, *The Latest Country Houses*, Bodley Head, 1984.
3 D. Spring, *The English Landed Estate in the Nineteenth Century: Its Administration*, Johns Hopkins Press, 1963, pp. 15–17.
4 ibid., p. 51.
5 For example, F.G. Emmison, *Archives and Local History*, Methuen, 1966.
6 M. Holmes, *The Country House Described. An Index to the Country Houses of Great Britain and Ireland*, 1986.
7 Royal Commission on Historical Manuscripts (HMC), *Guide to the Location of Collections Described in the Reports and Calendars Series*, HMSO, 1982.
8 R.J. Olney, 'The Portland Papers', *Archives*, vol. xix, no. 82, October 1989, pp. 78–87.

Chapter 1 **The aristocracy: landownership, status and title**

1 Burke's *Peerage and Baronetage*, 105th edition, 1975, p. 1909.
2 House of Lords Record Office, Hist.Coll.116.
3 J.V. Beckett, *The Aristocracy in England, 1660-1914*, Blackwell, 1986, p. 38.
4 M.L. Bush, *The English Aristocracy*, Manchester University Press, 1984, pp. 110–11.
5 G.R. Elton, *England Under the Tudors*, Methuen, 1955, pp. 258–9.
6 J.R. Wordie, *Estate Management in Eighteenth-Century England*, Royal Historical Society, 1982, pp. 9–10.
7 L. Stone, *Family and Fortune*, Oxford, 1973, pp. 209–10.
8 A.F. Upton, *Sir Arthur Ingram*, Oxford, 1961, pp. 23–45.
9 M.E. Finch, *The Wealth of Five Northamptonshire Families 1540–1640*, Northamptonshire Record Office, 1956, pp. 100–1.
10 M. Mauchline, *Harewood House*, David and Charles, 1974, pp. 14–15.
11 Finch, op. cit. pp. 38–9.
12 F.W. Steer, ed., *The Ashburnham Archives*, East Sussex County Council, 1955, pp. vi–xiii.
13 J.M.L. Booker, ed., *The Wiston Archives*, West Sussex County Council, 1975, p. vii.
14 A.A. Dibben, ed., *The Cowdray Archives*, West Sussex County Record Office, 1960, pp. xxviii–xxxii.

15 Steer, ed., op. cit., p. 14.

16 J.M. Robinson, *The Dukes of Norfolk*, Oxford, 1982, pp. 99–100.

17 S.C. Newton, ed., *The Londonderry Papers*, Durham County Council, 1969, p. 3.

18 R. Latham and W. Matthewson, eds., *The Diary of Samuel Pepys*, 11 vols., Bell and Hyman, 1970–83, vol. VI, pp. 138, 159.

19 S. Margerison, ed., 'Memorandum Book of Sir Walter Calverley, Bt.', in *Yorkshire Diaries and Autobiographies*, vol. II, Surtees Society, 1886, p. 113.

20 C.W. James, *Chief Justice Coke: His Family and Descendants at Holkham*, Country Life, 1929, pp. 80–2.

21 R.A.C. Parker, *Coke of Norfolk*, Oxford, 1975, pp. 61–3.

22 For a summary of the debate, see G.R. Rubin and D. Sugarman, eds., *Law, Economy and Society*, Abingdon: Professional Books, 1984, pp. 168–88.

23 B. English and J. Saville, *Strict Settlement: A Guide for Historians*, University of Hull Press, 1983, p. 19.

24 G.E. Mingay, *English Landed Society in the Eighteenth Century*, Routledge, 1963, pp. 32–5.

25 English and Saville, op. cit., pp. 34–6.

26 J. Davies, *Cardiff and the Marquesses of Bute*, University of Wales Press, 1981, p. 44.

27 *The Ancestor*, no. 1, April 1902, pp. 160–1.

28 National Trust, *Baddesley Clinton, Warwickshire*, 1986, pp. 40–1.

29 James, op. cit., Appendix 1.

30 J.M. Robinson and T. Woodcock, *The Oxford Guide to Heraldry*, Oxford, 1988, pp. 182–5.

31 Finch, op. cit., Appendix XI.

32 G. Blakiston, *Woburn and the Russells*, Hutchinsons, 1980, pp. 5–6.

33 Parker, op. cit., pp. 83–93.

34 R.W. Unwin, *Wetherby*, Leeds University Press for Wetherby Historical Trust, 1986, pp. 81–99.

35 *Loving Memory*, BBC 2, 1987.

Chapter 2 **Building, landscaping and improving**

1 G. Webb, ed., *The Complete Works of Sir John Vanbrugh*, vol. 4, Nonesuch Press, 1928, pp. 24 ff.

2 C. Maxwell, ed., *A Tour in Ireland made in the years 1776, 1777 & 1778 by Arthur Young*, CUP, 1925, p. 8.

3 G.R. Smith, *Without Touch of Dishonour: the Life and Death of Sir Henry Slingsby*, Roundwood Press, 1968, pp. 5, 53.

4 J.T. Cliffe, *The Yorkshire Gentry from the Reformation to the Civil War*, Athlone Press, 1969, p. 225.

5 T. Friedman, *James Gibbs*, Yale University Press, 1984, p. 108.

6 A. Fairfax-Lucy, *Mistress of Charlecote*, Gollancz, 1987, p. 36.

7 J. Franklin, *The Gentleman's Country House and its Plan, 1835–1914*, Routledge & Keegan Paul, 1981, p. 245.

8 M. Girouard, *The Victorian Country House*, Yale University Press, 1979, p. 415.

9 Beckett, op. cit., pp. 331–2.

10 D.N. Durant and P. Riden, *The Building of Hardwick Hall*, Part 2, Derbyshire Record Society, vol. 9, 1984, p. 158.

11 G.R. Batho, *The Household Papers of Henry Percy, 9th Earl of Northumberland (1564–1632)*, Camden Society, 3rd Series, vol. 93, 1962, p. 1.
12 K. Downes, *Sir John Vanbrugh, A Biography*, Sidgwick & Jackson, 1987, p. 334.
13 West Yorkshire Archive Service (WYAS), Leeds, Vyner, 2239.
14 ibid., TN/EA 12/11.
15 Downes, op. cit., p. 200.
16 I. Davies, 'Robert Davies of Croes Foel, Bersham', *Denbighshire Historical Society Transactions*, vol. 6, 1957, p. 37.
17 National Library, Dublin, MS 11466. An undated bill in estate accounts from 1714–42.
18 J. Woolfe and J. Gandon, *Vitruvius Britannicus*, 1771, plates 23 and 24.
19 WYAS, Leeds, Allerton Park 4 and Grimston Park.
20 A. Young, *A Six Months' Tour through the North of England*, 2nd edition, London, 1770–1, vol. 1, pp. 127–8.
21 R. Warner, *A Tour through the northern counties of England and the borders of Scotland*, London, 1802, p. 227.
22 WYAS, Leeds, TN/EA 3/18.
23 ibid., GR AC 291.
24 ibid., Notes on *Harewood House* by M. Mauchline.
25 ibid., HAR/Correspondence.
26 HMC, Salisbury MSS, vol. 21, p. 137.
27 G.S. Thomson, *Life in a Noble Household*, Cape, 1937, pp. 247, 254.
28 Yorkshire Archaeological Society, MSS 328.
29 Leeds Central Library, Local Studies Collection, F/YST 15/(2), and J. Badeslade and J. Roque, *Vitruvius Britannicus*, 1739, plates 55–6.
30 WYAS, Leeds, Ingilby of Ripley, Acc:2922.
31 National Trust, op. cit., p. 43.
32 WYAS, Leeds, TN/EA20/5A.
33 ibid., Allerton Park 8.
34 Humberside Record Office, Beverley (HROB), DDCC/145/6.
35 A.M.W. Stirling, *Annals of a Yorkshire House*, Bodley Head, 1911, vol. I, p. 251.
36 C. Murdoch, 'Some Yorkshire Innocents Abroad', National Register of Archives, Annual Report of the West Riding Northern Section, no. 10, 1967, p. 42.
37 J.J. Cartwright, ed., *The Wentworth Papers, 1705–39*, 1883, p. 26.
38 WYAS, Leeds, Vyner 286.
39 ibid., TN/EA/12/5.
40 Cartwright, op. cit., pp. 213, 279.
41 C. Ramsay, 'Temple Newsam: the formation of the eighteenth century library', *Leeds Arts Calendar*, no. 76, 1975, p. 5.
42 National Trust, *Kingston Lacy*, pp. 11–12.

Chapter 3 **The landed estate: management and improvement**

1 M.M. Postan, *The Medieval Economy and Society*, Penguin, 1972, p. 121.
2 Bush, op. cit., pp. 129–33.
3 B.A. Holderness, *Pre-Industrial England*, Dent, 1976, p. 77.
4 N.W. Alcock, *Old Title Deeds*, Phillimore, 1986, p. 69.
5 J. West, *Village Records*, Macmillan, 1962, pp. 30–1.
6 E. Huxley, *Gallipot Eyes*, Weidenfeld, 1976, pp. 179–80.

NOTES

7 Manorial Documents Register, Royal Commission on Historical Manuscripts, Quality House, Quality Court, Chancery Lane, London WC2A 1HP.

8 The Law of Property Act (1922) abolished the remnants of copyhold tenure and the remaining principal financial returns on manors, namely, the fines on entry to copyhold land. This effectively ended the role of manorial courts.

9 Lord Leconfield, *Petworth Manor in the Seventeenth Century*, Oxford, 1954, p. 31.

10 ibid., p. 32.

11 ibid., p. 59.

12 J.H. Bettey, *Rural Life in Wessex 1500–1900*, Alan Sutton, 1977, p. 109.

13 ibid., pp. 27–8.

14 L. Cantor, *The Changing English Countryside 1400–1700*, Routledge, 1987, p. 51.

15 Holderness, op. cit., pp. 57–8.

16 M. Overton, 'Agricultural Revolution? England 1540–1850', in A. Digby and C. Feinstein, eds., *New Directions in Social and Economic History*, Macmillan, 1989, p. 9.

17 Mingay, op. cit., p. 181.

18 J. Cottis, 'A Country Gentleman and his Estates *c.* 1729–68: Sir Mark Stuart Pleydell, Bart., of Coleshill, Berkshire', in C.W. Chalklin and J.R. Wordie, eds., *Town and Countryside: The English Landowner in the National Economy 1660–1860*, Unwin Hyman, 1989, p. 33.

19 F.G. Emmison, *Archives and Local History*, Phillimore, 1978, pp. 62–6.

20 D.V. Fowkes and G.R. Potter, eds., 'William Senior's Survey of the Estates of the First and Second Earls of Devonshire *c.* 1600–28', in *Derbyshire Record Society*, vol. XIII, 1968, pp. vii-xx; 27.

21 WYAS, Leeds, TN/C14/8.

22 ibid., Harewood Estate Papers.

23 C. Wandesford, *A Book of Instruction*, 79 (n.d.), cited in J.T. Cliffe, op. cit., pp. 32–3.

24 Wordie, op. cit., pp. 13–14.

25 WYAS, Leeds, Harewood Estate Papers.

26 ibid.

27 ibid.

28 C. Clay, 'Landlords and Estate Management in England', in J. Thirsk, ed., *The Agrarian History of England and Wales*, vol. 5, part 2, 1985, p. 215.

29 Cottis, op. cit., pp. 26–7.

30 Parker, op. cit., pp. 138–42.

31 ibid., pp. 2–3.

32 Chalklin and Wordie, op. cit., pp. 7–8.

33 J. Godber, 'The Marchioness Grey of Wrest Park', *Bedford Historical Record Society*, vol. 47, 1968, pp. 93–4.

34 *The London Chronicle*, July 3–5 1804, cited in A.M.W. Stirling, *Coke and His Friends* (n.d.), vol. 2, p. 31.

35 Beckett, op. cit., pp. 134–6.

36 Mingay, op. cit., p. 64.

37 G. Blakiston, *Woburn and the Russells*, Hutchinson, 1980, p. 112.

38 HROB, Burton Constable Papers, DDCC/154/5.

39 P. Roebuck, ed., 'Constables of Everingham Estate Correspondence 1726–1743', *Yorkshire Archaeological Society Record Series*, vol. CXXXVI, 1976, pp. 53, 139.

40 G. Firth, 'The Roles of a West Riding Land Steward 1773–1803', *Yorkshire Archaeological Journal* 51, 1979, pp. 105–16.

41 Spring, op. cit., pp. 92–5.

42 ibid., pp. 44–8.
43 HROB Burton Constable Papers, DDCC/144/20.
44 ibid., DDCC/144/5 and DDCC/144/18.
45 Sykes Papers, University of Hull, DDSY/101/77.
46 Wentworth Woolley Papers, University of Leeds, Box 65.
47 See W.B. Stephens, *Sources for English Local History*, Manchester University Press, 1973, pp. 127–8.
48 Wentworth Woolley Papers, University of Leeds, Box 65.
49 HROB Burton Constable Papers, DDCC/144/34.
50 Sykes Papers, University of Hull, DDSY/101/85.

Chapter 4 **The country house and the Industrial Revolution**

1 Bush, op. cit., p. 187.
2 Beckett, op. cit., p. 8.
3 J.R. Wordie, Introduction to Chalklin and Wordie, op. cit., p. 3.
4 J.R. Wordie, 'The Shropshire Mining Industry 1748–1803', in Chalklin and Wordie, op. cit., pp. 210–11.
5 M.B. Rowlands, 'Continuity and Change in an Industrializing Society: the Case of the West Midlands Industries', in P. Hudson, ed., *Regions and Industries*, CUP, 1989, p. 106.
6 Lord Leconfield, op. cit., p. 98.
7 R.V. Saville, 'Gentry Wealth on the Weald in the Eighteenth Century: The Fullers of Brightling Park', *Sussex Archaeological Collections*, 121, 1983, pp. 129–47.
8 M.C.L. Salt, 'The Fullers of Brightling Park', *Sussex Archaeological Collections*, 104, 1966, pp. 65–6.
9 D. Hey, *Yorkshire from AD 1000*, Longman, 1986, p. 153.
10 J. Wigfall, 'William Dickenson's Notebook', in *Hunter Archaeological Society*, vol. 2, 1924, pp. 189–200.
11 S.M. Jack, *Trade and Industry in Tudor and Stuart England*, Allen and Unwin, 1977, pp. 159–61.
12 ibid., pp. 162–3.
13 Spencer-Stanhope Papers, Letters on Iron Working 1778–1815, Sheffield City Archives, 60579/2.
14 D. Spring, 'English Landowners and Nineteenth Century Industrialism', in J.T. Ward and R.G. Wilson, eds., *Land and Industry*, David and Charles, 1971, pp. 32–8.
15 Wentworth Woolley Papers, University of Leeds, Box 33/10.
16 ibid., Box 33.
17 ibid., Box 33/12.
18 Rockingham Papers, Sheffield City Archives.
19 J.R. Wordie, 'Aristocrats and Entrepreneurs in the Shropshire Mining Industry 1748–1803', in Chalklin and Wordie, op. cit., pp. 191–212.
20 Mingay, op. cit., p. 195.
21 G. Mee, *Aristocratic Enterprise*, Blackie, 1975, p. xv.
22 ibid., p. 25.
23 Wentworth Woolley Papers, University of Leeds, Box 59/46/8.
24 Mingay, op. cit., p. 197.
25 Carlisle Papers, 1897.

26 Jack, op. cit., p. 197.
27 R.W. Unwin, 'The Aire and Calder Navigation, Part I: The Beginning of the Navigation', in *Bradford Antiquary*, Part XLII, 1964, pp. 53–8.
28 B.F. Duckham, 'The Fitzwilliams and the Navigation of the Yorkshire Derwent', in *Northern History*, vol. II, 1967.
29 Mingay, op. cit., p. 197.
30 Hey, op. cit., p. 215.
31 J.V. Beckett, *The East Midlands from AD 1000*, Longman, 1988, p. 149.
32 H. Malet, *Bridgewater: the Canal Duke*, Manchester University Press, 1977, *passim*.
33 Bettey, op. cit., p. 86.
34 J. Davies, op. cit., pp. 260–1.
35 J.T. Ward, 'West Riding landowners and the Railways', *Journal of Transport History*, 4, 1960.
36 E.H. Fowkes, 'Railway History and the Local Historian', *East Yorkshire Local History Society*, 1963, pp. 8–9.
37 Wentworth Woolley Papers, University of Leeds Box 59/35.
38 M. Beresford, *East End, West End: the Face of Leeds during Urbanisation 1684–1842*, Thoresby Society, vols. LX, LXI, 1988, p. 77.
39 W. White, *History, Gazetteer and Directory of the West Riding of Yorkshire*, 1837, vol. 1, p. 361.
40 E. Baines, *Yorkshire, Past and Present*, 1870, vol. 2, p. 431.
41 J. Springett, 'Landowners and urban development: the Ramsden Estate and nineteenth century Huddersfield', *Journal of Historical Geography*, 8, 1982, pp. 129–44.
42 E. Baines, *History, Directory and Gazetteer of the County of York*, 1822, vol. 1, p. 294.
43 J. Davies, op. cit., p. 13.
44 M.J. Daunton, *Coal Metropolis, Cardiff 1870–1914*, Leicester University Press, 1977, p. 22.
45 J. Davies, op. cit., p. 186.

Chapter 5   **The landowner in society: leadership and leisure**

1 WYAS, HAR, Housekeeping accounts, 203.
2 HMC, Carlisle, p. 85.
3 C. Greville, *The Greville Memoirs*, ed. L. Strachey & R. Fulford, Macmillan, 1938, vol. 5, p. 347.
4 'Report of the Mines Inspector for Yorkshire', 1845, p. 25, quoted in F. Machin, *The Yorkshire Miners*, NUM, 1958, p. 29.
5 Beckett, op. cit., p. 341n.
6 Leeds Central Library, Local Studies Collection, Posters for Sports and Pastimes, 1845.
7 Fairfax-Lucy, op. cit., pp. 134–5.
8 *Malton Messenger*, 28 March 1863.
9 National Library of Ireland, Domville Papers, MS 9391.
10 WYAS, Leeds, Ingilby Papers, 3068.
11 B.I. Coleman, *The Church of England in the Mid-Nineteenth century*. Historical Assn, 1980, pp. 18; 44n.
12 WYAS, Leeds, op. cit., 3006–7.
13 BL, Addl 31142, ff. 101–2.
14 Sheffield City Archives, Wentworth Woodhouse MSS, RI 1868 and 1871.

15   WYAS, Leeds, GC/MA/54.
16   J. McCann, ed., *Correspondence of the Dukes of Richmond & Newcastle 1724–50*, Sussex Record Society, vol. 73, 1984, p. 89.
17   WYAS, Leeds, Vyner, 5735, T/3.
18   ibid., TN/PO3/C/14.
19   HMC, Cowper, vol. 3, p. 79.
20   HMC, Salisbury, vol. 23, pp. 3–4.
21   University of Leeds, W.W. Box 33.
22   WYAS, Leeds, Radcliffe, 428.
23   Cf. below, pp. 153.
24   HMC, Middleton, pp. 539–40.
25   HMC, Various Collections, vol. 2, p. 82.
26   HMC, Middleton, pp. 424, 436.
27   V. Sackville-West, ed., *Diary of Lady Anne Clifford*, Heinemann, 1923, p. 57.
28   E.K. Berry, *Henry Ferrers, an early Warwickshire antiquary, 1550–1633*, Dugdale Society Occasional Papers no. 16, 1965, pp. 10–11.
29   E. MacLysaght, *The Kenmare MSS*, Irish University Press for Irish MSS Commission, 1942, p. 99.
30   ibid., p. 101.
31   WYAS, Leeds, Vyner, *Diary of Lady Amabel Yorke*, vol. 8, 1784–6.
32   J. Godber, op. cit., pp. 90–1.
33   WYAS, Leeds, TN, & BL Addl 22259.
34   BL, Addl 31152, ff. 84–5.
35   H. Whitbread, ed., *I know my own heart: the Diaries of Anne Lister 1791–1840*, Virago, pp. 117, 130, 283, 293.
36   PRO, HO 107, 2365.37.
37   HROB, DDCC/144/34.
38   WYAS, Leeds, TA 7/6.
39   University of Hull, DDSY/104/129.
40   WYAS, Leeds, VR/C/33/1.
41   HMC, Rutland, vol. 4, pp. 443, 513.
42   Margerison, op. cit., pp. 88–9.

Chapter 6   **Downstairs: servants in house and estate**

1   J.H. Jesse, *Memoirs of the Court of England; George Selwyn and his contemporaries*, Rice, Boston, n.d., vol. I, pp. 248–9.
2   BL, Addl MSS, 22237, f. 254.
3   WYAS, Leeds, Ramsden Papers, Rockingham Letters, vol. 2B.
4   L.G. Mitchell, ed., *The Purefoy Letters 1735–53*, Sidgwick & Jackson, 1973, p. 135.
5   WYAS, Leeds, TA 7/6.
6   Margerison, op. cit., pp. 102–3.
7   National Library of Ireland, Domville Papers, 11297 & 9391.
8   HMC, Rutland, vol. 4, pp. 308–9.
9   L.M. Munby, ed., *Early Stuart Household Accounts*, Herts Record Publications, 1986, pp. ix–x.
10   PRO, HO 107 2365.
11   A.S. Turberville, *History of Welbeck Abbey*, Faber & Faber, 1938–9, vol. 2, pp. 59–60.

12 Thomson, op. cit., pp. 315–16.

13 E.S. Turner, *What the butler saw*, Michael Joseph, 1962, pp. 72–3.

14 WYAS, Leeds, TN/EA3/18.

15 Sheffield City Archives, Elmhirst Muniments, 1143, f. 34.

16 HROB, DDCC/140/104.

17 University of Hull, DDSY/102/1.

18 M. Waterson, *The Servants' Hall*, Routledge & Kegan Paul, 1980, pp. 82, 158.

19 J. Burnett, *Useful Toil*, 1974, Penguin edn., p. 186.

20 Cf. above, p. 135.

21 Burnett, op. cit., p. 188.

22 J. Osborne, ed., *The Autobiography of Thomas Whythorne*, Oxford, Clarendon Press, 1961, p. 37.

23 Routledge, 1927 edn., p. 237.

24 Burnett, op. cit., p. 187.

25 Cf. above, pp. 109, 111.

26 'A booke of orders & rules by Anthony 2nd Viscount Montague', *Sussex Archaeological Collections*, vol. 7, 1854, p. 186.

27 Mitchell, op. cit., pp. 151–2.

28 T. Balston, ed., *The Housekeeping Book of Susanna Whatman 1776–1800*, Geoffrey Bles, 1956, p. 38.

29 WYAS, Leeds, TA 7/6.

30 Waterson, op. cit.

31 ibid., p. 108.

32 cf. above, pp. 146.

33 Waterson, op. cit., p. 190.

34 J.P. Cooper, ed., *The Wentworth Papers 1597–1628*, Camden Society, 4th series, vol. 12, 1973, p. 15.

35 Turner, op. cit., p. 26.

36 J. Lees Milne, *Earls of Creation*, Century-Hutchinson edn., p. 189.

37 S.J. Flower, *The Stately Homes of Britain*, Debrett, 1982, p. 175.

Chapter 7 **Changing fortunes: decline and renewal**

1 Spring, op. cit., p. 43.

2 Sotheby's Catalogue, *Thoresby Hall sale*, 31 May, 1 & 2 June 1989, p. 10.

3 T.W. Beastall, *A North Country Estate*, Phillimore, 1974, p. 200.

4 F.M.L. Thompson, *English Landed Society in the Nineteenth Century*, Routledge & Kegan Paul, 1963, pp. 304–6.

5 Spring, op. cit., p. 42.

6 Fairfax-Lucy, op. cit., p. 175.

7 ibid., pp. 157, 174.

8 Thompson, op. cit., pp. 276–7.

9 Beckett, op. cit., p. 464.

10 Thompson, op. cit., p. 293.

11 ibid., p. 319.

12 H.A. Clemenson, *English Country Houses and Landed Estates*, Croom Helm, 1982, p. 103.

13 C. Aslet, *The Last Country Houses*, Yale University Press, 1982, p. 33, quoting from

Beatrice Webb *Our Partnership*, 1948, pp. 412–13.

14   D. Wilson, *Rothschild*, Andre Deutsch, 1988, p. 229.

15   B. Short, *The Geography of England and Wales in 1910: An Evaluation of Lloyd George's 'Domesday' of Landownership*, Historical Geography Research Group, no. 22, 1989.

16   Thompson, op. cit., pp. 332–3.

17   F.W. Dawes, *Not in front of the Servants*, Hutchinson, 1984, p. 169.

18   M. Waterson, *The Country House Remembered*, Routledge & Kegan Paul, 1985, p. 30.

19   Clemenson, op. cit., pp. 136, 149.

20   ibid., pp. 135 & 140, and R. Sadler, 'Fall of the House', *Yorkshire Post*, 23 January 1986.

21   J. Cornforth, 'Country Houses in Britain – can they survive?', *Country Life*, 1974, pp. 3, 5–9.

22   D. Neave and E. Waterson, *Lost Houses of East Yorkshire*, 1988, in foreward by Marcus Binney, p. 3.

23   Burke's and Savills *Guide to Country Houses*, vol. 1, M. Bence-Jones, 'Ireland', 1978; vol. 2, P. Reid, 'Herefordshire, Worcestershire, Shropshire & Warwickshire', 1981; vol. 3, H. Montgomery Massingberd, 'East Anglia', 1986.

24   National Monuments Record, Fortress House, 23 Savile Row, London W1X 1AB; National Monuments Record of Scotland, 7 Coates Place, Edinburgh EH3 7AA.

25   National Register of Archives, Quality House, Quality Court, Chancery Lane, London WC2. Supplementary information about records located in Scotland can also be obtained from NRA (Scotland), PO Box 36, HM General Register House, Edinburgh EH1 3YY. In Northern Ireland information can be obtained from the Public Record Office of Northern Ireland, 66 Balmoral Avenue, Belfast BT9 6NY.

26   Waterson, op. cit., p. 242.

27   D.R. Mills, ed., *Twentieth Century Lincolnshire*, History of Lincolnshire Committee, 1989, pp. 12–14, yet Professor Cannadine was able to write his *Decline and Fall of the British Aristocracy* based entirely on printed sources.

28   Information kindly supplied by A.J. McDonald, Search Department, Public Record Office, Kew.

29   Cornforth, op. cit., p. 24.

30   John, Duke of Bedford, *A Silver Plated Spoon*, Cassell, 1959, p. 196.

COUNTRY HOUSE ARCHIVES

A select list of those country houses or associated gardens open to the public together with the name of the family most closely identified with them and the main location of their estate archives.

Glossary of abbreviations:

NT = National Trust, EH = English Heritage, CC = County Council, DC = District Council.

England

CRO = County Record Office, D = Dispersed, F = privately held, H = the house itself, BOD = Bodleian Library, Oxford, BL = British Library, U = University, RA = Royal Archives, Windsor, JRL = John Rylands Library, Manchester, SBT = Shakespeare Birthplace Trust, Stratford-upon-Avon, USAH = Huntington Library, USA.

The dates relate to the architecture of the houses.

Avon

SCRO = Somerset CRO, GCRO = Gloucestershire CRO.

Badminton House 17th cent.	Duke of Beaufort	H
Clevedon Court NT 12th–14th cents.	Elton family	SCRO
Dodington House 1796–1813	Codrington family	GCRO
Dyrham Park NT 1693	Blaythwayt family	GCRO

Bedfordshire

Luton Hoo 1767–20th cent.	Stuart/Wernher family	CRO
Woburn Abbey 17th–19th cents.	Russell family	CRO
Wrest Park House EH 1834–9	Lucas family	CRO

Berkshire

Basildon Park NT 18th cent.	Morrison family	CRO
Windsor Castle 12th–19th cents.	H M The Queen	PRO & RA

Buckinghamshire

Ascott NT 17th–20th cents.	Rothschild family	F
Chenies Manor 15th–16th cents.	Russell family	Beds CRO
Chichely Hall 18th cent.	Chester family	CRO
Claydon House NT 18th cent.	Verney family	H
Cliveden NT 1851	Astor family	BL
Dorney Court 1440	Palmer family	H
Hughenden Manor NT 19th cent.	Disraeli	BOD, BL & CRO
Nether Winchendon 16th–19th cents.	Bernard family	H & CRO
Stowe 18th cent.	Duke of Buckingham/School	USAH
Waddesdon Manor NT 19th cent.	Rothschild family	F
West Wycombe Park NT 18th cent.	Dashwood family	CRO
Wotton House 1704	Grenville family	USAH

Cambridgeshire

CRO = CRO, Cambridge, HCRO = CRO, Huntingdon.

Elton Hall 15th–19th cents.	Proby family	H
Hinchinbrooke 16th–19th cents.	Montagu family	HCRO
Island Hall 18th cent.	Baumgartner/Percy family	CRO
Kimbolton Castle 18th cent.	Montagu family	D/HCRO
Ramsay Abbey 19th cent.	Fellowes family	HCRO
Wimpole Hall NT 17th–19th cents.	Yorke family	BL & CRO

Cheshire

LivRO = Liverpool RO, GMCRO = Greater Manchester.

Adlington Hall 15th–16th cents.	Legh family	H
Capesthorne 19th cent.	Davenport family	JRL
Dunham Massey NT 18th cent.	De Gray family	JRL
Lyme Park NT 16th–19th cents.	Legh family	JRL, Liv RO and GMCRO
Peover Hall 16th–19th cents.	Mainwaring family	JRL
Rode Hall 18th–19th cents.	Wilbraham family	CRO
Tatton Park NT 15th–18th cents.	Egerton family	CRO & JRL

Cleveland

Ormesby Hall NT 18th cent.	Pennyman family	CRO

Cornwall

Antony NT 1711–1721	Carew Pole family	H
Cotehele NT 1485–1647	Edgcumbe family	CRO
Godolphin House 16th–17th cents.	Earls of Godolphin	CRO
Lanhydrock NT 17th–19th cents.	Robartes family	CRO

Mount Edgcumbe CC 16th–18th cents.	Edgcumbe family	CRO
Pencarrow 18th cent.	Molesworth family	H
Prideaux Place 16th cent.	Prideaux-Brune family	CRO
Trelowarren 16th–17th cents.	Vyvyan family	CRO
Trerice NT 16th cent.	Arundel family	F
Trewithen 18th cent.	Hawkins/Johnstone families	CRO

Cumbria

CCRO = CRO, Carlisle, KCRO = CRO, Kendal, LCRO = CRO, Lancashire.

Askham Hall	Lonsdale family	K & CCRO
Belle Isle 18th cent.	Curwen family	CCRO
Dalemain 16th–18th cents.	Hasell family	CCRO
Holker Hall 19th cent.	Cavendish family	LCRO
Hutton in the Forest 17th–19th cents.	Lord Inglewood	CCRO
Levens Hall 13th–17th cents.	Bagot family	H
Muncaster Castle 19th cent.	Pennington Ramsden family	CCRO
Naworth Castle 19th cent.	The Earl of Carlisle	CCRO
Sizergh Castle NT 14th–16th cents.	Strickland family	H

Derbyshire

Bolsover Castle EH 17th cent.	Cavendish family	Notts U
Calke Abbey NT 1701–3	Harper Crewe family	CRO
Chatsworth 17th–18th cents.	Cavendish family	H
Haddon Hall	Manners family	F
Hardwick Hall NT 16th cent.	Cavendish family	H
Kedleston Hall NT 1759–1765	Curzon family	H
Sudbury Hall NT 17th cent.	Venables-Vernon family	CRO

Devon

CRO = CRO, Exeter, WDRO = West Devon RO, Plymouth, NDRO = North Devon RO, Barnstaple.

Arlington Court NT 1822	Chichester family	NDRO
Bickleigh Castle 11th cent.	Carew family	CRO
Flete 16th–19th cents.	Mildmay family	F
Fursdon House 18th cent.	Fursdon family	H
Hartland Abbey 18th cent.	Stucley family	CRO
Killerton NT 18th cent.	Acland family	CRO
Powderham Castle 14th–18th cents.	Courtenay family	CRO
Saltram NT 16th–18th cents.	Parker family	WDRO
Sand 16th cent.	Huyshe family	CRO
Tapeley Park 17th–18th cents.	Christie family	NDRO
Tiverton Castle 12th–17th cents.	Giffard/West families	CRO
Torre Abbey BC 12th–18th cents.	Cary family	CRO
Ugbrooke 18th cent.	Clifford family	H

Dorset

Forde Abbey 12th–19th cents.	Prideaux family	CRO
Kingston Lacy NT 17th–19th cents.	Bankes family	CRO
Mapperton 16th–17th cents.	Montagu family	CRO
Melbury House 16th–19th cents.	Fox-Strangeways family	CRO
Sandford Orcas 16th cent.	Medlycott family	H
Sherborne Castle 17th–19th cents.	Digby family	H & CRO
Smedmore 17th/18th cents.	Mansel family	H

Durham

Raby Castle 14th–19th cents.	Neville/Vane Tempest families	H
Rokeby Park 1735	Morrit family	CRO

Essex

Audley End EH 17th–19th cents.	Neville family	CRO
Hedingham Castle 1140–18th cent.	Majendie family	CRO

Gloucestershire

Berkeley Castle 1153–16th cent.	Berkeley family	H
Chavenage 16th–19th cents.	Stephens family	CRO
Sudeley Castle 16th–19th cents.	Dent-Brocklehurst family	H & CRO
Westbury Court NT 17th cent.	Colchester-Wemyss family	CRO

Hampshire

Beaulieu Abbey and Palace House 12th–16th cents.	Douglas-Scott-Montagu family	Southampton U
Broadlands 18th cent.	Mountbatten family	Southampton U
Hinton Ampner NT 20th cent.	Dutton family	CRO
The Vyne NT 16th–19th Cents.	Chute family	CRO
Stratfield Saye House 17th–19th cents.	Duke of Wellington	Southampton U

Hereford and Worcester

BLA = Birmingham Public Library Archives Department, HCRO = CRO, Hereford, WCRO = CRO, Worcester.

Berrington Hall NT 1778–1781	Brydges family	HCRO
The Commandery 16th cent.	Wylde family	CRO
Croft Castle NT 14th–18th cents.	Croft family	H
Eastnor Castle 1812	Somers Cocks family	H
Hagley Hall 18th cent.	Lyttelton family	WCRO & BLA
Hanbury Hall NT *c.*1700	Vernon family	WCRO
Harvington Hall 16th–18th cents.	Packington/Throckmorton families	CRO

Hellen's 12th–16th cents.	Walwyn family	CRO
Moccas Court 18th cent.	Cornewall family	NLW
Packington 18th cent.	Lord Hampton	H & CRO

Hertfordshire

Ashbridge NT 19th cent.	Egerton family	CRO
Gorhambury House 1774–84	Grimston family	CRO & H
Hatfield House 1604–11	Cecil family	H
Hunsdon House 19th cent.	Calvert/Charrington families	CRO
Knebworth House 16th cent.	Lytton family	H & CRO
Moor Park Mansion DC 1720	Grosvenor family	F

Humberside

Burton Agnes Hall 1598–1610	Boynton family	Hull U
Burton Constable 1570	Chichester-Constable family	CRO
Carlton Towers 19th cent.	Beaumont family	CRO
Normanby Hall BC 19th cent.	Sheffield family	CRO
Sledmere 1751–1787	Sykes family	Hull U

Isle of Wight

Appledurcombe House EH 1701–1800 (ruins)	Worsley family	CRO
Nunwell House 17th–18th cents.	Oglander family	CRO
Osborne EH 19th cent.	Queen Victoria	RA

Kent

Broughton Monchelsea 16th cent.	Rudston family	H
Chiddingstone Castle 17th–19th cents.	Streatfeild family	CRO
Cobham Hall 19th cent.	Darnley family	CRO
Godinton Park 17th cent.	Toke family/Wyndham Green	CRO
Knole NT 15th–17th cents.	Sackville family	CRO
Leeds Castle 12th–16th cents.	Fairfax family	D
Lullingstone Castle 16th–18th cents.	Hart Dyke family	CRO
Penshurst Place 14th–19th cents.	Sidney family	CRO
Quex House 19th cent.	Powell Cotton family	CRO
Sissinghurst NT 16th cent.	Sackville West	CRO

Lancashire

Browsholme Hall 16th–19th cents.	Parker family	CRO
Gawthorpe Hall NT 17th–19th cents.	Shuttleworth family	CRO
Hoghton Tower 16th cent.	De Hoghton family	CRO
Rufford Old Hall NT 15th cent.	Hesketh family	CRO

Leicestershire

Belgrave Hall CC 1709–1713	Ellis family	CRO
Belvoir Castle 16th cent.–1816	Manners family	H
Quernby Hall 17th–18th cents.	de Lisle family	CRO
Stanford Hall 1690s	Cave family	CRO

Lincolnshire

Belton House NT 17th cent.	Cust family	CRO
Burghley House 16th cent.	Cecil family	CRO
Fulbeck Hall 18th cent.	Fane family	CRO
Gunby Hall NT 1700	Massingberd family	CRO

London

GLRO = Greater London RO

Chiswick House EH 1725	Earl of Burlington	F
Kenwood EH 18th cent.	Murray family	H & F
Ranger's House EH 18th cent.	Stanhope family	BL
Osterley Park NT 18th cent.	Child-Villiers family	GLRO
Syon House 16th–18th cents.	Cecil family	H

Merseyside

Croxteth Hall DC 16th–20th cents.	Molyneux family	Lancs CRO
Speke Hall NT 16th–19th cents.	Norris/Watt families	Liv RO

Norfolk

Blickling Hall NT 17th–18th cents.	Hobart/Kerr families	CRO
Felbrigg Hall NT 17th cent.	Windham/Ketton-Cremer families	BL & CRO
Holkham Hall 18th cent.	Coke family	H
Houghton Hall 18th cent.	Walpole family	CRO
Oxburgh Hall NT 15th cent.	Bedingfeld family	H
Sandringham House 19th cent.	H M The Queen	RA
Sheringham Park NT 19th cent.	Upcher family	CRO

Northamptonshire

Althorp 16th–19th cents.	Spencer family	BL & CRO
Boughton House 1749	Montagu-Douglas-Scott family	CRO
Canons Ashby NT 16th–18th cents.	Dryden family	CRO
Deene Park 16th–19th cents.	Brudenell family	CRO
Rockingham Castle 11th–19th cents.	Watson family	H

COUNTRY HOUSE ARCHIVES

Northumberland

Alnwick Castle 12th–19th cents.	Cecil family	H
Belsay Hall Castle EH 19th cent.	Middleton family	CRO
Cragside House NT 19th cent.	Watson-Armstrong family	CRO
Seaton Delaval Hall 18th cent.	Delaval family	CRO
Wallington Hall NT 17th–19th cents.	Trevelyan family	CRO

Nottinghamshire

Clumber NT house demolished	Duke of Newcastle	CRO
Holme Pierrepoint Hall 15th–19th cents.	Pierrepoint family	Notts U
Newstead Abbey CC 13th–19th cents.	Byron/Shaw families	CRO
Wollaton Hall CC 16th cent.	Willoughby family	CRO

Oxfordshire

Ashdown House NT 17th cent.	Craven family	Berks CRO
Blenheim Palace 18th cent.	Spencer-Churchill family	BL
Broughton Castle 13th–18th cents.	Fiennes family	CRO & H
Buscot Park NT 1780	Townsend/Campbell/Henderson	Berks CRO
Ditchley Park 18th cent.	Lee/Dillon families	CRO
Rousham Park 1635	Cottrell-Dormer family	H
Stonor Park 13th–18th cents.	Stonor family	H

Shropshire

Attingham Park NT 1785	Noel-Hill family	CRO
Condover Hall 16th cent.	Cholmondeley family	D
Dudmaston NT 17th–19th cents.	Wolryche-Whitmore family	CRO
Mawley Hall 18th cent.	Blount family	CRO
Weston Park 1671	The Earl of Bradford	CRO etc.

Somerset

Dunster Castle NT 13th–19th cents.	Luttrell family	CRO
Montacute House NT 16th–18th cents.	Phelips family	CRO

Staffordshire

Alton Towers 19th cent.	Talbot family	CRO etc.
Moseley Old Hall NT 16th cent.	Whitgreave family	CRO
Shugborough NT 17th–18th cents.	Anson family	CRO

Suffolk

BCRO = County Record Office, Bury St Edmunds, ICRO = County Record Office, Ipswich.

Euston Hall 18th cent.	Fitzroy family	BCRO
Helmingham Hall 15th cent.	Tollemache family	H & ICRO
Ickworth NT 1794	Hervey family	BCRO
Kentwell Hall 16th cent.	Bence family	D & ICRO
Melford Hall NT 1578	Hyde Parker family	H
Somerleyton Hall 19th cent.	Peto/Crossley families	ICRO

Surrey

Albury Park 19th cent.	Cecil family	F
Clandon Park NT 1730s	Onslow family	CRO
Claremont 1772	Clive family	NLW
Hatchlands NT 1758	Admiral Boscawen	F & CRO
Loseley House 16th cent.	More-Molyneux family	CRO

Sussex (East)

Brickwall House 17th cent.	Frewen family	CRO
Firle Place 16th–18th cents.	Gage family	CRO
Glynde Place 16th cent.	Brand family	CRO
Michelham Priory 16th cent.	Sackville family	CRO
Newick Park 16th–18th cents.	Hicks family	Hampshire CRO
Sheffield Park NT 18th–20th cents.	Holroyd family	CRO

Sussex (West)

Arundel Castle 19th cent.	Fitzalan-Howard family	H
Danny 16th–18th cents.	Campion family	E Sussex CRO
Goodwood House 17th–18th cents.	Gordon-Lennox family	CRO
Petworth House NT 17th–19th cents.	Wyndham family	H

Warwickshire

Arbury Hall 16th cent./1750s	Newdegate family	CRO
Baddesley Clinton NT 15th–19th cents.	Ferrers family	CRO
Charlecote Park NT 1550–19th cent.	Lucy family	CRO & H
Coughton Court NT 16th cent.	Throckmorton family	CRO
Farnborough Hall NT 18th cent.	Holbech family	CRO
Stoneleigh Abbey 14th–18th cents.	Leigh family	SBT
Upton House NT 1695	Child-Villiers family	CRO
Warwick Castle 14th–19th cents.	Greville family	CRO

COUNTRY HOUSE ARCHIVES

West Midlands

BLA = Birmingham Public Library Archives Department, WLA = Wolverhampton Library Archives Department.

Aston Hall CC 17th cent.	Holte family	BLA
Wightwick Manor NT 1887	Mander family	H & WLA

Wiltshire

Bowood 18th–20th cents.	The Earl of Shelburne	H
Chalcot House 18th–19th cents.	Phipps family	CRO
Charlton Park House 17th–18th cents.	Howard family	CRO
Corsham Court 16th–18th cents.	Methuen family	CRO
Lacock Abbey NT 1232	Talbot family	H & CRO
Littlecote 15th–16th cents.	Popham family etc.	CRO
Longleat 16th–19th cents.	Thynne family	H
Stourhead NT 1721–5	Hoare family	CRO
Tottenham House 18th–19th cents.	Bruce family	CRO
Wilton House 17th cent.	Herbert family	CRO

Yorkshire (North)

HCRO = Humberside CRO, NYCRO = North Yorkshire CRO, WYASL = West Yorkshire Archive Service, Leeds, YAS = Yorkshire Archaeological Society, Leeds.

Allerton Park 19th cent.	Stourton family	WYASL
Carlton Towers 19th cent.	Beaumont/Duke of Norfolk	HCRO
Castle Howard 17th–18th cents.	Howard family	H
Constable Burton 1768	Wyvill family	NYCRO
Fountains Abbey & Studley Royal NT	Vyner family	WYASL
Newby Hall 18th–19th cents.	Robinson/Vyner family	WYASL
Newburgh Priory 12th–18th cents.	Wombwell family	NYCRO
Norton Conyers 16th–18th cents.	Graham family	NYCRO
Nunnington Hall NT 16th–17th cents.	Graham family	NYCRO
Ripley Castle 14th–19th cents.	Ingilby family	WYASL
Skipton Castle 11th–17th cents.	Clifford family	YAS

Yorkshire (South)

D = Doncaster Archives Department.

Cannon Hall BC 18th cent.	Spencer-Stanhope family	H & CRO
Cusworth Hall BC 18th cent.	Battie Wrightson family	D & WYASL

Yorkshire (West)

WYASC = West Yorkshire Archive Service, Calderdale.

Bramham Park 18th/20th cents.	Lane Fox family	WYASL
Harewood House 18th cent.	Lascelles family	WYASL
Ledston Hall 17th cent.	Wheler family	WYASL
Lotherton Hall DC 1896–1903	Gascoigne family	WYASL
Nostell Priory NT 1733	Winn family	WYASL
Shibden Hall DC 15th cent.	Lister family	WYASC
Temple Newsam DC 16th–17th cents.	Ingram family	WYASL

Wales

NLW = National Library of Wales, UCNW = University College of North Wales.

Clwyd

Chirk Castle NT 1310	Myddleton family	NLW
Erddig NT 17th–18th cents.	Yorke family	CRO

Glamorgan

Cardiff Castle CC 1090–19th cent.	Stuart family	CRO

Gwynedd

Penrhyn Castle NT *c.*1820–1845	Dawkins-Pennant family	UCNW
Plas Newydd NT 18th cent.	Paget family	UCNW

Powys

Gregynog 19th cent.	Davies family	NLW
Powis Castle NT *c.*1200	Herbert family	NLW

Ireland

NLI = National Library of Ireland, PROI = Public Record Office of Ireland, TCD = Trinity College Dublin.

Dublin

Malahide Castle 15th–19th cents.	Talbot de Malahide family	BOD & PROI

Kerry

Muckross House 1839–1943	Herbert/Guiness/Bourne Vincent	PROI

Longford

Carriglas Manor 1837–1840	Lefroy family	TCD

Roscommon

Clonalis House 1878–1880	O'Conor family	H

Waterford

Lismore Castle 17th–19th cents.	Cavendish family	NLI

Northern Ireland

PRONI = Public Record Office of Northern Ireland.

Armagh

The Argory NT 19th cent.	Bond family	PRONI

Down

Mount Stewart House NT 18th–19th cents.	Vane-Tempest-Stewart family	PRONI

Fermanagh

Castle Coole NT 18th cent.	Lowry-Corry family	PRONI
Florence Court NT 18th cent.	Cole family	PRONI

Scotland

NLS = National Library of Scotland, SRO = Scottish Record Office.

Borders Region

Bowhill 19th cent.	Montagu-Douglas-Scott family	H
Floors Castle 18th–19th cents.	Duke of Roxburghe	H
Manderston 18th–20th cents.	Miller family	H
Mellerstain 18th cent.	Baillie family	H
Thirlestane Castle 16th–19th cents.	Maitland family	H
Traquair House 18th cent.	Maxwell Stuart family	H

Dumfries and Galloway Region

Drumlanrig Castle 1679–1691	Douglas family	H

Grampian Region

Castle Fraser NTS 1575–1636	Fraser family	H
Craigievar Castle NTS 1626	Forbes family	SRO
Duff House 18th cent.	Duff family	Aberdeen U
Haddo House 18th cent.	Gordon family	H
Leith Hall NTS 17th–19th cents.	Leith-Hay family	H

Highlands Region

Cawdor Castle 14th cent.	Earl of Cawdor	H
Dunrobin Castle 18th–19th cents.	Sutherland family	NLS

Lothian Region

Hopetoun House 18th cent.	Hope family	H
Lennoxlove 17th cent.	Duke of Hamilton	H

Strathclyde

Inverary Castle 18th cent.	Campbell family	H
Torosay Castle 19th cent.	Guthrie-James family	H

Tayside Region

Blair Atholl 13th–19th cents.	The Duke of Atholl	H
Glamis Castle 17th cent.	The Earls of Strathmore & Kinghorne	H

SELECT BIBLIOGRAPHY

ASLET, C., *The Last Country Houses*, Yale University Press, 1982.

BEARD, M., *English Landed Society in the Twentieth Century*, Routledge, 1989.

BECKETT, J.V., *The Aristocracy in England, 1660–1914*, Blackwell, 1986.

BELLAMY, L., and WILLIAMSON, T., *Property and Landscape*, Batsford, 1988.

BUSH, M.L., *The English Aristocracy*, Manchester University Press, 1984.

CANNADINE, D., *Lords and Landlords; The Aristocracy and the Towns 1774–1967*, Leicester University Press, 1980.

CANNADINE, D., *The Decline and fall of the British Aristocracy*, Yale University Press, 1990.

CLEMENSON, H.A., *English Country Houses and Landed Estates*, Croom Helm, 1982.

CLIFFE, J.T., *The Yorkshire Gentry from the Reformation to the Civil War*, Athlone Press, 1969.

CORNFORTH, J., *Country Houses in Britain – can they survive?*, Country Life, 1974.

DAVIES, J., *Cardiff and the Marquesses of Bute*, University of Wales Press, 1981.

FAIRFAX-LUCY, A., ed, *Mistress of Charlecote*, Gollancz, 1987.

GIROUARD, M., *Life in the English Country House*, Yale University Press, 1978.

GIROUARD, M., *The Victorian Country House*, Yale University Press, 1979.

JACKSON-STOPS, G., *The Treasure Houses of Britain*, Yale University Press, 1985.

MINGAY, G.E., *English Landed Society in the Eighteenth Century*, Routledge, 1963.

ROBINSON, J.M., *The English Country Estate*, National Trust, 1988.

ROEBUCK, P., *Yorkshire Baronets 1640–1760*, Oxford, 1980.

SPRING, D., *The English Landed Estate in the Nineteenth Century: Its Administration*, Johns Hopkins Press, 1963.

THOMPSON, F.M.L., *English Landed Society in the Nineteenth Century*, Routledge & Kegan Paul, 1963.

WATERSON, M., *The Servant's Hall*, Routledge & Kegan Paul, 1980.

WATERSON, M., (ed) *The Country House Remembered*, Routledge & Kegan Paul, 1985.

WILLIAMSON, B., *Using Archives at National Trust Properties*, 1985.

WORDIE, J.R., *Estate Management in Eighteenth Century England*, Royal Historical Society, 1982.

INDEX

INDEX